Copyright © 2009 by Nova Science Publishers, Inc.

All rights reserved. No part of this book may be reproduced, stored in a retrieval system or transmitted in any form or by any means: electronic, electrostatic, magnetic, tape, mechanical photocopying, recording or otherwise without the written permission of the Publisher.

For permission to use material from this book please contact us:
Telephone 631-231-7269; Fax 631-231-8175
Web Site: http://www.novapublishers.com

NOTICE TO THE READER

The Publisher has taken reasonable care in the preparation of this book, but makes no expressed or implied warranty of any kind and assumes no responsibility for any errors or omissions. No liability is assumed for incidental or consequential damages in connection with or arising out of information contained in this book. The Publisher shall not be liable for any special, consequential, or exemplary damages resulting, in whole or in part, from the readers' use of, or reliance upon, this material.

Independent verification should be sought for any data, advice or recommendations contained in this book. In addition, no responsibility is assumed by the publisher for any injury and/or damage to persons or property arising from any methods, products, instructions, ideas or otherwise contained in this publication.

This publication is designed to provide accurate and authoritative information with regard to the subject matter covered herein. It is sold with the clear understanding that the Publisher is not engaged in rendering legal or any other professional services. If legal or any other expert assistance is required, the services of a competent person should be sought. FROM A DECLARATION OF PARTICIPANTS JOINTLY ADOPTED BY A COMMITTEE OF THE AMERICAN BAR ASSOCIATION AND A COMMITTEE OF PUBLISHERS.

LIBRARY OF CONGRESS CATALOGING-IN-PUBLICATION DATA

Available upon request.

ISBN: 978-1-60692-512-6

Published by Nova Science Publishers, Inc. ✢ New York

Contents

Preface		vii
Chapter 1	Executive Summary	1
Chapter 2	Introduction	21
Chapter 3	History of the Current Regulatory Framework	25
Chapter 4	Short-Term Recommendations	63
Chapter 5	Intermediate-Term Recommendations	73
Chapter 6	The Optimal Regulatory Structure	111
Chapter 7	Conclusion	151
Appendix		153
References		173
Index		187

PREFACE*

The mission of the Department of the Treasury ("Treasury") focuses on promoting economic growth and stability in the United States. Critical to this mission is a sound and competitive financial services industry grounded in robust consumer protection and stable and innovative markets. Financial institutions play an essential role in the U.S. economy by providing a means for consumers and businesses to save for the future, to protect and hedge against risks, and to access funding for consumption or organize capital for new investment opportunities. A number of different types of financial institutions provide financial services in the United States: commercial banks and other insured depository institutions, insurers, companies engaged in securities and futures transactions, finance companies, and specialized companies established by the government. Together, these institutions and the markets in which they act underpin economic activity through the intermediation of funds between providers and users of capital. This is an edited and excerpted edition.

This intermediation function is accomplished in a number of ways. For example, insured depository institutions provide a vehicle to allocate the savings of individuals. Similarly, securities companies facilitate the transfer of capital among all types of investors and investment opportunities. Insurers assist in the financial intermediation process by providing a means for individuals, companies, and other financial institutions to protect assets from various types of losses. Overall, financial institutions serve a vitally important function in the U.S. economy by allowing capital to seek out its most productive uses in an efficient matter. Given the economic significance of the U.S. financial services sector, Treasury considers the structure of its regulation worthy of examination and reexamination.

---

* Excerpted from The Department of the Treasury Report "Blueprint for a Modernized Financial Regulatory Structure" dated March 2008.

Chapter 1

EXECUTIVE SUMMARY

The mission of the Department of the Treasury ("Treasury") focuses on promoting economic growth and stability in the United States. Critical to this mission is a sound and competitive financial services industry grounded in robust consumer protection and stable and innovative markets.

Financial institutions play an essential role in the U.S. economy by providing a means for consumers and businesses to save for the future, to protect and hedge against risks, and to access funding for consumption or organize capital for new investment opportunities. A number of different types of financial institutions provide financial services in the United States: commercial banks and other insured depository institutions, insurers, companies engaged in securities and futures transactions, finance companies, and specialized companies established by the government. Together, these institutions and the markets in which they act underpin economic activity through the intermediation of funds between providers and users of capital.

This intermediation function is accomplished in a number of ways. For example, insured depository institutions provide a vehicle to allocate the savings of individuals. Similarly, securities companies facilitate the transfer of capital among all types of investors and investment opportunities. Insurers assist in the financial intermediation process by providing a means for individuals, companies, and other financial institutions to protect assets from various types of losses. Overall, financial institutions serve a vitally important function in the U.S. economy by allowing capital to seek out its most productive uses in an efficient matter. Given the economic significance of the U.S. financial services sector, Treasury considers the structure of its regulation worthy of examination and reexamination.

Treasury began this current study of regulatory structure after convening a conference on capital markets competitiveness in March 2007. Conference participants, including current and former policymakers and industry leaders, noted that while functioning well, the U.S. regulatory structure is not optimal for promoting a competitive financial services sector leading the world and supporting continued economic innovation at home and abroad. Following this conference, Treasury launched a major effort to collect views on how to improve the financial services regulatory structure.

In this report, Treasury presents a series of "short-term" and "intermediate-term" recommendations that could immediately improve and reform the U.S. regulatory structure. The short-term recommendations focus on taking action now to improve regulatory coordination and oversight in the wake of recent events in the credit and mortgage markets. The intermediate recommendations focus on eliminating some of the duplication of the U.S. regulatory system, but more importantly try to modernize the regulatory structure applicable to certain sectors in the financial services industry (banking, insurance, securities, and futures) within the current framework.

Treasury also presents a conceptual model for an optimal regulatory framework. This structure, an objectives-based regulatory approach, with a distinct regulator focused on one of three objectives—market stability regulation, safety and soundness regulation associated with government guarantees, and business conduct regulation—can better react to the pace of market developments and encourage innovation and entrepreneurialism within a context of enhanced regulation. This model is intended to begin a discussion about rethinking the current regulatory structure and its goals. It is not intended to be viewed as altering regulatory authorities within the current regulatory framework. Treasury views the presentation of a tangible model for an optimal structure as essential to its mission to promote economic growth and stability and fully recognizes that this is a first step on a long path to reforming financial services regulation.

The current regulatory framework for financial institutions is based on a structure that developed many years ago. The regulatory basis for depository institutions evolved gradually in response to a series of financial crises and other important social, economic, and political events: Congress established the national bank charter in 1863 during the Civil War, the Federal Reserve System in 1913 in response to various episodes of financial instability, and the federal deposit insurance system and specialized insured depository charters (e.g., thrifts and credit unions) during the Great Depression. Changes were made to the regulatory system for insured depository institutions in the intervening years in response to other financial crises (e.g., the thrift crises of the 1980s) or as enhancements (e.g., the Gramm-Leach-Bliley Act of 1999 ("GLB Act")); but, for the most part the underlying structure resembles what existed in the 1930s. Similarly, the bifurcation between securities and futures regulation, was largely established over seventy years ago when the two industries were clearly distinct.

In addition to the federal role for financial institution regulation, the tradition of federalism preserved a role for state authorities in certain markets. This is especially true in the insurance market, which states have regulated with limited federal involvement for over 135 years. However, state authority over depository institutions and securities companies has diminished over the years. In some cases there is a cooperative arrangement between federal and state officials, while in other cases tensions remain as to the level of state authority. In contrast, futures are regulated solely at the federal level.

Historically, the regulatory structure for financial institutions has served the United States well. Financial markets in the United States have developed into world class centers of capital and have led financial innovation. Due to its sheer dominance in the global capital markets, the U.S. financial services industry for decades has been able to manage the inefficiencies in its regulatory structure and still maintain its leadership position. Now, however, maturing foreign financial markets and their ability to provide alternate sources of capital and financial innovation in a more efficient and modern regulatory system are pressuring the U.S. financial services industry and its regulatory structure. The United States can no longer rely on the strength of its historical position to retain its preeminence in the global markets. Treasury believes it must ensure that the U.S. regulatory structure does not inhibit the continued growth and stability of the U.S.

financial services industry and the economy as a whole. Accordingly, Treasury has undertaken an analysis to improve this regulatory structure.

Over the past forty years, a number of Administrations have presented important recommendations for financial services regulatory reforms.[1] Most previous studies have focused almost exclusively on the regulation of depository institutions as opposed to a broader scope of financial institutions. These studies served important functions, helping shape the legislative landscape in the wake of their release. For example, two reports, *Blueprint for Reform: The Report of the Task Group on Regulation of Financial Services* (1984) and *Modernizing the Financial System: Recommendations for Safer, More Competitive Banks* (1991), laid the foundation for many of the changes adopted in the GLB Act.

In addition to these prior studies, similar efforts abroad inform this Treasury report. For example, more than a decade ago, the United Kingdom conducted an analysis of its financial services regulatory structure, and as a result made fundamental changes creating a tri-partite system composed of the central bank (i.e., Bank of England), the finance ministry (i.e., H.M. Treasury), and the national financial regulatory agency for all financial services (i.e., Financial Services Authority). Each institution has well-defined, complementary roles, and many have judged this structure as having enhanced the competitiveness of the U.K. economy.

Australia and the Netherlands adopted another regulatory approach, the "Twin Peaks" model, emphasizing regulation by objective: One financial regulatory agency is responsible for prudential regulation of relevant financial institutions, and a separate and distinct regulatory agency is responsible for business conduct and consumer protection issues. These international efforts reinforce the importance of revisiting the U.S. regulatory structure.

THE NEED FOR REVIEW

Market conditions today provide a pertinent backdrop for this report's release, reinforcing the direct relationship between strong consumer protection and market stability on the one hand and capital markets competitiveness on the other and highlighting the need for examining the U.S. regulatory structure.

Prompting this Treasury report is the recognition that the capital markets and the financial services industry have evolved significantly over the past decade. These developments, while providing benefits to both domestic and global economic growth, have also exposed the financial markets to new challenges.

Globalization of the capital markets is a significant development. Foreign economies are maturing into market-based economies, contributing to global economic growth and stability and providing a deep and liquid source of capital outside the United States.

Unlike the United States, these markets often benefit from recently created or newly developing regulatory structures, more adaptive to the complexity and increasing pace of innovation. At the same time, the increasing interconnectedness of the global capital markets poses new challenges: an event in one jurisdiction may ripple through to other jurisdictions.

In addition, improvements in information technology and information flows have led to innovative, risk-diversifying, and often sophisticated financial products and trading strategies. However, the complexity intrinsic to some of these innovations may inhibit investors and other market participants from properly evaluating their risks. For instance, securitization allows the holders of the assets being securitized better risk management opportunities and a new source of capital funding; investors can purchase products with reduced transactions costs and at targeted risk levels. Yet, market participants may not fully understand the risks these products pose.

The growing institutionalization of the capital markets has provided markets with liquidity, pricing efficiency, and risk dispersion and encouraged product innovation and complexity. At the same time, these institutions can employ significant degrees of leverage and more correlated trading strategies with the potential for broad market disruptions. Finally, the convergence of financial services providers and financial products has increased over the past decade. Financial intermediaries and trading platforms are converging. Financial products may have insurance, banking, securities, and futures components.

These developments are pressuring the U.S. regulatory structure, exposing regulatory gaps as well as redundancies, and compelling market participants to do business in other jurisdictions with more efficient regulation. The U.S. regulatory structure reflects a system, much of it created over seventy years ago, grappling to keep pace with market evolutions and, facing increasing difficulties, at times, in preventing and anticipating financial crises.

Largely incompatible with these market developments is the current system of functional regulation, which maintains separate regulatory agencies across segregated functional lines of financial services, such as banking, insurance, securities, and futures. A functional approach to regulation exhibits several inadequacies, the most significant being the fact that no single regulator possesses all of the information and authority necessary to monitor systemic risk, or the potential that events associated with financial institutions may trigger broad dislocation or a series of defaults that affect the financial system so significantly that the real economy is adversely affected. In addition, the inability of any regulator to take coordinated action throughout the financial system makes it more difficult to address problems related to financial market stability.

Second, in the face of increasing convergence of financial services providers and their products, jurisdictional disputes arise between and among the functional regulators, often hindering the introduction of new products, slowing innovation, and compelling migration of financial services and products to more adaptive foreign markets. Examples of recent inter-agency disputes include: the prolonged process surrounding the development of U.S. Basel II capital rules, the characterization of a financial product as a security or a futures contract, and the scope of banks' insurance sales.

Finally, a functional system also results in duplication of certain common activities across regulators. While some degree of specialization might be important for the regulation of financial institutions, many aspects of financial regulation and consumer protection regulation have common themes. For example, although key measures of financial health have different terminology in banking and insurance—capital and surplus respectively—they both serve a similar function of ensuring the financial strength and ability of financial institutions to meet their obligations. Similarly, while there are specific differences across institutions, the goal of most consumer protection regulation is to ensure consumers receive adequate information regarding the terms of financial transactions and industry complies with appropriate sales practices.

RECOMMENDATIONS

Treasury has developed each and every recommendation in this report in the spirit of promoting market stability and consumer protection. Following is a brief summary of these recommendations.

Short-Term Recommendations

This section describes recommendations designed to be implemented immediately in the wake of recent events in the credit and mortgage markets to strengthen and enhance market stability and business conduct regulation. Treasury views these recommendations as a useful transition to the intermediate-term recommendations and the proposed optimal regulatory structure model. However, each recommendation stands on its own merits.

President's Working Group on Financial Markets

In the aftermath of the 1987 stock market decline an Executive Order established the President's Working Group on Financial Markets ("PWG"). The PWG includes the heads of Treasury, the Federal Reserve, the Securities and Exchange Commission ("SEC"), and the Commodity Futures Trading Commission ("CFTC") and is chaired by the Secretary of the Treasury. The PWG was instructed to report on the major issues raised by that stock market decline and on other recommendations that should be implemented to enhance market integrity and maintain investor confidence. Since its creation in 1988, the PWG has remained an effective and useful inter-agency coordinator for financial market regulation and policy issues.

Treasury recommends the modernization of the current PWG Executive Order in four different respects to enhance the PWG's effectiveness as a coordinator of financial regulatory policy.

First, the PWG should continue to serve as an ongoing inter-agency body to promote coordination and communication for financial policy. But the PWG's focus should be broadened to include the entire financial sector, rather than solely financial markets.

Second, the PWG should facilitate better inter-agency coordination and communication in four distinct areas: mitigating systemic risk to the financial system, enhancing financial market integrity, promoting consumer and investor protection, and supporting capital markets efficiency and competitiveness.

Third, the PWG's membership should be expanded to include the heads of the Office of the Comptroller of the Currency ("OCC"), the Federal Deposit Insurance Corporation ("FDIC"), and the Office of Thrift Supervision ("OTS"). Similarly, the PWG should have the ability to engage in consultation efforts, as might be appropriate, with other domestic or international regulatory and supervisory bodies.

Finally, it should be made clear that the PWG should have the ability to issue reports or other documents to the President and others, as appropriate, through its role as the coordinator for financial regulatory policy.

Mortgage Origination

The high levels of delinquencies, defaults, and foreclosures among subprime borrowers in 2007 and 2008 have highlighted gaps in the U.S. oversight system for mortgage origination. In recent years mortgage brokers and lenders with no federal supervision originated a substantial portion of all mortgages and over 50 percent of subprime mortgages in the United States. These mortgage originators are subject to uneven degrees of state level oversight (and in some cases limited or no oversight).

However, the weaknesses in mortgage origination are not entirely at the state level. Federally insured depository institutions and their affiliates originated, purchased, or distributed some problematic subprime loans. There has also been some debate as to whether the OTS, the Federal Reserve, the Federal Trade Commission ("FTC"), state regulators, or some combination of all four oversees the affiliates of federally insured depository institutions.

To address gaps in mortgage origination oversight, Treasury's recommendation has three components.

First, a new federal commission, the Mortgage Origination Commission ("MOC"), should be created. The President should appoint a Director for the MOC for a four to six- year term. The Director would chair a seven-person board comprised of the principals (or their designees) of the Federal Reserve, the OCC, the OTS, the FDIC, the National Credit Union Administration, and the Conference of State Bank Supervisors. Federal legislation should set forth (or provide authority to the MOC to develop) uniform minimum licensing qualification standards for state mortgage market participants. These should include personal conduct and disciplinary history, minimum educational requirements, testing criteria and procedures, and appropriate license revocation standards. The MOC would also evaluate, rate, and report on the adequacy of each state's system for licensing and regulation of participants in the mortgage origination process. These evaluations would grade the overall adequacy of a state system by descriptive categories indicative of a system's strength or weakness. These evaluations could provide further information regarding whether mortgages originated in a state should be viewed cautiously before being securitized. The public nature of these evaluations should provide strong incentives for states to address weaknesses and strengthen their own systems.

Second, the authority to draft regulations for national mortgage lending laws should continue to be the sole responsibility of the Federal Reserve. Given its existing role, experience, and expertise in implementing the Truth in Lending Act ("TILA") provisions affecting mortgage transactions, the Federal Reserve should retain the sole authority to write regulations implementing TILA in this area.

Finally, enforcement authority for federal laws should be clarified and enhanced. For mortgage originators that are affiliates of depository institutions within a federally regulated holding company, mortgage lending compliance and enforcement must be clarified. Any lingering issues concerning the authority of the Federal Reserve (as bank holding company regulator), the OTS (as thrift holding company regulator), or state supervisory agencies in conjunction with the holding company regulator to examine and enforce federal mortgage laws with respect to those affiliates must be addressed. For independent mortgage originators, the sector of the industry responsible for origination of the majority of subprime loans in recent years, it is essential that states have clear authority to enforce federal mortgage laws including the TILA provisions governing mortgage transactions.

Liquidity Provisioning by the Federal Reserve

The disruptions in credit markets in 2007 and 2008 have required the Federal Reserve to address some of the fundamental issues associated with the discount window and the overall provision of liquidity to the financial system. The Federal Reserve has considered alternative ways to provide liquidity to the financial system, including overall liquidity issues associated with non-depository institutions. The Federal Reserve has used its authority for the first time since the 1930s to provide access to the discount window to non-depository institutions.

The Federal Reserve's recent actions reflect the fundamentally different nature of the market stability function in today's financial markets compared to those of the past. The Federal Reserve has balanced the difficult tradeoffs associated with preserving market stability and considering issues associated with expanding the safety net.

Given the increased importance of non-depository institutions to overall market stability, Treasury is recommending the consideration of two issues. First, the current temporary liquidity provisioning process during those rare circumstances when market stability is threatened should be enhanced to ensure that: the process is calibrated and transparent; appropriate conditions are attached to lending; and information flows to the Federal Reserve through on-site examination or other means as determined by the Federal Reserve are adequate. Key to this information flow is a focus on liquidity and funding issues. Second, the PWG should consider broader regulatory issues associated with providing discount window access to non-depository institutions.

Intermediate-Term Recommendations

This section describes additional recommendations designed to be implemented in the intermediate term to increase the efficiency of financial regulation. Some of these recommendations can be accomplished relatively soon; consensus on others will be difficult to obtain in the near term.

Thrift Charter

In 1933 Congress established the federal savings association charter (often referred to as the federal thrift charter) in response to the Great Depression. The federal thrift charter originally focused on providing a stable source of funding for residential mortgage lending. Over time federal thrift lending authority has expanded beyond residential mortgages. For example, Congress broadened federal thrifts' investment authority in the 1980s and permitted the inclusion of non-mortgage assets to meet the qualified-thrift lender test in 1996.

In addition, the role of federal thrifts as a dominant source of mortgage funding has diminished greatly in recent years. The increased residential mortgage activity of government-sponsored enterprises ("GSEs") and commercial banks, as well as the general development of the mortgage-backed securities market, has driven this shift.

Treasury recommends phasing out and transitioning the federal thrift charter to the national bank charter as the thrift charter is no longer necessary to ensure sufficient residential mortgage loans are made available to U.S. consumers. With the elimination of the federal thrift charter the OTS would be closed and its operations would be assumed by the OCC. This transition should take place over a two-year period.

Federal Supervision of State-Chartered Banks

State-chartered banks with federal deposit insurance are currently subject to both state and federal supervision. If the state-chartered bank is a member of the Federal Reserve System, the Federal Reserve administers federal oversight. Otherwise, the FDIC oversees state-chartered banks.

The direct federal supervision of state-chartered banks should be rationalized. One approach would be to place all such banking examination responsibilities for state-chartered banks with federal deposit insurance with the Federal Reserve.

Another approach would be to place all such bank examination responsibilities for state-chartered banks with federal deposit insurance with the FDIC.

Any such shift of supervisory authority for state-chartered banks with federal deposit insurance from the Federal Reserve to the FDIC or vice versa raises a number of issues regarding the overall structure of the Federal Reserve System. To further consider this issue, Treasury recommends a study, one that examines the evolving role of Federal Reserve Banks, to make a definitive proposal regarding the appropriate federal supervisor of state-chartered banks.

Payment and Settlement Systems Oversight

Payment and settlement systems are the mechanisms used to transfer funds and financial instruments between financial institutions and between financial institutions and their customers. Payment and settlement systems play a fundamental and important role in the economy by providing a range of mechanisms through which financial institutions can easily settle transactions. The United States has various payment and settlement systems, including large-value and retail payment and settlement systems, as well as settlement systems for securities and other financial instruments.

In the United States major payment and settlement systems are generally not subject to any uniform, specifically designed, and overarching regulatory system. Moreover, there is no defined category within financial regulation focused on payment and settlement systems. As a result, regulation of major payment and settlement systems is idiosyncratic, reflecting choices made by payment and settlement systems based on options available at some previous time.

To address the issue of payment and settlement system oversight, a federal charter for systemically important payment and settlement systems should be created and should incorporate federal preemption. The Federal Reserve should have primary oversight responsibilities for such payment and settlement systems, should have discretion to designate a payment and settlement system as systemically important, and should have a full range of authority to establish regulatory standards.

Insurance

For over 135 years, states have primarily regulated insurance with little direct federal involvement. While a state-based regulatory system for insurance may have been appropriate over some portion of U.S. history, changes in the insurance marketplace have increasingly put strains on the system.

Much like other financial services, over time the business of providing insurance has moved to a more national focus even within the state-based regulatory structure. The inherent nature of a state-based regulatory system makes the process of developing national products cumbersome and more costly, directly impacting the competitiveness of U.S. insurers.

There are a number of potential inefficiencies associated with the state-based insurance regulatory system. Even with the efforts of the National Association of Insurance Commissioners ("NAIC") to foster greater uniformity through the development of model laws and other coordination efforts, the ultimate authority still rests with individual states. For insurers operating on a national basis, this means not only being subject to licensing requirements and regulatory examinations in all states where the insurer operates, but also operating under different laws in each state.

In addition to a more national focus today, the insurance marketplace operates globally with many significant foreign participants. A state-based regulatory system creates increasing tensions in such a global marketplace, both in the ability of U.S.-based firms to compete abroad and in allowing greater participation of foreign firms in U.S. markets.

To address these issues in the near term, Treasury recommends establishing an optional federal charter ("OFC") for insurers within the current structure. An OFC structure should provide for a system of federal chartering, licensing, regulation, and supervision for insurers, reinsurers, and insurance producers (i.e., agents and brokers). It would also provide that the current state-based regulation of insurance would continue for those not electing to be regulated at the national level. States would not have jurisdiction over those electing to be federally regulated. However, insurers holding an OFC could still be subject to some continued compliance with other state laws, such as state tax laws, compulsory coverage for workers' compensation and individual auto insurance, as well as the requirements to participate in state mandatory residual risk mechanisms and guarantee funds.

An OFC would be issued to specify the lines of insurance that each national insurer would be permitted to sell, solicit, negotiate, and underwrite. For example, an OFC for life insurance could also include annuities, disability income insurance, long-term care insurance, and funding agreements. On the other hand, an OFC for property and casualty insurance could include liability insurance, surety bonds, automobile insurance, homeowners, and other specified lines of business. However, since the nature of the business of life insurers is very different from that of property and casualty insurers, no OFC would authorize an insurer to hold a license as both a life insurer and a property and casualty insurer.

The establishment of an OFC should incorporate a number of fundamental regulatory concepts. For example, the OFC should ensure safety and soundness, enhance competition in national and international markets, increase efficiency in a number of ways, including the elimination of price controls, promote more rapid technological change, encourage product innovation, reduce regulatory costs, and provide consumer protection.

Treasury also recommends the establishment of the Office of National Insurance ("ONI") within Treasury to regulate those engaged in the business of insurance pursuant to an OFC. The Commissioner of National Insurance would head ONI and would have specified regulatory, supervisory, enforcement, and rehabilitative powers to oversee the organization, incorporation, operation, regulation, and supervision of national insurers and national agencies.

While an OFC offers the best opportunity to develop a modern and comprehensive system of insurance regulation in the short term, Treasury acknowledges that the OFC debate in Congress is difficult and ongoing. At the same time, Treasury believes that some aspects of the insurance segment and its regulatory regime require immediate attention. In particular, Treasury recommends that Congress establish an Office of Insurance Oversight ("OIO") within Treasury. The OIO through its insurance oversight would be able to focus immediately on key areas of federal interest in the insurance sector.

The OIO should be established to accomplish two main purposes. First, the OIO should exercise newly granted statutory authority to address international regulatory issues, such as reinsurance collateral. Therefore, the OIO would become the lead regulatory voice in the promotion of international insurance regulatory policy for the United States (in consultation with the NAIC), and it would be granted the authority to recognize international regulatory bodies for specific insurance purposes. The OIO would also have authority to ensure that the NAIC and state insurance regulators achieved the uniform implementation of the declared U.S. international insurance policy goals. Second, the OIO would serve as an advisor to the Secretary of the Treasury on major domestic and international policy issues. Once Congress passes significant insurance regulatory reform, the OIO could be incorporated into the OFC framework.

Futures and Securities

The realities of the current marketplace have significantly diminished, if not entirely eliminated, the original reason for the regulatory bifurcation between the futures and securities markets. These markets were truly distinct in the 193 0s at the time of the enactment of the Commodity Exchange Act and the federal securities laws. This bifurcation operated effectively until the 1970s when futures trading soon expanded beyond agricultural commodities to encompass the rise and eventual dominance on non-agricultural commodities.

Product and market participant convergence, market linkages, and globalization have rendered regulatory bifurcation of the futures and securities markets untenable, potentially harmful, and inefficient. To address this issue, the CFTC and the SEC should be merged to provide unified oversight and regulation of the futures and securities industries.

An oft-cited argument against the merger of the CFTC and the SEC is the potential loss of the CFTC's principles-based regulatory philosophy. Treasury would like to preserve the market benefits achieved in the futures area. Accordingly, Treasury recommends that the SEC undertake a number of specific actions, within its current regulatory structure and under its current authority, to modernize the SEC's regulatory approach to accomplish a more seamless merger of the agencies. These recommendations would reflect rapidly evolving market dynamics. These steps include the following:

- The SEC should use its exemptive authority to adopt core principles to apply to securities clearing agencies and exchanges. These core principles should be modeled after the core principles adopted for futures exchanges and clearing organizations under the Commodity Futures Modernization Act ("CFMA"). By imbuing the SEC with a regulatory regime more conducive to the modern marketplace, a merger between the agencies will proceed more smoothly.
- The SEC should issue a rule to update and streamline the self-regulatory organization ("SRO") rulemaking process to recognize the market and product innovations of the past two decades. The SEC should consider streamlining and expediting the SRO rule approval process, including a firm time limit for the SEC to publish SRO rule filings and more clearly defining and expanding the type of rules deemed effective upon filing, including trading rules and administrative rules. The SEC should also consider streamlining the approval for any securities products common to the marketplace as the agency did in a 1998 rulemaking vis-à-vis certain derivatives securities products. An updated, streamlined, and expedited approval process will allow U.S. securities firms to remain competitive with the over-the-counter markets and international institutions and increase product innovation and investor choice.
- The SEC should undertake a general exemptive rulemaking under the Investment Company Act of 1940 ("Investment Company Act"), consistent with investor protection, to permit the trading of those products already actively trading in the U.S. or foreign jurisdictions. Treasury also recommends that the SEC propose to Congress legislation that would expand the Investment Company Act by permitting registration of a new "global" investment company.

These steps should help modernize the SEC's regulation prior to the merger of the CFTC and the SEC. Legislation merging the CFTC and the SEC should not only call for a structural merger, but also a process to merge regulatory philosophies and to harmonize securities and futures regulations and statutes. The merger plan should also address certain key aspects:

- Concurrent with the merger, the new agency should adopt overarching regulatory principles focusing on investor protection, market integrity, and overall financial system risk reduction. This will help meld the regulatory philosophies of the agencies. Legislation calling for a merger should task the PWG with drafting these principles.
- Consistent with structure of the CFMA, all clearing agency and market SROs should be permitted by statute to self-certify all rulemakings (except those involving corporate listing and market conduct standards), which then become effective upon filing. The SEC would retain its right to abrogate the rulemakings at any time. By limiting self-certified SRO rule changes to non-retail investor related rules, investor protection will be preserved.
- Several differences between futures regulation and federal securities regulation would need to be harmonized. These include rules involving margin, segregation, insider

trading, insurance coverage for broker-dealer insolvency, customer suitability, short sales, SRO mergers, implied private rights of action, the SRO rulemaking approval process, and the agency's funding mechanism. Due to the complexities and nuances of the differences in futures and securities regulation, legislation should establish a joint CFTC-SEC staff task force with equal agency representation with the mandate to harmonize these differences. In addition, the task force should be charged with recommending the structure of the merged agency, including its offices and divisions.

Finally, there has also been a continued convergence of the services provided by broker-dealers and investment advisers within the securities industry. These entities operate under a statutory regime reflecting the brokerage and investment advisory industries as they existed decades ago. Accordingly, Treasury recommends statutory changes to harmonize the regulation and oversight of broker-dealers and investment advisers offering similar services to retail investors. In that vein, the establishment of a self-regulatory framework for the investment advisory industry would enhance investor protection and be more cost-effective than direct SEC regulation. Thus, to effectuate this statutory harmonization, Treasury recommends that investment advisers be subject to a self-regulatory regime similar to that of broker-dealers.

Long-Term Optimal Regulatory Structure

While there are many possible options to reform and strengthen the regulation of financial institutions in the United States, Treasury considered four broad conceptual options in this review. First, the United States could maintain the current approach of the GLB Act that is broadly based on functional regulation divided by historical industry segments of banking, insurance, securities, and futures. Second, the United States could move to a more functional-based system regulating the activities of financial services firms as opposed to industry segments. Third, the United States could move to a single regulator for all financial services as adopted in the United Kingdom. Finally, the United States could move to an objectives-based regulatory approach focusing on the goals of regulation as adopted in Australia and the Netherlands.

After evaluating these options, Treasury believes that an objectives-based regulatory approach would represent the optimal regulatory structure for the future. An objectives-based approach is designed to focus on the goals of regulation in terms of addressing particular market failures. Such an evaluation leads to a regulatory structure focusing on three key goals:

- Market stability regulation to address overall conditions of financial market stability that could impact the real economy;
- Prudential financial regulation to address issues of limited market discipline caused by government guarantees; and
- Business conduct regulation (linked to consumer protection regulation) to address standards for business practices.

More closely linking the regulatory objectives of market stability regulation, prudential financial regulation, and business conduct regulation to regulatory structure greatly improves regulatory efficiency. In particular, a major advantage of objectives-based regulation is that regulatory responsibilities are consolidated in areas where natural synergies take place, as opposed to the current approach of dividing these responsibilities among individual regulators. For example, a dedicated market stability regulator with the appropriate mandate and authority can focus broadly on issues that can impact market stability across all types of financial institutions. Prudential financial regulation housed within one regulatory body can focus on common elements of risk management across financial institutions. A dedicated business conduct regulator leads to greater consistency in the treatment of products, eliminates disputes among regulatory agencies, and reduces gaps in regulation and supervision.

In comparison to other regulatory structures, an objectives-based approach is better able to adjust to changes in the financial landscape than a structure like the current U.S. system focused on industry segments. An objectives-based approach also allows for a clearer focus on particular goals in comparison to a structure that consolidates all types of regulation in one regulatory body. Finally, clear regulatory dividing lines by objective also have the most potential for establishing the greatest levels of market discipline because financial regulation can be more clearly targeted at the types of institutions for which prudential regulation is most appropriate.

In the optimal structure three distinct regulators would focus exclusively on financial institutions: a market stability regulator, a prudential financial regulator, and a business conduct regulator. The optimal structure also describes the roles of two other key authorities, the federal insurance guarantor and the corporate finance regulator.

The optimal structure also sets forth a structure rationalizing the chartering of financial institutions. The optimal structure would establish a federal insured depository institution ("FIDI") charter for all depository institutions with federal deposit insurance; a federal insurance institution ("FII") charter for insurers offering retail products where some type of government guarantee is present; and a federal financial services provider ("FFSP") charter for all other types of financial services providers. The market stability regulator would have various authorities over all three types of federally chartered institutions. A new prudential regulator, the Prudential Financial Regulatory Agency ("PFRA"), would be responsible for the financial regulation of FIDIs and FIIs. A new business conduct regulator, the Conduct of Business Regulatory Agency ("CBRA"), would be responsible for business conduct regulation, including consumer protection issues, across all types of firms, including the three types of federally chartered institutions. More detail regarding the responsibilities of these regulators follows.

Market Stability Regulator – The Federal Reserve

The market stability regulator should be responsible for overall issues of financial market stability. The Federal Reserve should assume this role in the optimal framework given its traditional central bank role of promoting overall macroeconomic stability. As is the case today, important elements of the Federal Reserve's market stability role would be conducted through the implementation of monetary policy and the provision of liquidity to the financial system. In addition, the Federal Reserve should be provided with a different, yet critically important regulatory role and broad powers focusing on the overall financial system and the three types of federally chartered institutions (i.e., FIIs, FIDIs, or FFSPs). Finally, the Federal Reserve should oversee the payment and settlement system.

In terms of its recast regulatory role focusing on systemic risk, the Federal Reserve should have the responsibility and authority to gather appropriate information, disclose information, collaborate with the other regulators on rule writing, and take corrective actions when necessary in the interest of overall financial market stability. This new role would replace its traditional role as a supervisor of certain banks and all bank holding companies.

Treasury recognizes the need for enhanced regulatory authority to deal with systemic risk. The Federal Reserve's responsibilities would be broad, important, and difficult to undertake. In a dynamic market economy it is impossible to fully eliminate instability through regulation. At a fundamental level, the root causes of market instability are difficult to predict, and past history may be a poor predictor of future episodes of instability. However, the Federal Reserve's enhanced regulatory authority along with clear regulatory responsibilities would complement and attempt to focus market discipline to limit systemic risk.[2]

A number of key long-term issues should be considered in establishing this new framework. First, in order to perform this critical role, the Federal Reserve must have detailed information about the business operations of PFRA- and CBRA-regulated financial institutions and their respective holding companies. Such information will be important in evaluating issues that can have an impact on overall financial market stability.

The other regulators should be required to share all financial reports and examination reports with the Federal Reserve as requested. Working jointly with PFRA, the Federal Reserve should also have the ability to develop additional information-reporting requirements on issues important to overall market stability.

The Federal Reserve should also have the authority to develop information-reporting requirements for FFSPs and for holding companies with federally chartered financial institution affiliates. In terms of holding company reporting requirements, such reporting should include a requirement to consolidate financial institutions onto the balance sheet of the overall holding company and at the segmented level of combined federally chartered financial institutions. Such information-reporting requirements could also include detailed reports on overall risk management practices.

As an additional information-gathering tool, the Federal Reserve should also have the authority to participate in PFRA and CBRA examinations of federally chartered entities, and to initiate such examinations targeted on practices important to market stability. Targeted examinations of a PFRA- or CBRA-supervised entity should occur only if the information the Federal Reserve needs is not available from PFRA or CBRA and should be coordinated with PFRA and CBRA.

Based on the information-gathering tools described above, the Federal Reserve should publish broad aggregates or peer group information about financial exposures that are important to overall market stability. Disseminating such information to the public could highlight areas of risk exposure that market participants should be monitoring. The Federal Reserve should also be able to mandate additional public disclosures for federally chartered financial institutions that are publicly traded or for a publicly traded company controlling such an institution.

Second, the type of information described above will be vitally important in performing the market stability role and in better harnessing market forces. However, the Federal Reserve should also have authority to provide input into the development of regulatory policy and to undertake corrective actions related to enhancing market stability. With respect to regulatory policy, PFRA and CBRA should be required to consult with the Federal Reserve prior to adopting or modifying regulations affecting market stability, including capital requirements for PFRA-regulated institutions and chartering requirements for CBRA-regulated institutions, and supervisory guidance regarding areas important to market stability (e.g., liquidity risk management, contingency funding plans, and counterparty risk management).

With regard to corrective actions, if after analyzing the information described above the Federal Reserve determines that certain risk exposures pose an overall risk to the financial system or the broader economy, the Federal Reserve should have authority to require corrective actions to address current risks or to constrain future risk-taking. For example, the Federal Reserve could use this corrective action authority to require financial institutions to limit or more carefully monitor risk exposures to certain asset classes or to certain types of counterparties or address liquidity and funding issues.

The Federal Reserve's authority to require corrective actions should be limited to instances where overall financial market stability was threatened. The focus of the market stability regulator's corrective actions should wherever possible be broadly based across particular institutions or across asset classes. Such actions should be coordinated and implemented with the appropriate regulatory agency to the fullest extent possible. But the Federal Reserve would have residual authority to enforce compliance with its requirements under this authority.

Third, the Federal Reserve's current lender of last resort function should continue through the discount window. A primary function of the discount window is to serve as a complementary tool of monetary policy by making short-term credit available to insured depository institutions to address liquidity issues. The historic focus of Federal Reserve discount window lending reflects the relative importance of banks as financial intermediaries and a desire to limit the spread of the federal safety net. However, banks' somewhat diminished role and the increased role of other types of financial institutions in overall financial intermediation may have reduced the effectiveness of this traditional tool in achieving market stability.

To address the limited effectiveness of discount window lending over time, a distinction could be made between "normal" discount window lending and "market stability" discount window lending. Access to normal discount window funding for FIDIs—including borrowing under the primary, secondary, and seasonal credit programs—could continue to operate much as it does today. All FIDIs would have access to normal discount window funding, which would continue to serve as a complementary tool of monetary policy by providing a mechanism to smooth out short-term volatility in reserves, and providing some degree of liquidity to FIDIs. Current Federal Reserve discount window policies regarding collateral, above market pricing, and maturity should remain in place. With such policies in place, normal discount window funding would likely be used infrequently.

In addition, the Federal Reserve should have the ability to undertake market stability discount window lending. Such lending would expand the Federal Reserve's lender of last resort function to include non-FIDIs. A sufficiently high threshold for invoking market stability discount window lending (i.e., overall threat to financial system stability) should be established. Market stability discount window lending should be focused wherever possible on broad types of institutions as opposed to individual institutions. In addition, market stability discount window lending would have to be supported by Federal Reserve authority to collect information from and conduct examinations of borrowing firms in order to protect the Federal Reserve (and thereby the taxpayer).

Prudential Financial Regulator

The optimal structure should establish a new prudential financial regulator, PFRA. PFRA should focus on financial institutions with some type of explicit government guarantees associated with their business operations. Most prominent examples of this type of government guarantee in the United States would include federal deposit insurance and state-established insurance guarantee funds. Although protecting consumers and helping to maintain confidence in the financial system, explicit government guarantees often erode market discipline, creating the potential for moral hazard and a clear need for prudential regulation. Prudential regulation in this context should be applied to individual firms, and it should operate like the current regulation of insured depository institutions, with capital adequacy requirements, investment limits, activity limits, and direct on-site risk management supervision. PFRA would assume the roles of current federal prudential regulators, such as the OCC and the OTS.

A number of key long-term issues should be considered in establishing the new prudential regulatory framework. First, the optimal structure should establish a new FIDI charter. The FIDI charter would consolidate the national bank, federal savings association, and federal credit union charters and should be available to all corporate forms, including stock, mutual, and cooperative ownership structures. A FIDI charter should provide field preemption over state laws to reflect the national nature of financial services. In addition, to obtain federal deposit insurance a financial institution would have to obtain a FIDI charter. PFRA's prudential regulation and oversight should accompany the provision of federal deposit insurance. The goal of establishing a FIDI charter is to create a level playing field among all types of depository institutions where competition can take place on an economic basis rather than on the basis of regulatory differences.

Activity limits should be imposed on FIDIs to serve the traditional prudential function of limiting risk to the deposit insurance fund. A starting place could be the activities that are currently permissible for national banks.

PFRA's regulation regarding affiliates should be based primarily at the individual FIDI level. Extending PFRA's direct oversight authority to the holding company should be limited as long as PFRA has an appropriate set of tools to protect a FIDI from affiliate relationships. At a minimum, PFRA should be provided the same set of tools that exists today at the individual bank level to protect a FIDI from potential risks associated with affiliate relationships. In addition, consideration should be given to strengthen further PFRA's authority in terms of limiting transactions with affiliates or requiring financial support from affiliates. PFRA should be able to monitor and examine the holding company and the FIDI's affiliates in order to ensure the effective implementation of these protections. With these added protections in place, from the perspective of protecting a FIDI, activity restrictions on affiliate relationships are much less important.

Holding company regulation was designed to protect the assets of the insured depository institution and to prevent the affiliate structure from threatening the assets of the insured institution. However, some market participants view holding company supervision as intended to protect non-bank entities within a holding company structure. In the optimal structure, PFRA will focus on the original intent of holding company supervision, protecting the assets of the insured depository institution; and a new market stability regulator will focus on broader systemic risk issues.

Second, to address the inefficiencies in the state-based insurance regulatory system, the optimal structure should establish a new FII charter. Similar to the FIDI charter, a FII charter should apply to insurers offering retail products where some type of government guarantee is present. In terms of a government guarantee, in the long run a uniform and consistent federally established guarantee structure, the Federal Insurance Guarantee Fund ("FIGF"), could accompany a system of federal oversight, although the existing state-level guarantee system could remain in place. PFRA would be responsible for the financial regulation of FIIs under the same structure as FIDIs.

Finally, some consideration should focus on including GSEs within the traditional prudential regulatory framework. Given the market misperception that the federal government stands behind the GSEs' obligations, one implication of the optimal structure is that PFRA should not regulate the GSEs. Nonetheless, given that the federal government has charged the GSEs with a specific mission, some type of prudential regulation would be necessary to ensure that they can accomplish that mission. To address these challenging issues, in the near term, a separate regulator should conduct prudential oversight of the GSEs and the market stability regulator should have the same ability to evaluate the GSEs as it has for other federally chartered institutions.

Business Conduct Regulator

The optimal structure should establish a new business conduct regulator, CBRA. CBRA should monitor business conduct regulation across all types of financial firms, including FIIs, FIDIs, and FFSPs. Business conduct regulation in this context includes key aspects of consumer protection such as disclosures, business practices, and chartering and licensing of certain types of financial firms. One agency responsible for all financial products should bring greater consistency to areas of business conduct regulation where overlapping requirements currently exist. The business conduct regulator's chartering and licensing function should be different than the prudential regulator's financial oversight responsibilities. More specifically, the focus of the business conduct regulator should be on providing appropriate standards for firms to be able to enter the financial services industry and sell their products and services to customers.

A number of key long-term issues should be considered in establishing the new business conduct regulatory framework.

First, as part of CBRA's regulatory function, CBRA would be responsible for the chartering and licensing of a wide range of financial firms. To implement the chartering function, the optimal structure should establish a new FFSP charter for all financial services providers that are not FIDIs or FIIs. The FFSP charter should be flexible enough to incorporate a wide range of financial services providers, such as broker-dealers, hedge funds, private equity funds, venture capital funds, and mutual funds. The establishment of a FFSP charter would result in the creation of appropriate national standards, in terms of financial capacity, expertise, and other requirements, that must be satisfied to enter the business of providing financial services. For example, these standards would resemble the net capital requirements for broker-dealers for that type of FFSP charter. In addition to meeting appropriate financial requirements to obtain a FFSP charter, these firms would also have to remain in compliance with appropriate standards and provide regular updates on financial conditions to CBRA, the Federal Reserve, and the public as part of their standard public disclosures. CBRA would also oversee and regulate the business conduct of FIDIs and FIIs.

Second, the optimal structure should clearly specify the types of business conduct issues where CBRA would have oversight authority. In terms of FIDIs' banking and lending, CBRA should have oversight responsibilities in three broad categories: disclosure, sales and marketing practices (including laws and regulations addressing unfair and deceptive practices), and anti-discrimination laws. Similar to banking and lending, CBRA should have the authority to regulate FIIs' insurance business conduct issues associated with disclosures, business practices, and discrimination. CBRA's main areas of authority would include disclosure issues related to policy forms, unfair trade practices, and claims handling procedures.

In term of business conduct issues for FFSPs, such as securities and futures firms and their markets, CBRA's focus would include operational ability, professional conduct, testing and training, fraud and manipulation, and duties to customers (e.g., best execution and investor suitability).

Third, CBRA's responsibilities for business conduct regulation in the optimal structure would be very broad. CBRA's responsibilities would take the place of those of the Federal Reserve and other insured depository institution regulators, state insurance regulators, most aspects of the SEC's and the CFTC's responsibilities, and some aspect of the FTC's role.

Given the breadth and scope of CBRA's responsibilities, some aspect of self-regulation should form an important component of implementation. Given its significance and effectiveness in the futures and securities industry, the SRO model should be preserved. That model could be considered for other areas, or the structure could allow for certain modifications, such as maintaining rule writing authority with CRBA, while relying on an SRO model for compliance and enforcement.

Finally, the proper role of state authorities should be established in the optimal structure. CBRA would be responsible for setting national standards for a wide range of business conduct laws across all types of financial services providers. CBRA's national standards would apply to all financial services firms, whether federally or state-chartered. In addition, field preemption would be provided to FIDIs, FIIs, and FFSPs, preempting state business conduct laws directly relating to the provision of financial services.

In the optimal structure, states would still retain clear authority to enact laws and take enforcement actions against state-chartered financial service providers. In considering the future role of the states vis-à-vis federally chartered institutions, the optimal structure seeks to acknowledge the existing national market for financial products, while at the same time preserving an appropriate role for state authorities to respond to local conditions. Two options should be considered to accomplish that goal. First, state authorities could be given a formalized role in CBRA's rulemaking process as a means of utilizing their extensive local experience. Second, states could also play a role in monitoring compliance and enforcement.

Federal Insurance Guarantee Corporation

The FDIC should be reconstituted as the Federal Insurance Guarantee Corporation ("FIGC") to administer not only deposit insurance, but also the FIGF (if one is created and valid reasons to leave this at the state level exist as discussed in the report). The FIGC should function primarily as an insurer in the optimal structure. Much as the FDIC operates today, the FIGC would have the authority to set risk-based premiums, charge ex- post assessments, act as a receiver for failed FIDIs or FIIs, and maintain some back-up examination authority over those institutions. The FIGC will not possess any additional direct regulatory authority.

Corporate Finance Regulator

The corporate finance regulator should have responsibility for general issues related to corporate oversight in public securities markets. These responsibilities should include the SEC's current responsibilities over corporate disclosures, corporate governance, accounting oversight, and other similar issues. As discussed above, CBRA would assume the SEC's current business conduct regulatory and enforcement authority over financial institutions.

CONCLUSION

The United States has the strongest and most liquid capital markets in the world. This strength is due in no small part to the U.S. financial services industry regulatory structure, which promotes consumer protection and market stability. However, recent market developments have pressured this regulatory structure, revealing regulatory gaps and redundancies. These regulatory inefficiencies may serve to detract from U.S. capital markets competitiveness.

In order to ensure the United States maintains its preeminence in the global capital markets, Treasury sets forth the aforementioned recommendations to improve the regulatory structure governing financial institutions. Treasury has designed a path to move from the current functional regulatory approach to an objectives-based regulatory regime through a series of specific recommendations. The short-term recommendations focus on immediate reforms responding to the current events in the mortgage and credit markets. The intermediate recommendations focus on modernizing the current regulatory structure within the current functional system.

The short-term and intermediate recommendations will drive the evolution of the U.S. regulatory structure towards the optimal regulatory framework, an objectives-based regime directly linking the regulatory objectives of market stability regulation, prudential financial regulation, and business conduct regulation to the regulatory structure. Such a framework best promotes consumer protection and stable and innovative markets.

Chapter 2

INTRODUCTION

The mission of the Department of the Treasury ("Treasury") focuses on promoting economic growth and stability in the United States. Critical to this mission is a sound and competitive financial services industry grounded in robust consumer protection and stable and innovative markets.

Financial institutions play an essential role in the U.S. economy by providing a means for consumers and businesses to save for the future, to protect and hedge against risks, and to access funding for consumption or organize capital for new investment opportunities. A number of different types of financial institutions provide financial services in the United States: commercial banks and other insured depository institutions, insurers, companies engaged in futures and securities transactions, finance companies, and specialized companies established by the government. Together, these institutions and the markets in which they act underpin economic activity through the intermediation of funds between providers and users of capital.

This intermediation function is accomplished in a number of ways. For example, insured depository institutions provide a vehicle to allocate the savings of individuals. Similarly, securities companies facilitate the transfer of capital among all types of investors and investment opportunities. Insurers assist in the financial intermediation process by providing a means for individuals, companies, and other financial institutions to protect assets from various types of losses. Overall, financial institutions serve a vitally important function in the U.S. economy by allowing capital to seek out its most productive uses in an efficient matter. Given the economic significance of the U.S. financial services sector, Treasury considers the structure of its regulation worthy of examination and reexamination.

Treasury began this current study of regulatory structure after convening a conference on capital markets competitiveness in March 2007. Conference participants, including current and former policymakers and industry leaders, noted that while functioning well, the U.S. regulatory structure is not optimal for promoting a competitive financial services sector leading the world and supporting continued economic innovation at home and abroad. Following this conference, Treasury launched a major effort to collect views on how to improve the financial services regulatory structure.

Over the past forty years, a number of Administrations have presented important recommendations for financial services regulatory reforms.[3] Most previous studies have focused almost exclusively on the regulation of depository institutions as opposed to a broader scope of financial institutions. These studies served important functions, helping shape the legislative landscape in the wake of their release. For example, two reports, *Blueprint for Reform: The Report of the Task Group on Regulation of Financial Services* (1984) and *Modernizing the Financial System: Recommendations for Safer, More Competitive Banks* (1991), laid the foundation for many of the changes adopted in the Gramm-Leach-Bliley Act of 1999 ("GLB Act").

In addition to these prior studies, similar efforts abroad inform this Treasury report. For example, more than a decade ago, the United Kingdom ("U.K.") conducted an analysis of its financial services regulatory structure, and as a result made fundamental changes creating a tri-partite system composed of the central bank (i.e., Bank of England), the finance ministry (i.e., H.M. Treasury), and the national financial regulatory agency for all financial services (i.e., Financial Services Authority). Each institution has well-defined, complementary roles, and many have judged this structure as having enhanced the competitiveness of the U.K. economy.

Australia and the Netherlands adopted another regulatory approach, the "Twin Peaks" model, emphasizing regulation by objective: One financial regulatory agency is responsible for prudential regulation of relevant financial institutions, and a separate and distinct regulatory agency is responsible for business conduct and consumer protection issues. These international efforts reinforce the importance of revisiting the U.S. regulatory structure.

Market conditions today provide a pertinent backdrop for this report's release, reinforcing the direct relationship between strong consumer protection and market stability on the one hand and capital markets competitiveness on the other and highlighting the need for examining the U.S. regulatory structure.

Prompting this Treasury report is the recognition that the capital markets and the financial services industry have evolved significantly over the past decade. These developments, while providing benefits to both domestic and global economic growth, have also exposed the financial markets to new challenges.

Globalization of the capital markets is a significant development. Foreign economies are maturing into market-based economies, contributing to global economic growth and stability and providing a deep and liquid source of capital outside the United States. Unlike the United States, these markets often benefit from recently created or newly developing regulatory structures, more adaptive to the complexity and increasing pace of innovation. At the same time, the increasing interconnectedness of the global capital markets poses new challenges: an event in one jurisdiction may ripple through to other jurisdictions.

In addition, improvements in information technology and information flows have led to innovative, risk-diversifying, and often sophisticated financial products and trading strategies. However, the complexity intrinsic to some of these innovations may inhibit investors and other market participants from properly evaluating their risks. For instance, securitization allows the holders of the assets being securitized better risk management opportunities and a new source of capital funding; investors can purchase products with reduced transactions costs and at targeted risk levels. Yet, market participants may not fully understand the risks these products pose.

The growing institutionalization of the capital markets has provided markets with liquidity, pricing efficiency, and risk dispersion and has encouraged product innovation and complexity. At the same time, these institutions can employ significant degrees of leverage and more correlated trading strategies with the potential for broad market disruptions. Finally, the convergence of financial services providers and financial products has increased over the past decade. Financial intermediaries and trading platforms are converging. Financial products may have insurance, banking, securities, and futures components.

These developments are pressuring the U.S. regulatory structure, exposing regulatory gaps as well as redundancies, and compelling market participants to do business in other jurisdictions with more efficient regulation. The U.S. regulatory structure reflects a system, much of it created over seventy years ago, grappling to keep pace with market evolutions and, facing increasing difficulties, at times, in preventing and anticipating financial crises.[4]

Largely incompatible with these market developments is the current system of functional regulation, which maintains separate regulatory agencies across segregated functional lines of financial services, such as banking, insurance, securities, and futures. A functional approach to regulation exhibits several inadequacies, the most significant being the fact that no single regulator has all of the information and authority necessary to monitor systemic risk, or the potential that events associated with financial institutions may trigger broad dislocation or a series of defaults that affect the financial system so significantly that the real economy is adversely affected. In addition, the inability of any regulator to take coordinated action throughout the financial system makes it more difficult to address problems related to financial market stability.

Second, in the face of increasing convergence of financial services providers and their products, jurisdictional disputes arise between and among the functional regulators, often hindering the introduction of new products, slowing innovation, and compelling migration of financial services and products to more adaptive foreign markets. Examples of recent inter-agency disputes include: the prolonged process surrounding the development of U.S. Basel II capital rules, the characterization of a financial product as a futures or a security contract, and the scope of banks' insurance sales.

Finally, a functional system also results in duplication of certain common activities across regulators. While some degree of specialization might be important for the regulation of financial institutions, many aspects of financial regulation and consumer protection regulation have common themes. For example, although key measures of financial health have different terminology in banking and insurance (i.e., capital and surplus, respectively) they both serve a similar function of ensuring the financial strength and ability of financial institutions to meet their obligations. Similarly, while there are specific differences across institutions, the goal of most consumer protection regulation is to ensure consumers receive adequate information regarding the terms of financial transactions and industry complies with appropriate sales practices.

In this report, Treasury presents a series of "short-term" and "intermediate-term" recommendations that could immediately improve and reform the U.S. regulatory structure. The short-term recommendations focus on taking action now to improve regulatory coordination and oversight in the wake of recent events in the credit and mortgage markets. The intermediate recommendations focus on eliminating some of the duplication of the U.S. regulatory system, but more importantly try to modernize the regulatory structure applicable to certain sectors in the financial services industry (i.e., banking, insurance, securities, and futures) within the current framework.

Treasury also presents a conceptual model for an optimal regulatory structure. This structure, an objectives-based regulatory approach, with a distinct regulator focused on one of three objectives (i.e., market stability regulation, safety and soundness regulation associated with government guarantees, and business conduct regulation) can better react to the pace of market developments and encourage innovation and entrepreneurialism within a context of enhanced regulation. This model is intended to begin a discussion about rethinking the current regulatory structure and its goals. It is not intended to be viewed as altering regulatory authorities within the current regulatory framework. Treasury views the presentation of a tangible model for an optimal structure as essential to its mission to promote economic growth and stability and fully recognizes that this is a first step on a long path to reforming financial services regulation.

In preparing this report, Treasury requested public comment on a variety of issues relating to financial services regulation. In October 2007, Treasury published a request for public comment in the Federal Register on both general issues related to financial regulation as well as specific issues related to depository institutions, futures and securities markets, and insurance. The notice is attached hereto at Appendix A. The more than 200 responses received are publicly available.[5]

The amount and variety of comments are testimony to the importance and broad interest that these issues provoke. Investors, domestic and global financial institutions, trade associations, regulators, academics, and other market participants have provided comments. Submissions generally included thoughtful and detailed suggestions addressing both the issues raised by Treasury in the request and additional topics which the respondents believed merited attention. The wide variety of views also highlights the diversity of thought regarding financial regulation. The high quality of the comments engendered a healthy discussion among all those involved in the development of this report. Treasury reviewed every comment letter submitted for this study.

Chapter 3

HISTORY OF THE CURRENT REGULATORY FRAMEWORK

BROAD OVERVIEW OF THE U.S. FINANCIAL SERVICES SECTOR

Broadly speaking, the U.S. financial services sector provides four major types of financial services. Each of these services can be delivered by different types of financial services providers, and their financial products can and generally do include features from more than one type of financial service. It is also important to note that nonfinancial services firms also generally provide financial services, although in a manner that is incidental to the function of their non-financial business.

The first major type of financial service that is widely utilized is payment and liquidity products. While these products range from consumer checking accounts to large-value aggregate payment systems between major institutions, they all share the basic function of providing and pervasively dispersing funds throughout the economy so as to facilitate the many purchase and sale transactions within the economy. These payment and liquidity products generally are expected to accomplish their functions within a short period of time with a maximum duration of a few days, and to provide readily usable money to the intended recipient.

A second major form of financial services is the many types of credit products, all of which generally have in common the transfer of funds subject to repayment between two or more parties. Credit products are extremely diverse in nature, and are provided by a very wide array of financial services firms including but not limited to depository institutions, insurers, and securities firms. Credit products can be intended for end-users or be in the form of wholesale products intended for further distribution through financial intermediaries. Historically, credit products are closely related to payment products, given the fact that banknotes originated as a debt obligation issued by the monetary authority for which repayment, typically in specie, could be demanded. Credit products exist with a diversity of tenors, or periods for repayment, and while many exist in forms that are readily negotiable for sale to third-parties, others exist in forms that are only readily usable by the original parties to the indebtedness.

Investment products are a third major form of financial services product and exist to provide a hoped-for level of economic return for one party, while often providing a different purpose to the counterparty (e.g., additional of capital, an extension of credit, etc.). Investment products are provided by a variety of financial firms and are characterized by their readily negotiable nature and the functions that they perform. Investment products include a wide variety of securities, as well as certain banking products like time deposits, insurance company products, and investment products from other types of financial services.

Finally, the fourth major form of financial services are products that transfer financial risk. Examples of these include insurance products, futures products, some securities, as well as other types of financial services products. These products all serve to transfer financial risk between and among different parties and can be provided by a variety of different financial services firms, including insurers and futures firms. It is important to note that these products generally only transfer financial risks, with other forms of risk not transferred through this process.

DEPOSITORY INSTITUTION REGULATION AND HISTORY

Introduction

The depository institution regulatory system in the United States is complex and layered: a product of history and tradition rather than a product of any coherent institutional design. This regulatory system developed to ensure the financial soundness and safety of the regulated institutions and of the banking system as a whole, thus affording protections to depositors and to the public.

The basic license allowing depository institutions to operate is called a charter. Depository institutions can generally obtain charters at the federal or state level under the U.S. "dual banking system," which is a dual chartering system. Depending on their intended focus, depository institutions also possess some flexibility in selecting among several types of charters, including a basic commercial charter, a thrift charter, a credit union charter, or an industrial loan company charter ("ILC"). The existence of the dual federal and state chartering system and alternative charter types provides a depository institution some flexibility in selecting its primary regulator and the regulatory regime governing its operations.

At the federal level, five agencies simultaneously divide and share regulatory and examination authority:

- The Office of the Comptroller of the Currency ("OCC");
- The Board of Governors of the Federal Reserve System ("Federal Reserve");
- The Federal Deposit Insurance Corporation ("FDIC");
- The Office of Thrift Supervision ("OTS"); and
- The National Credit Union Administration ("NCUA").

The jurisdictional boundaries among these federal depository institution regulators often blur and their responsibilities significantly overlap, with the exception of the NCUA.

In this highly fragmented system, a complicated web of multiple federal and state banking and other statutes, as well as various agency regulations, govern depository institutions.

Overview of Key Developments and Legislation in the Regulation of Depository Institutions in a Historical Context

The history of depository institutions in the United States and their regulation is closely tied to the history of the nation as a whole. In addition to reflecting the United States' rich history and tradition of federalism, depository institution regulation reflects the competing priorities and personalities that shaped American history, rather than any overarching rationale in its design.

The early struggles between the first federally chartered banks and state-chartered banks were important to American history. The first Secretary of the Treasury, Alexander Hamilton, strove to establish a federally chartered bank, and that bank disappeared when Congress declined to renew its charter. President Andrew Jackson later attacked the second bank chartered by Congress and ultimately succeeded in eliminating the bank. While the federally chartered bank with its regional branches was the premier bank during portions of its existence in the early nineteenth century, hundreds of state- authorized or state-chartered banks also sprang up during this period. The states specifically chartered some of these banks, but many incorporated under state law without any special charter from the state legislature. As the second federally chartered bank approached its demise in the 1830s, these state-chartered banks flourished from 1829 to 1837. When these banks, often lacking even rudimentary internal governance or any form of governmental regulation, contributed to a financial panic in 1837, states like New York began to expand their banking oversight through more formal banking commissions and reserve requirements. The individual states remained the sole source of depository bank charters until the Civil War.

The National Bank Act of 1863 and the Creation of the "Dual Banking System"

The dual banking system emerged when Congress, seeking to finance its Civil War debt and ensure financial stability, passed the National Bank Act of 1863. This law created a federal bank charter and established the OCC as the office in charge of chartering and overseeing the newly created national banks. The national bank system, instrumental in the emergence of a single national currency, was expected to replace the state bank system. In 1866, Congress attempted to force state banks to convert to federal charters by imposing a punitive tax on bank notes issued by state-chartered banks, but the greater usage of checking accounts as payment instruments allowed state-chartered banks to continue to exist, although the loss of seigniorage income was significant.

The Federal Reserve Act of 1913

In the post-Civil War period, the national bank system suffered from periods of severe illiquidity, runs on deposits, and panics, the worst of which hit the U.S. economy in 1907. In response, Congress passed the Federal Reserve Act of 1913, which created the Federal Reserve System, and was designed to prevent bank runs and panics by providing liquidity support to commercial banks. In the early 1930s, during the Great Depression, Congress authorized the Federal Reserve to begin to formulate and implement national monetary policy. The Federal Reserve System is made up of the Board of Governors, the twelve regional Federal Reserve Banks, and the Federal Open Market Committee.

The Federal Reserve Act also gave the Federal Reserve regulatory and supervisory authority with respect to commercial banks that are members of the Federal Reserve System. Thus, this statute applied directly to both national banks and state member banks, although states continued to charter banks with all corporate powers granted by the state.

The Great Depression Legislation

Following a temporary contraction during World War I and post-war inflation, the U.S. economy rebounded in the 1920s, which led cash-rich U.S. banks to expand their lending and securities activities. However, after the stock market crash of 1929 and the subsequent Great Depression, massive bank failures prompted Congress to enact a series of legislative acts which strongly shaped the current U.S. depository institution regulatory system.

The key statute, focused on the commercial banks, was the Banking Act of 1933. Four sections of that statute, known as the Glass-Steagall Act, mandated the strict separation of commercial and investment banking. The Glass-Steagall Act generally prohibited national banks from directly underwriting and dealing in securities other than certain government debt securities, prohibited any entity engaged in investment banking from receiving deposits, and prohibited Federal Reserve member banks from affiliating or having interlocking management with any entity "engaged principally" in the securities business.

During this same period, Congress also took action in the mortgage finance arena by passing legislation designed to support and regulate the thrift (or savings and loan) industry, which focused principally on taking deposits and making residential mortgage loans. Up to that time, only states chartered and oversaw thrifts. The Federal Home Loan Bank Act of 1932 ("FHLB Act") created the Federal Home Loan Bank ("FHLB") System, twelve cooperatively owned regional banks that borrowed funds on behalf of state-chartered members and were overseen by the Federal Home Loan Bank Board ("FHLBB"). The following year, the Home Owners' Loan Act of 1933 ("HOLA") granted the FHLBB the authority to charter and regulate federal thrifts.

Congress also moved to establish a federal charter for credit unions, passing the Federal Credit Union Act in 1934, making it possible to charter a credit union anywhere in the United States. Credit unions, a relatively recent development, first appeared in the United States in the early 1900s as state-chartered entities; unique in that they were required to focus on depositors (called "members") in a certain group or geography, and to be cooperatively owned by those depositors.

In both the commercial banking and thrift arenas, Congress created systems of deposit insurance, overseen by separate regulators to ensure that banks and thrifts participating in their respective deposit insurance systems met certain minimum standards for institutional safety and soundness. The Banking Act of 1933 created the FDIC to regulate participants in the commercial bank deposit insurance system, while the National Housing Act of 1934 created the Federal Savings and Loan Insurance Corporation ("FSLIC") to regulate participants in the thrift deposit insurance system. The creation of these deposit insurers further complicated the division of responsibilities among the federal bank regulators.

The Bank Holding Company Act of 1956 and Savings and Loan Holding Company Act of 1967

Although prohibiting affiliations between commercial and investment banks, the Glass-Steagall Act did not explicitly prohibit affiliations between banks and other types of commercial entities. As a result, many non-financial companies began acquiring commercial banks under a holding company structure.

Congress responded by enacting the Bank Holding Company Act of 1956 ("BHC Act"), explicitly prohibiting bank holding companies ("BHCs") controlling multiple U.S. commercial banks from engaging in activities other than banking, managing banks, or activities "closely related" to banking through affiliates. The BHC Act also prohibited BHCs from making interstate bank acquisitions unless authorized by state law, and gave the Federal Reserve the power to regulate and supervise all BHCs. Amendments to the BHC Act in 1970 extended regulation to one-bank holding companies and prohibited commercial banks from "tying" their products or services to other products or services offered by their non-bank affiliates.

When concerns emerged regarding the thrifts' enjoyment of competitive advantages in comparison with commercial banks due to these BHC Act requirements, Congress responded by enacting the similar Savings and Loan Holding Company ("SLHC") Act of 1967 ("SLHC Act"). The SLHC Act gave similar authority to monitor holding companies' non-depository institution-related businesses. Unlike BHCs, however, SLHCs owning only one thrift were subject to less extensive regulation, including fewer restrictions on commercial activities.

The Savings and Loan Crisis and Related Legislation

In the 1970s and 1980s, a combination of macroeconomic conditions and de-regulation contributed to significant losses at thrifts across the United States and resulted in a significant new round of reform legislation.

In the Banking Acts of 1933 and 1935, Congress granted the Federal Reserve the authority to place deposit-rate ceilings on banks.[6] Deposit rate ceilings were also imposed upon thrift institutions in the 1960s. The deposit-rate ceiling acted as a price ceiling on deposits and the advent of money market mutual funds afforded current and prospective depositors other avenues to save and invest their funds.

This situation was one of the key factors resulting in the passage of the Depository Institutions Deregulation and Monetary Control Act of 1980, which eased the deposit-rate ceilings imposed upon banks and thrifts.[7] With deposit rates deregulated and floating, thrifts needed to generate greater return on newly acquired assets in order to remain profitable and retain and attract depositors.

In response, Congress passed the Garn-St Germain Depository Institutions Act of 1982 ("Garn-St Germain Act"). This legislation removed certain business and investment restrictions imposed on thrifts, permitting them to invest some funds in commercial real estate and other riskier assets. The unintended consequence was that many thrifts began to invest aggressively in shopping malls, office buildings, and even more speculative investments like junk bonds, windmill farms, and oil operations. Fraud and insider abuses only contributed to an already unstable situation. By the end of the 1980s, a combination of unsound investments and poor oversight contributed to the failure of hundreds of thrifts, ultimately leading to a U.S. government bailout at a cost of $160 billion.

As a response to the large number of thrift failures and the attendant high cost to the government, Congress enacted two key pieces of legislation. The Financial Institutions Reform, Recovery, and Enforcement Act of 1989 ("FIRREA") terminated the FSLIC and the FHLBB and created the OTS. The OTS was modeled after the OCC and designated as an office within the Department of the Treasury ("Treasury"). FIRREA gave the OTS authority to charter federal thrifts and to regulate federal and most state-chartered thrifts and their holding companies. FIRREA also created a fund within the FDIC to replace the FSLIC fund and established the Federal Housing Finance Board to regulate the Federal Home Loan Bank System. FIRREA importantly also established the Resolution Trust Corporation ("RTC") to manage failed bank and thrift assets. As the crisis came to an end, the RTC was transferred to the Savings Association Insurance Fund in 1995.

In 1991, Congress took a further step to address the perceived problems of lax regulatory oversight during the thrift crisis by passing the Federal Deposit Insurance Corporation Improvement Act ("FDICIA"). FDICIA established a system of capital-based prompt corrective action ("PCA"), which eliminated various discretionary powers granted to regulators and instead imposed requirements on regulators to act upon regulated institutions' failure to meet certain prescribed tests. FDICIA required regulators to create capitalization categories and risk-based capital measures. Additionally, FDICIA mandated a system of least cost resolution for failed banks and thrifts.

In 1994, Congress passed the Riegle-Neal Interstate Banking and Branching Efficiency Act ("Riegle -Neal Act"), repealing the prohibitions on interstate bank and branch acquisitions, thereby providing banks more of the advantages already enjoyed by thrifts.

The Gramm-Leach-Bliley Act of 1999

The strict separations of commercial and investment banking, and of banking and commerce, embodied primarily in the activity restrictions under the Glass-Steagall Act and the BHC Act, fostered intense policy debate and criticism for decades. The GrammLeach-Bliley Act of 1999 ("GLB Act") relaxed the activity restrictions for commercial banking organizations. The GLB Act repealed the Glass-Steagall Act's prohibitions on certain affiliations and management interlocks between banks and securities firms, and significantly expanded the permissible activities of BHCs by establishing a financial holding company ("FHC") structure, allowing qualifying institutions to participate in commercial banking, full-scale securities underwriting and dealing, insurance underwriting, and merchant banking all under one holding company.

To facilitate the continuing evolution of the financial services industry, the GLB Act authorized FHCs to engage in activities that the Federal Reserve, in consultation with Treasury, determines to be "financial in nature" or "incidental" to a financial activity, as well as activities that the Federal Reserve determines to be "complementary" to a financial activity. The GLB Act provided similar authority to banks' qualifying "financial subsidiaries" but prohibited certain principal activities. The GLB Act provided that the Federal Reserve would regulate FHCs; however, a primary financial regulator would functionally regulate each of the financial affiliates, whether insurance, futures, or securities.

At the same time, the GLB Act furthered the convergence between commercial banks and thrifts by eliminating the ability of non-grandfathered SLHCs owning a single thrift institution to avoid SLHC regulation and affiliate with commercial entities.

Key Types of Depository Institution Charters, Overlap in Business Activities, and Industry Structure

Commercial Banks

A commercial bank charter, the charter most familiar to the public, allows a depository institution to participate across a broad range of banking and financial activities. Establishing a federally chartered "national" bank requires filing an application with the only federal bank chartering authority, the OCC, which conducts a thorough review of each application and grants a charter upon compliance with all statutory and regulatory criteria. Each state has similar statutory requirements for chartering banks, including an application, a review process, and decision-making standards.

The OCC regulates and examines national banks as the primary regulator. In addition, all national banks must obtain federal deposit insurance, which subjects them to examination by the FDIC in all aspects concerning their status as federally insured banks. National banks also are required to become members of the Federal Reserve System.

For state-chartered banks, membership in the Federal Reserve System, which allows them to access the Federal Reserve System's payments and liquidity facilities, is optional. State-chartered banks choosing the Federal Reserve System (i.e., "state member banks") become subject to regulation and examination by the Federal Reserve as their primary federal regulator and must obtain federal deposit insurance.

As a general matter, any commercial bank that seeks to accept retail deposits (i.e., deposits in an amount less than $100,000) must obtain federal deposit insurance before commencing such deposit-taking activities. State-chartered banks, regardless of their Federal Reserve System membership status, all have federally insured deposits and, therefore, are subject to FDIC examination. In addition, the FDIC is the primary federal regulator for the insured state-chartered banks that are not members of the Federal Reserve System (i.e., "state non-member banks").

Bank Holding Companies and Financial Holding Companies

The BHC Act defines BHCs as entities owning or controlling one or more U.S. commercial banks. Although the definition of "control" for purposes of determining whether an entity is a BHC is very complicated and fact-dependent, as a general matter, the most common form of control is ownership of 25 percent or more of any class of voting shares of a U.S. bank or company. All BHCs must register with the Federal Reserve and are subject to extensive regulation and examination by the Federal Reserve, which administers the key statute governing BHCs' formation and activities, the BHC Act. The

BHC Act effectively prohibits BHCs from conducting any business activities other than banking, controlling or managing banks, and activities "closely related" to banking.

FHCs are formed when a BHC satisfies certain capital and management criteria and files the requisite election with the Federal Reserve. As discussed above, the GLB Act amended the BHC Act to permit FHCs to engage in a wider range of activities that are "financial in nature," including insurance, securities underwriting and dealing, and merchant banking. Being a subset of BHCs, all FHCs remain subject to the Federal Reserve's regulation and examination.

Thrifts

Historically, thrifts (or savings and loans) are depository institutions focused on providing mortgage lending to residential customers. Legislation in the 1930s established a federal charter, a federal regulator, and a liquidity facility for thrifts, which were originally chartered and regulated by the states. Congress also established a thrift insurance fund similar to that of banks. After concluding that lax federal and state oversight had contributed to the savings and loan crisis of the 1980s, Congress replaced the then-existing thrift regulator with the OTS, housed within Treasury. Congress also moved the thrift insurance fund into the FDIC.

Over the years, thrifts began to expand the focus of their activities, though they maintained a significant housing focus. To address this trend, Congress established the qualified thrift lender ("QTL") test in the Competitive Equality Banking Act of 1987 ("CEBA"), in order to keep the thrift industry focused on the provision of residential mortgage loans to U.S. consumers. Qualifying as a QTL, which became a requirement to maintain many of the benefits special to thrifts, required that at least 65 percent of an institution's portfolio assets be qualified thrift investments, primarily residential mortgages and related investments.

Credit Unions

Credit unions, tax-exempt financial institutions owned by their depositors, typically focus on a range of services offered by commercial banks, but generally in a more limited scope. Credit unions usually offer savings and checking accounts, online banking, and credit cards to depositors. As a general rule, credit unions may accept as depositors only those individuals identified in a credit union's articulated field of membership, such as working in the same profession or living in the same community.

A number of rules, generally more restrictive than those applicable to other types of depository institutions, govern credit unions. Rules may limit the amount of interest that a credit union can charge on a loan and the length of time that a loan may extend, cap the share of lending that can go to commercial borrowers, with certain exceptions, and restrict fund investment, causing them to focus principally on government and agency securities or other highly secure instruments.

Industrial Loan Companies

Industrial Loan Companies ("ILCs") are financial institutions that can be owned by commercial firms. ILCs operate much like commercial banks except that they can avoid BHC regulation, and the commerce-banking barrier, by one of three ways: having less than $100 million in total assets, not accepting demand deposits, or not having changed control since 1987.

Although not BHCs, ILCs are FDIC insured and supervised. ILCs also must abide by the Federal Reserve Act's requirements limiting bank transactions with affiliates. In addition to FDIC oversight, ILCs are subject to home state regulatory supervision. Utah, California, and Nevada charter most ILCs.

While originally taking the form of consumer finance companies without deposit taking authority, today ILCs generally have the same powers as state commercial banks due to chartering states' expanding ILCs' powers.

Federal Regulatory Agencies with Oversight of Depository Institutions

Five federal regulatory agencies oversee depository institutions with frequently overlapping responsibilities and jurisdictional boundaries: the OCC, the OTS, the Federal Reserve, the FDIC, and the NCUA. Congress created each of these agencies in response to a significant event in the nation's financial history. Not dependent on federal appropriations for funding, these agencies finance their operations through fees and assessments on their regulated entities, deposit insurance premiums paid to the FDIC, and the Federal Reserve's open market operations and seigniorage income.

Office of the Comptroller of the Currency
The National Bank Act of 1863, authorizing the creation of the national bank system, established the OCC as the oldest federal banking agency. The OCC, an office located within Treasury, charters, regulates, and examines all national banks and federally licensed branches and agencies of non-U.S. banks. The Comptroller of the Currency, appointed by the President for a five-year term, subject to Senate confirmation, heads the OCC.

As the chartering agency, the OCC has regulatory and examination responsibility over national banks and promulgates rules, legal interpretations, and corporate decisions concerning bank applications, activities, investments, community development activities, and other aspects of national bank operations. The OCC's bank examiners conduct on- site examinations of national banks and examine bank operations. With broad enforcement powers, the OCC may take various actions against national banks that fail to comply with laws and regulations or otherwise engage in unsound banking practices, remove officers and directors of such banks, negotiate agreements to change banking practices, issue cease and desist orders, and impose monetary fines.

Office of Thrift Supervision
The OTS, a relatively recent creation, plays a role for federally chartered thrifts similar to that of the OCC for national banks. Under HOLA, the OTS charters federal thrifts and regulates and examines federal and state thrifts (except FDIC-supervised state savings banks) and their holding companies. The OTS, like the OCC, is an independent office within Treasury but is subject to the general oversight of the Secretary of the

Treasury. The President appoints the Director of the OTS for a five-year term, subject to Senate confirmation.

As the primary regulator of thrifts, the OTS issues rules, legal interpretations, and corporate decisions concerning nearly all aspects of thrift operations. Like the OCC, by statute the OTS possesses the authority to establish uniform rules preempting state laws and regulations.

Federal Reserve

The Federal Reserve System, the independent U.S. central bank, consists of twelve regional statutorily established Federal Reserve Banks, each of which effectively performs functions of a central bank for its geographic region. The Board of Governors, located in Washington and composed of seven members appointed by the President to fourteen year terms and confirmed by the Senate, oversees the Federal Reserve System.

The Federal Reserve has the principal responsibility for formulating and executing national monetary and credit policy, fulfilled primarily through its open market operations, reserve requirements for depository institutions, and discount window lending program.

In addition to conducting monetary and credit policy, the Federal Reserve has significant bank regulatory and examination responsibilities. Most importantly, the Federal Reserve functions as the primary federal regulator of state member banks, the regulator of BHCs, the regulator and supervisor of the U.S. operations of foreign banks, and the regulator of foreign activities of member banks.

Federal Deposit Insurance Corporation

The FDIC administers the federal deposit insurance system under the Federal Deposit Insurance Act ("FDIA"). A five-member Board of Directors heads the FDIC: the President appoints three members, including the chair, for six-year terms, subject to Senate confirmation, and the other two members are the Comptroller of the Currency and the Director of OTS.

The FDIC insures deposits up to $100,000 per depositor per depository institution, with a separate coverage for retirement accounts up to $250,000. The agency monitors risks to the deposit insurance fund and possesses a wide range of enforcement powers with respect to insured institutions, including the right to terminate insurance coverage of any institution engaged in unsafe or unsound practices.

The FDIC has backup regulatory and examination authority over all depositary institutions that it insures, and serves as the primary federal regulator of insured state non-member banks and state savings banks. In addition, the FDIC plays a key role in administering the process of resolution of failed institutions and, as a practical matter, serves as the receiver or conservator for all FDIC-insured depository institutions. Initially limited in its focus to commercial banks, with the transfer of the Savings Association Insurance Fund to the FDIC, the FDIC in the 1980s was given backup examination authority over thrifts (in addition to ILCs).

National Credit Union Administration

The NCUA, an independent agency created in 1970, charters and supervises federal credit unions and insures savings in federal and most state-chartered credit unions across the country through the National Credit Union Share Insurance Fund. The President appoints the Chair and two other members of the board for a six-year term, subject to Senate confirmation.

The Regulatory Process

System of Controls and Regulations

The main principles and tools of federal depository institution regulation and examination may be grouped broadly around the key public policies underlying the system in general: protecting financial stability, ensuring the safety and soundness of federally insured depository institutions, maintaining an efficient and competitive financial system, and protecting consumers. These principles and tools frequently overlap, as many regulatory provisions are designed to serve more than one policy objective.

For instance, some of the most important regulatory principles serving the goal of an efficient and competitive banking system include limitations on banks' insider lending practices, oversight of business reorganizations and changes in control of banks, restrictions on banks' ability to "tie" their services to non-banking products, and nationwide deposit caps. These provisions aim at ensuring wide availability of credit by preventing banks from abusing their substantial economic power.

Consumer Protections

The Federal Reserve possesses general consumer protection authority over depository institutions at the federal level, with individual agency authority in some cases. The primary federal regulator and the states oversee enforcement.

To protect consumers, Congress over the years has enacted several important statutes applicable to all lenders:

- The Truth in Lending Act ("TILA"), which requires that credit terms for both credit card and mortgage transactions be disclosed in a meaningful way so consumers can compare credit terms more readily and knowledgeably.
- The Home Ownership and Equity Protection Act ("HOEPA"), which amended TILA to prohibit unfair or deceptive acts for mortgage lending.
- The Federal Trade Commission Act ("FTC Act"), which prohibits unfair and deceptive acts or practices affecting commerce.
- The Equal Credit Opportunity Act, which prohibits unlawful discrimination in any aspect of a credit transaction.
- The Real Estate Settlement Procedures Act, which governs information disclosures for the home-buying process.

Federal banking regulators also ensure that banks and thrifts comply with other statutes relating to privacy, fair housing, community reinvestment, credit reporting, electronic funds transfers, and saving account disclosures. This system of various statutory and regulatory provisions requiring banks to provide full and timely disclosure of material terms of consumer banking products and to protect the security and privacy of consumers' personal information primarily achieves the policy goal of consumer protection.

The Federal Reserve has sole authority to write regulations implementing TILA and HOEPA. These rules issued by the Federal Reserve apply to all mortgage lenders but are enforced by the various bank regulators depending on the type of depository institution. In addition, the FTC Act provides sole rulemaking authority to the Federal Reserve for banks regarding unfair or deceptive acts or practices, while giving the OTS and the NCUA rulemaking authority for thrifts and credit unions, respectively. On the other hand, the GLB Act's privacy provisions authorize each of the federal banking agencies to write rules for its supervised entities, although each of the agencies must "consult and coordinate" with one another. The GLB Act's insurance customer protection provisions require the federal banking agencies to determine jointly appropriate regulations.

Coordination

Numerous formal and informal mechanisms facilitate coordination among the federal depository institution regulators and between federal and state regulators. Among them are the Federal Financial Institutions Examination Council ("FFIEC"), the streamlined supervision provisions of the GLB Act, agreements between federal and state examiners, and the President's Working Group on Financial Markets ("PWG").

Congress established the FFIEC in 1978 to formalize an interagency coordinating committee created by the agencies during the mid-1970s. The FFIEC, comprising the OCC, the Federal Reserve, the FDIC, the OTS, the NCUA, and the Conference of State Bank Supervisors, works to establish uniform principles and standards and report forms for depository institution examinations. States participate in the FFIEC through a five- member Liaison Committee.

The GLB Act codified the concept of functional regulation of depository institutions, securities firms, futures firms, and insurers. To minimize duplication and promote coordination, the GLB Act streamlines the Federal Reserve's supervisory authority over functionally regulated affiliates of BHCs. For example, the Federal Reserve must defer to functional regulators' examinations to the fullest extent possible. The GLB Act expressly encourages information sharing between the Federal Reserve and state insurance regulators, and between federal depository institution regulators and state insurance regulators.

Established in 1988 by Executive Order to address the October 1987 stock market decline, the PWG serves to enhance the integrity, efficiency, orderliness, and competitiveness of U.S. financial markets and to maintain investor protections against fraud, manipulation, and other abuses. The PWG is chaired by the Secretary of the Treasury and includes the heads of the Federal Reserve, the Commodity Futures Trading Commission ("CFTC"), and the Securities and Exchange Commission ("SEC"). Other federal financial supervisors such as the OCC and Federal Reserve Bank of New York are included in discussions as appropriate. The PWG serves as a forum to discuss and coordinate public policy issues but has no regulatory or examination authority.

FUTURES REGULATION AND HISTORY

Introduction

Federal and industry regulators carry out the regulation of futures markets in the United States under the Commodity Exchange Act ("CEA"). In general, states do not have authority to regulate futures markets. The fundamental aims of futures market regulation resemble those of securities regulation: to help protect market users and the public from fraud and manipulation and to ensure fair and orderly markets.

Although undefined in statute, a "future" or "futures contract" generally refers to a highly standardized agreement between two parties to buy and sell a specific asset at a specified price before or upon some set future date. The first futures contracts focused on agricultural commodities. Today, futures contracts involve a vast array of assets, including agricultural products (except onions), financial instruments and indexes, energy products, and metals.

Background – Futures Regulation before the Commodity Exchange Act

The organized trading of futures on agricultural commodities in the United States dates back to the middle of the nineteenth century. In 1848, a group of commodities merchants, who began to trade so-called "to arrive" contracts, formally established the Chicago Board of Trade. As in the case of the securities markets, self-regulation of the futures markets preceded federal regulation. The first significant federal law to regulate futures was the Future Trading Act of 1921 ("Future Trading Act"), but the following year the U.S. Supreme Court determined the law to be unconstitutional because of its improper taxing of futures not traded on designated contract markets (i.e., those traded off-exchange). Later, in 1922, Congress enacted the Grain Futures Act, which, rather than taxing off-exchange trading of futures contracts, invoked the interstate commerce clause to ban such transactions. The U.S. Supreme Court later upheld the Grain Futures Act as constitutional.

The Future Trading Act and the Grain Futures Act established certain precedents in the regulation of futures markets persisting to this day. Among the most important are the notions that the regulator should be empowered to designate exchanges or boards of trade that meet certain requirements as "contract markets" (i.e., officially recognized trading venues for futures contracts) and that off-exchange trading of futures is illegal. Today, the basic premise remains that the trading of futures contracts, whenever intermediaries are involved, must be conducted on designated contract markets. However, recent amendments to the CEA, the statute that today governs commodity and futures markets, have significantly relaxed some trading restrictions.

Also, given that the first futures contracts involved agricultural commodities (the Future Trading Act and the Grain Futures Act specifically authorized futures only on selected grains), the Department of Agriculture ("USDA") possessed initial federal jurisdiction over futures markets. The Secretary of Agriculture oversaw futures regulation until 1975[8].

Although the USDA no longer has authority over futures markets (and although the bulk of modern futures trading is in non-agricultural assets), an agricultural tie remains through the Senate and House Agriculture Committees' oversight of the CFTC, the federal agency overseeing futures regulation.

The Commodity Exchange Act and the Commodity Futures Trading Commission

Origin and Early Developments

Replacing the precursor Grain Futures Act, the CEA in 1936 broadened the types of commodities on which futures contracts could trade. Apart from the grains already permitted, the CEA expanded the list of enumerated commodities to include cotton, rice, butter, eggs, and Irish potatoes. The transactions still had to take place on an organized exchange. Over the ensuing three decades, numerous amendments to the CEA continued to add more and more covered commodities to the list. In addition, the Commodity Exchange Authority, the predecessor agency of the CFTC, gradually acquired or exercised additional regulatory powers, including the ability to investigative and enforce authorities, and the ability to set minimum financial standards for futures commission merchants.

Landmark reform of the CEA arrived with the enactment of the Commodity Futures Trading Commission Act of 1974 ("CFTC Act"). First, the CFTC Act moved the authority over the futures markets from the Secretary of Agriculture to a newly created independent federal agency, the CFTC. In addition to transferring to the CFTC the powers of its predecessor agency, Congress conferred upon the CFTC exclusive jurisdiction over "contracts for the sale of a commodity for future delivery" and options on such contracts. The CFTC's exclusive jurisdiction for all assets, not just with respect to enumerated agricultural commodities, remains in place today. In addition, the CFTC Act authorized the creation of national futures associations, or self-regulatory organizations ("SROs"), for the futures industry.

In 1975, the CFTC, with its new authority over futures markets, approved the first futures contracts on financial assets, including the Chicago Board of Trade's futures contract on Government National Mortgage Association certificates, and the Chicago Mercantile Exchange's futures contract on 90-day U.S. Treasury bills. In the years ahead, the growth of financial futures and other financial derivatives, coupled with the increasingly complicated issue of what exactly a future is, would test the limits of the CFTC's exclusive jurisdiction.

In particular, the emergence of innovative financial instruments such as swaps, stock-index futures, and other derivative instruments, some of which were traded off-exchange, began to introduce uncertainty as to where the line between futures regulation and securities regulation should be drawn. In 1981, for example, the CFTC and the SEC negotiated an agreement that divided jurisdiction and regulatory responsibility over stock index futures among the two agencies. This jurisdictional agreement, known as the Shad-Johnson Accord, was later codified in the Futures Trading Act of 1982, and resulted in a statutory ban on single-stock futures and narrow-based stock index futures that lasted almost 20 years. Subsequently, the CFTC in 1989 issued a policy statement concerning swaps in which it identified certain transactions that it would decline to regulate as futures or futures options. Also, the Futures Trading Practices Act of 1992 provided the CFTC the authority to exempt certain off-exchange, or over-the-counter ("OTC") transactions, from most provisions of the CEA. The following year, the CFTC began using this new authority to exempt certain swap agreements, hybrid instruments, and certain OTC energy contracts.

None of these statutory amendments or CFTC actions, however, addressed the fundamental question of whether or not swaps and other derivative instruments were indeed futures contracts or futures options. Lacking such clarification, and coupled with the CEA's exchange-trading requirement and the CFTC's exclusive jurisdiction, the legal uncertainty in the area of financial derivatives continued to swell. In 1998, following a legislative moratorium preventing the CFTC from taking additional regulatory action in the area of OTC derivatives, Congress asked the President's Working Group on Financial Markets ("PWG") to conduct a study of OTC derivatives markets and to develop legislative recommendations. In 1999 the PWG issued its report, *Over-the-Counter Derivatives Markets and the Commodity Exchange Act* ("1999 PWG Report"), and the unanimous recommendations advanced in that report became the basis for some of the most significant reforms to the derivatives markets since the CFTC's creation.

The Commodity Futures Modernization Act of 2000

The Commodity Futures Modernization Act of 2000 ("CFMA"), amending the CEA, took as its starting point the recommendations in the 1999 PWG Report on OTC derivatives. Most fundamentally, the PWG had concluded that the trading of OTC financial derivatives between certain sophisticated counterparties (which mainly includes regulated financial institutions, state and local governments, and certain businesses, pension funds, high net worth individuals, and other institutions) should largely be excluded, as opposed to exempted, from the CEA. The primary justifications for recommending exclusion for such transactions were a determination that most OTC financial derivatives (e.g., interest rate swaps) were not susceptible to manipulation and that the counterparties in such transactions did not need the same protections as smaller, unsophisticated market participants who relied on intermediaries to conduct their transactions.

The CFMA excluded a broad range of transactions from most provisions of the CEA, thereby providing much needed legal certainty for the burgeoning OTC derivatives markets. In general, the exclusions provided by the CFMA depended, as did the PWG recommendations, upon the types of assets being traded, the sophistication of the counterparties, and where and how the transactions were executed. The CFMA created several new definitions to facilitate the exclusions:

- Excluded commodity: generally includes financial assets such as securities and currencies, interest rates, exchange rates, economic measures or indexes of risk, return, or value, and contingencies beyond the control of the parties.
- Eligible contract participant: the main type of sophisticated investor that includes financial institutions, registered market professionals (e.g., broker-dealers and futures commission merchants), other institutional investors, and certain high net worth individuals.
- Eligible commercial entity: a certain eligible contract participant (as defined above) that deals in one or more commodities as part of their business.

- Trading facility: a catch-all term for either a physical or electronic facility where multiple participants are able to trade with each other through mutually available bids and offers.

Thus the CFMA excluded from most provisions of the CEA, including the antifraud provisions, the following:

- Agreements, contracts, and transactions in excluded commodities
  o between eligible contract participants that are not executed on a trading facility; or
  o between eligible contract participants, on a principal-to-principal basis, and executed on an electronic trading facility.
- Agreements, contracts, and transactions in assets, other than agricultural commodities, between eligible contract participants are subject to individual negotiation by the parties and are not executed on a trading facility.

In addition, the CFMA excluded transactions in hybrid instruments that are (as determined by a "predominance test") chiefly securities, and electronic trading facilities that limit trading to certain types of transactions that are otherwise excluded.

However, the CFMA went further than (and actually contradicted) the PWG recommendations in this area by exempting certain transactions in exempt commodities. The CFMA also defined exempt commodities to mean a commodity that is not an excluded commodity or an agricultural commodity. In practice, exempt commodities include mainly metals and energy products. Under the CFMA, agreements, contracts, and transactions in exempt commodities are exempt from most provisions of the CEA (but not including the antifraud provisions or other powers of the CFTC) if they are between eligible contract participants and not executed on a trading facility or if they are between eligible commercial entities on a principal-to-principal basis and traded on an electronic trading facility.

In addition to addressing swap transactions, the CFMA also included several other important aspects:

- It clarified the CFTC's jurisdiction over certain retail foreign currency transactions.
- It repealed the eighteen year-old Shad-Johnson ban on single-stock futures and other security future products and implemented a system of "coordinated regulation" for such products.
- It provided legal certainty that products offered by banks would not be regulated as futures contracts.

The CFMA also codified a regulatory relief proposal developed by the CFTC. In early 2000, the CFTC proposed a "New Regulatory Framework" in an effort to modernize the regulatory structure of the U.S. futures markets. In November 2000, the CFTC approved rules implementing this framework, but the CFMA superseded this action and the rules were withdrawn. In large part, the CFMA borrowed from the CFTC's framework and created a three-tiered structure for the trading of derivatives that distinguishes among markets based on the types of contracts traded and the sophistication of the market participants. The upper tier resembles a traditional futures exchange (with some important modifications), while the two lower tiers are permitted to operate largely outside of the CEA.

The Commodity Futures Trading Commission

The CFTC Act established the CFTC as an independent federal agency with exclusive jurisdiction over the futures markets. The executive structure of the CFTC is similar to that of the SEC. The Commission consists of five Commissioners, appointed to staggered five-year terms by the President, with the advice and consent of the Senate.

The President also designates one of the Commissioners to serve as Chairman, but unlike the SEC, the Senate must separately confirm this designation.

Regulated Entities – Markets, Clearing Organizations, Intermediaries, SROs

Until the year 2000 it had been a fairly consistent principle in the federal regulation of U.S. futures markets that futures transactions had to occur on registered or regulated exchanges and that off-exchange trading of futures were appropriately banned. This requirement became especially pronounced following the creation of the CFTC by the CFTC Act of 1974 and the concurrent expansion of the term commodity to include almost any conceivable agricultural, physical, financial, and intangible interest (e.g., interest rates) or contingency asset (except onions). In sharp contrast to the founding model of futures regulation, today's futures markets are characterized by a risk-based, tiered approach to regulation.

Markets

The CFMA prompted a comprehensive overhaul of both the structure and the regulation of U.S. futures markets. Previously, the regulatory approach to futures trading in the United States was "one-size-fits-all." As a result, all trading occurred on regulated exchanges and all futures and options were generally subject to the same rules and regulations without regard to differences in the underlying assets or the types of participants in a given market segment.

A fundamental achievement of the CFMA was to consider the differences in products and market participants and to create a structure that provided a specific intensity of regulatory oversight that corresponded with the needs of the markets. The new risk-based, tiered structure included designated contract markets ("DCMs"), derivatives transaction execution facilities, and exempt markets, all of which are differentiated based upon the types of products offered and market participants. In addition, the CFMA moved the regulation of futures markets away from a purely prescriptive rules-based approach and toward a system that relies more on compliance with principles. DCMs, for example, must comply with specific "core principles" designed to elicit minimum standards of market behavior and integrity while permitting flexibility in the implementation of the standards.

Designated Contract Markets

DCMs are essentially the traditional organized futures exchanges or boards of trade. They may be open-outcry exchanges with physical trading floors or electronic exchanges. Since DCMs may list for trading futures or options contracts on any type of asset, index, or instrument, they are able to offer the widest range of products for trading compared to other market types. But DCMs generally must allow access to all types of traders, including retail market participants, and therefore they are subject to the highest level of CFTC regulatory oversight.

Exchanges must apply to the CFTC to receive the DCM designation. In general, in order to qualify for a designation as a contract market by the CFTC, the exchange must demonstrate to the CFTC in its application that it satisfies several standards for designation. These include such criteria as the ability to prevent market manipulation, rules to ensure fair and equitable trading, rules for the operation of the trade execution facility, financial integrity of transactions, public access to rules and contract specifications, and the ability to obtain the information necessary to perform its other required functions.

In addition, to maintain their status DCMs must demonstrate ongoing compliance with eighteen core principles that were established in the CFMA.[9] Although the DCMs, through their self-regulatory programs, are responsible for ensuring their own compliance with the core principles, the CFTC conducts regular reviews of each DCM's adherence to the designation standards, the core principles, and other requirements. However, as part of the more streamlined approach to futures regulation, DCMs are permitted to list new contracts and to implement new rules or rule amendments through a self-certification process.

Exempt Markets

Exempt markets are the least regulated trading facilities established by the CFMA. However, because they are exempt from most requirements of the CEA and most CFTC oversight, they face the highest restrictions on the types of commodities that may be traded and who may participate. Exempt markets are not registered with, or designated, recognized, or in any way officially sanctioned by the CFTC and are prohibited from representing otherwise.

There are two types of exempt markets: exempt boards of trade and exempt commercial markets. Exempt boards of trade must limit trading to transactions between eligible contract participants and for which the underlying asset has a nearly inexhaustible deliverable supply, a deliverable supply that is unlikely to be susceptible to manipulation, or has no cash market. Exempt commercial markets must limit trading to agreements, contracts, and transactions in *exempt commodities* (e.g., metals and energy commodities) executed on a principal-to-principal basis between eligible commercial entities. Exempt markets may not trade futures or options on any security.

Qualifying transactions on exempt markets are not subject to the CFTC's regulatory or enforcement jurisdiction, except for certain antifraud and manipulation provisions. Exempt markets must, however, notify the CFTC of the market's intention to operate in reliance on an exemption. Moreover, if the exempt market is determined by the CFTC to be performing a price setting function for a particular commodity, not only for its own market but for other key markets in that commodity, it may be required to make public certain pricing and trade information.

Clearing Organizations

The CFMA amended the CEA to require derivatives clearing organizations ("DCOs") to register with the CFTC in order to clear commodity futures and options. A DCO is a clearinghouse or other similar entity that serves a specific purpose:

- It enables each party to an agreement, contract, or transaction to substitute the credit of the clearing organization.
- It arranges or provides on a multilateral basis for settlement or netting of obligations resulting from the transactions.
- It otherwise provides services or arrangements that mutualize or transfer credit risk among the participants in the clearing organization.

The term DCO specifically excludes some types of entities, including those that provide settlement or netting on a bilateral basis, or settlement or netting of cash payments through an interbank payment system.

A clearinghouse that seeks to provide clearing services for commodity futures and options traded on a DCM or a derivatives transaction execution facility must register with the CFTC as a DCO and comply on an ongoing basis with fourteen core principles (established under the CFMA).[10] A DCO may also clear agreements, contracts, and transactions that are excluded or exempted from the CEA, or any other OTC derivative instruments. DCOs that limit their clearing services to such excluded or exempted agreements, contracts, or transactions need not register with the CFTC, but they may do so on a voluntary basis, in which case they would need to comply with the core principles for DCOs. DCOs that are registered with the SEC under the securities laws and only clear security futures are also not required to register with the CFTC, but may do so voluntarily.

Intermediaries

The CFTC oversees a number of types of intermediaries, market participants that act on behalf of other persons in trading futures and options. Intermediaries perform a variety of trading, advisory, and other services for market participants, including:

- Futures commission merchants ("FCMs");
- Introducing brokers;
- Commodity pool operators;
- Commodity trading advisers; and
- Floor brokers and floor traders.

In general, intermediaries must register with the CFTC unless an exemption or exclusion applies. Intermediaries' registrations generally are continuous, but annual updates usually are required. Under the CEA and the CFTC's regulations, intermediaries are subject to a wide range of disclosure, reporting, recordkeeping, and ethical requirements, depending on the nature of their activities. Intermediaries are also generally subject to rules governing certain aspects of their interactions with other market participants and customers, such as the treatment of customer funds. Some intermediaries are subject to capital requirements to help ensure the fulfillment of obligations to customers and counterparties.

Self-Regulatory Organizations

In addition to the CFTC, SROs oversee designated and registered futures and options markets and intermediaries in those markets. The designated contract markets (i.e., boards of trade or exchanges) themselves as well as the National Futures Association ("NFA"), a registered futures association overseeing FCMs, serve as SROs.

The NFA (which is not affiliated with any particular market) and the exchange SROs generally have responsibilities to help promote market integrity, protect investors, and enforce financial requirements, sales, and trading practices for their members. To carry out these functions, the NFA and the exchanges develop and enforce rules and other programs under the CFTC's oversight. The NFA also conducts arbitration and dispute resolution functions for industry participants and processes the registrations of FCMs.

SECURITIES REGULATION AND HISTORY

Introduction

Federal, state, and industry regulators, operating under the authorities of a myriad of state and federal laws, carry out securities regulation in the United States. Modern securities regulation fundamentally aims to help protect investors from fraud and to maintain fair and orderly markets. The securities regulatory system, like the banking system, is a product of historical development rather than of a single overarching rationale. As a result, it reflects the accumulation of decades of legislative and regulatory developments that have largely expanded, rather than streamlined, the set of laws, rules, and procedures that apply to securities markets and market participants.

Blue Sky Laws—Securities Regulation by the States

Background—Fifty State Securities Regulators

Private agreements among market participants in the United States during the late eighteenth century form the origins of securities regulation. However, as early as the mid- 1 800s, the first legislative efforts to regulate securities began at the state level in order to help protect investors from fraud. The earliest state laws tended to be limited in scope and often applied only to the stock issued by companies of specific industries, such as railroads, mining, or utilities. In 1911, Kansas enacted the first modern securities law requiring the registration of most new securities issues offered within the state as well as the licensing of persons engaged in the securities business. Over the next few years, many other states enacted securities laws either identical to or largely based upon the Kansas statute.

Today, all fifty states, the District of Columbia, the U.S. Virgin Islands, and Puerto Rico have statutes regulating securities transactions. State regulatory agencies are generally organized as either independent state securities commissions or as divisions in larger state financial services regulatory departments. These agencies, headed either by appointed individuals or by career state government employees, generally administer and enforce these laws, known as "blue sky" laws.

Three Basic Elements of State Securities Laws: Registration of Securities, Registration of Securities Professionals, and Enforcement

State securities laws typically include two basic requirements: the registration of securities and the registration and supervision of securities firms and professionals. In addition, state securities statutes commonly include provisions that prohibit securities fraud and that give state authorities the power to enforce those provisions.

Unless a state exemption applies, an issuer must register its securities prior to sale with the appropriate state agency. Originally, most states' securities regulation was essentially a form of "merit" regulation in which the state securities administrator wielded broad, subjective discretion in determining the securities permitted to be registered. Today, however, most states no longer evaluate individual securities offerings on their subjective merits and have put in place a disclosure-based approach more closely modeled on the federal securities laws.

To guard against fraud, each state requires the registration or licensing of securities professionals who conduct business in the particular state, unless an exception applies, including brokerage firms, individual broker-dealers' sales associates, and other intermediaries, advisers, and agents. State securities regulators often condition securities professionals' registration on the fulfillment of certain requirements, such as demonstrating their knowledge and understanding of state laws and regulations. State securities laws also typically require securities professionals to maintain certain books and records, and to submit to regulatory examination.

State laws also generally include civil and criminal liabilities and most have provisions permitting private causes of action for victims of alleged securities fraud. State securities regulators may investigate investor complaints and pursue potential cases of securities fraud. These investigations may result in sanctions such as fines and penalties on violators, including payment of restitution to harmed investors.

The Need for Coordination and Uniformity

The various state securities laws share broad goals and requirements, such as the protection of investors against fraud and the registration of securities offerings and securities professionals.

Prior to the enactment of the federal securities law and in order to address the divergence of state securities laws, the National Conference of Commissioners on Uniform State Laws ("NCCUSL") approved a Uniform Sale of Securities Act in 1929 ("1929 Act"). However, only a handful of states adopted the 1929 Act before Congress passed the Securities Act of 1933 ("Securities Act"), which not only rendered the NCCUSL's initial effort obsolete, but also created an entirely new need for state and federal coordination.

In 1956, the NCCUSL promulgated a second Uniform Securities Act ("1956 Act"), by which time a full complement of six separate federal securities laws were in force. A majority of states eventually enacted the 1956 Act, either in its entirety or with selected provisions added or omitted. In 1985, the 1956 Act was revised, but only six states adopted the amendments. Most recently, in 2002, the NCCUSL approved a fourth

Uniform Securities Act ("2002 Act"), adopted by thirteen states and the U.S. Virgin Islands. The 2002 Act outlines state authority for the registration of securities, the registration and supervision of broker-dealers, investment advisers, and other securities professionals, and enforcement, investigatory, and subpoena powers consistent with federal law.

Another important driving force for state regulatory uniformity, the North American Securities Administrators Association Inc. ("NASAA"), representing all state securities regulators in the United States, works to coordinate the regulatory and enforcement actions of its members. NASAA, founded in 1919, has issued numerous "statements of policy" and "model rules" on various securities matters, and has developed a series of "uniform forms," intended to standardize state securities regulation. NASAA also attempts to coordinate state legislative and regulatory initiatives with Congress and the SEC.

Federal Intervention

When passing the first federal securities law, the Securities Act, Congress deliberately included a provision that saved state securities laws from preemption. State laws continued to diverge and the complexity of securities regulation, from a national perspective, increased. Ultimately, despite efforts by the states to promote uniformity in implementation and interpretation of state laws, Congress had to address the states' perceived failure to standardize the interstate regulation of securities and securities professionals.

In 1996, Congress passed the National Securities Markets Improvement Act ("NSMIA") in an effort to reduce complexity and duplicative regulation among state and federal securities regulators, as well as to promote efficiency and capital formation in the national securities markets. To achieve this, NSMIA, among other things, amended the federal securities laws to preempt many state securities laws.

NSMIA created a category of federal "covered securities" exempted from state registration requirements, and which included securities listed (or approved for listing) on national securities exchanges, mutual fund shares, commercial paper, and government or municipal securities, among others. Similarly, NSMIA substantially curtailed states' rulemaking and supervisory authority over broker-dealers. Though states could still require broker-dealer registration, the SEC and the National Association of Securities Dealers ("NASD"), a SRO, would carry out most broker-dealer regulation. NSMIA also divided the regulation of investment advisers between state and federal regulators, limiting state regulation to those advisers with less that $25 million under management. NSMIA did, however, preserve states' jurisdiction to investigate fraud and unlawful conduct by a broker-dealer with respect to securities transactions.

The NSMIA preemptions effectively limited state securities law registration requirements to a narrow class of small securities offerings, such as those offered only on an intrastate basis, and reduced state authority over securities professionals. Nevertheless, NSMIA did call for continued coordination and cooperation among state and federal securities regulators. The changes in NSMIA prompted the NCCUSL to draft the 2002 Act.

Federal Securities Laws and the Securities and Exchange Commission

Overview of the Federal Securities Laws

Of the three levels of securities regulation in the United States (i.e., federal, state, or industry self-regulation), federal regulation emerged last. Federal securities regulation today encompasses numerous, sweeping statutes and countless regulations, all administered by the SEC and enforced by the SEC with the states. The Securities Act and the Securities Exchange Act of 1934 ("Exchange Act"), together with the Investment Company Act of 1940 ("Investment Company Act") and the Investment Advisers Act of 1940 ("Advisers Act"), form the core of federal securities regulation.

Securities Act of 1933

This first federal securities law, like its precursors in state law, prohibits securities fraud and requires either the registration or an exemption from registration of securities offered for public sale. However, in contrast to "merit" regulation, the Securities Act generally permits the registration of securities upon the satisfaction of required disclosures of important financial and other information. In general, companies issuing securities for sale to the public must file registration statements and prospectuses with the SEC that include a detailed description of the securities being offered, information about the issuer's business and management, and audited financial statements. These disclosures, made available to the public, allow investors to decide whether or not to purchase a particular security.

Securities Exchange Act of 1934

Whereas the Securities Act focuses on the issuance and initial registration of securities, the Exchange Act focuses on transactions in securities and the regulation of the securities industry. The Exchange Act created the SEC and established its sweeping authority over the nation's securities markets. The Exchange Act went far beyond state securities laws by giving the SEC the authority not only to register, regulate, and supervise securities professionals, including broker-dealers and transfer agents, but also the power to regulate and oversee national securities exchanges and securities associations, clearing agencies, and industry SROs. This power included the authority to approve (and, implicitly, to reject) rules of the exchanges and SROs. In addition, the Exchange Act established a system of securities registration and ongoing public disclosure through required annual, quarterly, and other reports. Numerous amendments over the years have added additional authorities and responsibilities, including the regulation of tender offers, the prohibition of insider trading, and a mandate to establish a "national market system." In addition, the SEC has authority under the Exchange Act to establish accounting standards for the preparation of reports and audited financial statements required by the Securities Act and the Exchange Act, although the SEC generally defers to the generally accepted accounting principles ("U.S. GAAP") set by the independent Financial Accounting Standards Board.

Investment Company Act of 1940

Congress passed the Investment Company Act in response to the growing popularity of investment companies and their management expertise and diversification possibilities among investors and a finding by the SEC that such companies could affect the "national public interest." There are generally three types of investment companies: open-end funds (e.g., most mutual funds), closed-end funds, and unit investment trusts.[11] The Investment Company Act governs many aspects of investment companies (e.g., organization, governance, capital structure, disclosure practices, and valuation methodologies) and requires SEC registration, although numerous exemptions are available. Upon selling their first shares, and subsequently on a regular basis, registered investment companies must make periodic public disclosures regarding their financial condition, investment policies, fees, and other company information. Registered investment companies are prohibited from engaging in fraudulent, deceptive, or manipulative practices and certain investment activities, such as using borrowed funds to buy securities (i.e., purchasing on margin) or selling borrowed securities in the belief that they can be bought back at a later time at a lower price (i.e., short-selling).

Investment Advisers Act of 1940

Though far narrower in scope, the Advisers Act imposes registration and other requirements on investment advisers, firms or individuals, providing investment advice to investors for compensation. In essence, the Advisers Act seeks to protect investors and compel fair practices by advisers by broadly prohibiting fraud and deception, preventing the misuse of nonpublic information, and regulating investment advisory contracts, including the terms of compensation, among other requirements. The Advisers Act also gives the SEC authority to require advisers to maintain certain books and records. Like other federal securities laws, the Advisers Act provides several exemptions from its registration requirements, but it also gives the SEC broad discretion to exempt any person or transaction from any or all provisions of the Advisers Act as long as the exemption is consistent with the protection of investors and purposes of the Advisers Act.

Sarbanes-Oxley Act of 2002

The Sarbanes-Oxley Act aimed to restore investor confidence in the securities markets following the accounting scandals at Enron, WorldCom and other companies. The Sarbanes-Oxley Act created a new regulator for the auditing profession, the Public Company Accounting Oversight Board ("PCAOB"), and enhanced corporate responsibility and financial disclosures, provided more stringent standards for auditor independence, and significantly increased criminal penalties for various types of fraud and "white-collar" crimes. The Sarbanes-Oxley Act led to numerous additional requirements for public companies, including executive certifications of financial statements, accelerated reporting requirements, and management reports and auditor attestation on internal controls over financial reporting, among many others.

Other Federal Securities Laws

The Trust Indenture Act of 1939 ("Trust Indenture Act") governs trust indentures, the special agreements or contracts between certain issuers of publicly offered debt securities and bondholders. Though narrow in purpose, the Trust Indenture Act supplements federal securities laws to help protect the rights of investors in debt securities.

The Securities and Exchange Commission

The Exchange Act created the SEC, an independent, administrative agency of the federal government. In particular, the SEC has broad authority to enforce the federal securities laws and to promulgate rules for the national securities markets. Federal securities laws give the SEC a three-fold mandate: to protect investors, to maintain the integrity and stability of markets, and to promote efficiency in capital formation.

Not until the stock market crash of 1929 and the subsequent events of the Great Depression did sentiment begin to solidify around the need for a federal regulator to protect investors and oversee the securities markets. The SEC is led by five Commissioners, one of whom serves as Chairman, who serve staggered five-year terms and are appointed by the President after the advice and consent of the Senate. Under the Chairman's leadership, the Commissioners guide overall SEC policy by interpreting federal securities laws, proposing new rules as market developments or congressional mandates warrant, amending existing rules, and overseeing and approving SEC enforcement actions.

Regulated Entities – Markets and Clearing, Broker-Dealers, SROs, and Others

Whereas the Securities Act focuses on the issuance of securities and their initial registration, the Exchange Act is primarily concerned with the secondary market and trading of securities through broker-dealers and other market professionals. This system has evolved significantly over the years in response to numerous changes in market structure and practices.

Markets and Clearing

The Exchange Act regulates the secondary markets where most public equity trading occurs. The Exchange Act regulates the two basic types of secondary equity markets: exchange markets as "national securities exchanges" and dealer markets as "national securities associations." The traditional stock exchanges (e.g., NYSE Euronext) are examples of auction-style national securities exchanges. There are no registered national securities associations in operation today. However, the NASDAQ, which is today a national securities exchange, was originally established as a dealer-centered national securities association.

The Exchange Act and the SEC's rules require the registration of securities exchanges, mandate some of the types of rules that securities exchanges are required to adopt, and require that their operating procedures and governance structures meet minimum public interest standards. The basic approach to regulation of trading on the exchanges, including the regulation of market participants such as specialists and broker-dealers, is through self-regulation with oversight by the SEC. Exchanges must file rule proposals with the SEC, for example, which then publishes the proposals for public review and comment. The SEC may then approve, modify, or disallow the proposed rules. The exchanges are also subject to other laws and SEC rules regarding, for example, their use and extension of margin, the prevention of manipulation, and restrictions on short selling.

The Exchange Act also provides for the regulation of securities clearing agencies, which provide clearing, netting and settlement, and central counterparty services for transactions in the securities markets. Securities clearing agencies generally are SROs subject to SEC oversight.

Brokers-Dealers and Other Intermediaries

The principal category of intermediary in the securities markets is the broker-dealer. Essentially, a broker is a firm or individual who acts as an intermediary between buyers and sellers of securities, usually charging a commission for these services. A dealer is a firm or person who is in the business of buying and selling securities for its own account, either directly or through a broker. Many firms operate as both brokers and dealers.

The Exchange Act prohibits any person from acting as a broker or dealer unless they are registered with the SEC or an exemption applies. The Exchange Act provides, for example, broad exceptions from the definitions of broker and dealer for certain securities-related activities traditionally conducted by banks. Moreover, even if it is required, the SEC may deny registration if it finds that registration requirements are not satisfied. The SEC also has authority to set standards for operational ability and professional conduct, and can establish requirements for testing and training as prerequisites for entering the industry.

Beyond registration, the Exchange Act and the SEC's rules and regulations impose a broad set of requirements on broker-dealers, including specialists and market-makers. In general, broker-dealers are subject to regulations concerning fraud and manipulation, protection from excessive risk and insolvency, and duties to customers. Broker-dealers are also subject to antifraud provisions of the Exchange Act as well as SEC regulations that define acceptable practices. The Exchange Act also authorizes the SEC to establish rules regulating the financial soundness of broker-dealers. Thus, broker-dealers are subject to various record-keeping requirements and the SEC's net capital rules. Broker- dealers' duties to their customers include rules covering best execution and investor suitability rules, among others. Broker-dealers may also be barred from the industry for certain misconduct or for certain violations of SEC, exchange, or SRO rules.

A special category of broker-dealers are those that specialize in the trading and dealing in government securities, as defined in the Exchange Act. Prior to the enactment of the Government Securities Act of 1986 ("GSA"), government securities brokers and dealers were exempt from registration and regulation under the securities laws. The GSA imposed new requirements on government securities brokers and dealers, including a requirement to register with the SEC and a system of regulation that includes recordkeeping, net capital requirements, and large position reporting rules. Rulemaking authority under the GSA resides with Treasury and enforcement resides with the SEC.

The Exchange Act also generally requires broker-dealers, including government securities broker-dealers, to be members of a registered national securities exchange or national securities association. Today, nearly all broker-dealers in the United States are members of the Financial Industry Regulatory Authority ("FINRA"), a SRO formed in 2007 by the merger of the NASD and the regulatory and enforcement units of the New York Stock Exchange. Thus, in addition to the Exchange Act and SEC rules and regulations, broker-dealers are subject to the rules and oversight of the exchange or the securities association (or both) of which they are members.

Self-Regulatory Organizations

The federal system of securities regulation relies to a great extent upon self-regulation by various segments of the securities markets. Indeed, self-regulation in the securities industry preceded both state and federal regulation, and today all of the exchanges in operation (e.g., the stock exchanges, options exchanges, and exchanges that trade security futures products[12]) effectively perform self-regulatory functions. With the enactment of the securities laws and the creation of the SEC, federal regulation was laid on top of, that is, in addition to, the system of regulation already in place in the markets.

Over the years, amendments to the securities laws authorized the creation of additional SROs for the industry. The Maloney Act of 1938, for example, authorized the SEC to register national securities associations to act as self-regulatory bodies for brokers and dealers.

In general, SROs have broad authority to impose governance standards, set rules, and undertake enforcement and disciplinary proceedings with respect to their members. However, the activities of the SROs are subject to SEC oversight. For example, the SEC must approve SRO rulemakings, prior to their being enacted, and the SEC may in some instances require that the SROs establish specific rules. In addition, most market participants must be members of the SRO for their segment of the securities market.

Other Entities

Public Companies

Public companies are a primary source of securities, issuing both debt and equity securities into the public securities markets. Public companies that list their securities on public markets are subject to a wide variety of securities law obligations, as well as the exchanges' financial requirements and listing standards.

Consolidated Supervised Entities

In 2004, the SEC implemented a voluntary program to regulate certain major U.S. securities firms on a consolidated or group-wide basis. The groups in the program, referred to as consolidated supervised entities ("CSEs"), are firms predominantly engaged in the securities business and have one or more large broker-dealer units. The aim of the CSE program is to enable the SEC to monitor and respond to problems in the group-wide structure while offering a less-restrictive regulatory environment for the individual firms. If the CSE group contains an affiliate that is regulated by another functional regulator, such as a banking regulator, the SEC defers to that regulator's oversight authority over the affiliate. Under the program, the CSEs are required to maintain a system of internal controls, adequate capital, and sufficient liquidity to ensure that they can meet any obligatory cash commitments, even in a stressed environment. For its part, the SEC must approve the CSEs' internal controls systems, examine and monitor the implementation of internal controls, and generally monitor the CSEs for financial and operational weaknesses. Further, the SEC has broad authority to require the CSEs to increase their holdings of regulatory capital or expand their liquidity pools if weaknesses develop or as market conditions may dictate.

Credit Rating Agencies

Credit rating agencies are independent entities that issue credit ratings on securities and other instruments offered by public companies, banks, governments, and other issuers. As a result, credit rating agencies serve as an integral part of the securities markets. Previously, under the SEC's regulations, credit rating agencies could apply to receive a designation as a nationally recognized statistical rating organization ("NRSRO"), but they were not subject to SEC regulation. The Credit Rating Agency Reform Act of 2006, however, gave the SEC the authority to register and oversee rating agencies as NRSROs. Registered NRSROs are subject to, among other duties and authorities, ongoing disclosure and recordkeeping requirements and SEC examination.

Auditors

The Sarbanes-Oxley Act created the PCAOB to register and inspect public company auditors. The PCAOB, subject to SEC oversight, also sets auditing standards for public companies and has enforcement authority for compliance with its rules and other provisions of the Sarbanes-Oxley Act.

INSURANCE REGULATION AND HISTORY

Background

Insurance is a financial product in which the consumer converts the uncertainty of financial loss of an unforeseen event, including its amount and timing, into a certain business cost (i.e., the premium) which is predictable over time. Insurance involves risk shifting, which occurs when a person facing the possibility of an economic loss transfers some or all of the financial consequences of the potential loss to an insurer. Insurance also involves risk distribution, which can involve the spreading of loss among policyholders or the party assuming the risk can distribute his potential liability in part among others.

Unlike banks, futures firms, securities firms, and other financial institutions regulated primarily at the federal level or on a dual federal and state basis, the states primarily regulate insurers. The constitutional and statutory allocation of power over insurance regulation between the federal government and the states has a complex evolution.

Before 1850, U.S. insurers were subject to little regulatory supervision other than through their corporate state charters. In 1851, the New Hampshire Legislature created a full-time board of insurance commissioners. Massachusetts and Vermont followed in 1852, New York in 1859, and Rhode Island in 1865. In 1869, in *Paul v. Virginia*,[13] the U.S. Supreme Court set out the constitutional basis for the primacy of the states in insurance regulation, holding that the issuance of an insurance policy was not a transaction in commerce. As a result, the federal government lacked authority to regulate insurance under the Commerce Clause of the U.S. Constitution. This decision was also the basis to exempt insurers from the later-enacted antitrust laws.

State insurance regulation at the time of the *Paul* decision varied with degrees of regulatory authority and some states lacked an established insurance department. After the

Paul decision, the existing state insurance regulators, in an effort to coordinate regulation of multi-state insurers, formed the National Association of Insurance Commissioners ("NAIC") in 1871. The concept of state insurance regulation then quickly expanded to all of the other states, each with its own chief insurance regulator, generally referred to as the "commissioner." Today, state governors appoint most commissioners, although in eleven states commissioners are elected.

With its influence increasing over the years, the NAIC currently serves as an organization for the commissioners from all fifty states, the District of Columbia, and the five U.S. territories. The NAIC provides its members a forum for exchanging information, coordinating regulatory activities, and developing uniform policy through model laws and regulations for state adoption (although the individual states frequently change the model laws, if and when adopted).

In 1944, placing in jeopardy the future of state insurance regulation, the U.S. Supreme Court overturned the *Paul* decision in *United States v. South-Eastern Underwriters Association*.[14] The U.S. Supreme Court held that insurance was indeed "interstate commerce," and thus subject to federal regulation. Not only did the decision signify that the federal government possessed the authority to regulate insurance, but it also meant that all of the various federal laws regulating interstate commerce, including the Sherman Antitrust Act, the Clayton Act, and the FTC Act, were applicable to insurers. The insurance industry, state insurance commissioners, and the NAIC urged Congress to pass legislation overriding the U.S. Supreme Court's decision and return insurance regulatory authority to the states.

In 1945, Congress passed the McCarran-Ferguson Act ("McCarran-Ferguson"), which returned the regulatory jurisdiction over "the business of insurance" (a broadly interpreted term) to the states, while generally exempting the business of insurance from most federal antitrust law. In passing McCarran-Ferguson, Congress affirmed the public interest in the continued state regulation and taxation of insurance. McCarran-Ferguson also provided the insurance industry with a general exemption from federal laws unless such laws specified applicability to insurance. Congress has not substantially modified this concept, sometimes referred to as the "reverse preemption" of state insurance law over federal law.

Post McCarran-Ferguson Legislation

In a few instances since McCarran-Ferguson, Congress has somewhat narrowed the reverse preemption granted to the states. In 1974, Congress enacted the Employee Retirement Income Security Act ("ERISA") that established regulatory requirements for employer-sponsored retirement plans, as well as other benefits such as medical, life, and disability insurance. ERISA established federal reporting requirements for such plans, as well as fiduciary standards for the management of assets used to support employer-sponsored benefits. ERISA's substantive requirements preempted any otherwise applicable state insurance regulations. The Department of Labor administers and enforces ERISA and this regulation has had a significant impact on the design of employee group insurance programs.

Twenty-five years later, Congress specifically reaffirmed McCarran-Ferguson and preserved state insurance regulation in the GLB Act. The GLB Act, noted for removing the barriers preventing banks, securities firms, and insurers from affiliating and competing with each other, provided clear authority for banks to affiliate with insurers through a financial holding company. However, the GLB Act placed a new federal mandate on states to achieve a prescribed degree of uniformity, or reciprocity, in insurer producer licensing by a certain date or confront federal intervention in the form of a federal preemptive insurance sales force licensing system, called the National Association of Registered Agents and Brokers ("NARAB").

In other more recent actions, Congress further involved itself in insurance regulation. After the September 11, 2001 terrorist attacks, Congress in 2002 enacted the Terrorism Risk Insurance Act ("TRIA") to provide property and casualty insurers with a federal backstop program for catastrophic losses resulting from a terrorist act. TRIA also preempted some aspects of state insurance regulation and imposed a number of federal conditions and requirements on insurers that are required to participate in the program.

These congressional developments reflect the radical differences of the insurance marketplace today from that of even a few years ago. Industry consolidation, globalization, the advent of e-commerce, and the accelerating integration of financial services are only a few of the trends driving the marketplace.

Fundamentals of State Insurance Regulation

State insurance regulation consists of two broad categories:

- Solvency or financial regulation, which focuses on preventing insurer insolvencies and mitigating consumer losses upon insolvencies.
- Consumer protection or market regulation, which focuses on such anti-consumer practices as deceptive advertising, unfair policy terms, or discriminatory or unfair treatment of policyholders.

Some regulatory functions relate to both. For example, company licensing will generally focus on the financial stability and capitalization of the applicant company, though it will also review the insurer's management and organizers for any past record of customer abuse or unfair dealing. Similarly, policy form review focuses on customer fairness, though in some cases such review can also include the pricing of the coverage and making sure an insurer is not undertaking commitments potentially threatening its solvency.

Solvency Regulation

There are many examples of the various aspects of state solvency regulation: the requirements of financial reporting based on statutory accounting principles ("SAP"), risk-based capital ("RBC") rules, financial examinations, statements of actuarial opinions, asset adequacy analysis, and the regulation of insurers' reserves and investments. These regulatory functions are prudential in nature, although state insurance regulators do not generally employ that term, as do the European Union and international regulators.

Following the failure of several major life insurers, the NAIC developed the RBC requirements in the 1990s in order to supplement the generally low and varying capital requirements found in the various state insurance laws. The NAIC-developed RBC requirements, related to an insurer's size and reflecting the risk of an insurer's activities, are uniform among the states. At the heart of the RBC system is total adjusted capital: the insurer's statutory net worth (i.e., assets minus liabilities) plus the insurer's asset valuation reserve. The state insurance commissioner compares the insurer's total adjusted capital to five "RBC levels," including the "red flag" level indicating possible solvency concerns to be addressed internally, and the "mandatory control level" requiring the state regulator to take action to protect policyholders. RBC data, considered by state insurance commissioners to be a regulatory tool and not to be used as a means to rank insurers, are not public information.

State liquidation laws rather than federal bankruptcy laws govern insurers. When seizing or "taking over" an insurer, the state regulator aims first to rehabilitate or sell the company. If unfeasible, then the regulator must institute receivership or liquidation proceedings in a state court. Depending upon the weakness of the insurer's financial condition, the regulator may find it necessary to recommend that the court approve significant changes in the insurer's previously issued insurance policies. For example, the state regulator may recommend the reduction of the minimum interest rate guaranteed in policies, or the modification of non-cancellable policies with guaranteed rates to guaranteed renewable policies, subject to rate increases.

Past Problems in Solvency Regulation

The financial impairment and state receivership or rehabilitation of several major insurers in the 1980s called into serious question state insurance solvency regulation. A 1987 Government Accountability Office ("GAO") report[15] estimated approximately 140 insurer insolvencies from 1969 through 1986 (42 percent of which occurred after 1983) and noted that the number of insurers designated for regulatory attention due to troubling financial conditions increased from 132 to 590 between 1978 and 1986. A 1989 GAO report[16] reviewed the monitoring of property and casualty insurer solvency and found nine major regulatory problems that needed remedying. In 1990, Representative John Dingell, Chairman of the Subcommittee on Oversight and Investigations of the House Committee on Energy and Commerce, issued *Failed Promises: Insurance Company Insolvencies*, a report finding "seriously deficient" state regulation of insurer solvency and noting the resulting significant and increasing costs to the public. Representative Dingell subsequently introduced legislation to create a dual federal and state system for solvency regulation, with a federal guarantee fund for nationally certified insurers. However, Congress never moved the proposed legislation.

Efforts of States to Address Solvency Regulatory Problems

Following these congressional and GAO findings in the late 1980s and early 1990s, state insurance commissioners, acting through the NAIC, quickly moved to improve state solvency regulation. The NAIC established a NAIC Accreditation Program ("Accreditation Program") requiring an independent review of each state's insurance regulatory agency to assess compliance with certain designated NAIC Financial Regulation Standards. These standards, including RBC requirements, apply to the financial regulation of all insurers operating in more than one state. Requiring such uniform standards in the Accreditation Program assures that an accredited state has sufficient authority and resources to effectively regulate its multi-state insurers. The NAIC accredits for a five-year period, subject to annual review, those states determined to have met the required standards. Currently, with the exception of New York, which rejected adopting one of the required model laws, all states and the District of Columbia have received accreditation.

The NAIC itself exercises some direct oversight of the Financial Regulation Standards by monitoring the financial performance of nationally significant companies through its Financial Analysis Division. This division reports potential solvency problems to an NAIC working group which then conducts peer review and queries the lead state regulator as to the insurer's financial condition and any regulatory actions taken. The NAIC also maintains a financial database, analyzes the data, and scores companies in order to assist states in prioritizing companies for further review. In 2004, the NAIC adopted a "Risk-Focused Surveillance Framework" in an effort to formalize a structure for evaluating and assessing all the risks inherent in an insurer's operations (e.g., market risk, underwriting risk, strategic risk, catastrophe risk, and liquidity risk). The details of such a proposed framework are still under development.

In 2001, the GAO, which had been critical of state insurance solvency regulation in the early 1 990s, was asked by Representative Dingell to review the NAIC's progress in improving and modernizing the state insurance regulatory processes. The GAO reported[17] that in response to the pressures from the GLB Act's NARAB proposal and the insurance industry's increasing competition with banking and securities firms, the NAIC was working to implement a streamlined reciprocal licensing system to allow agents and brokers to conduct business in more than one state after satisfying a single state's licensing requirements. The GAO report also cited other NAIC initiatives such as the development of a more uniform and efficient approach for bringing new products to market ("speed to market"), but concluded that "[a]t present, both the timely completion and degree of success for many of NAIC's financial modernization initiatives remain uncertain." In 2001, the GAO also issued a report on the NAIC's accreditation program,[18] recommending potential NAIC actions to strengthen the Accreditation Program. These recommendations included the strengthening of the focus on chartering and change of ownership, implementing new on-site review team procedures for all relevant examination information, and ensuring the Accreditation Program's flexibility to adjust for the time and scope of on-site visits. The NAIC responded to the GAO report by documenting already-planned improvements to further enhance the strength of the Accreditation Program, and pledging to give the GAO's recommendations for further improvements "serious consideration." The effectiveness of the NAIC's implementation of all of the GAO's recommended improvements to the Accreditation Program is unclear at this point.

State Guarantee Funds

No federal guarantee exists for insurance policyholders similar to that which is provided to most bank customers by the FDIC. Instead, individual state guarantee funds provide whatever guarantees may be available. Under this state-based system, developed in the 1 960s, all licensed insurers in a state automatically become members of that state's guarantee fund. Upon the occurrence of an insurer insolvency in a particular state, that state's guarantee fund assesses fees on all licensed insurers, generally on a post-event basis, to pay all or a portion of policyholders' outstanding claims. This insolvency guarantee mechanism is an important component of the current state regulatory system's solvency regulation. In 1969, the NAIC adopted a model guarantee fund act for property and liability insurance and in 1970 a similar model for life and health insurance. The wave of insurer insolvencies in the 1980s spurred on the guarantee fund movement and by 1992 all states had enacted guarantee fund legislation. On a cumulative basis, state guarantee funds have thus far paid policyholders of insolvent insurers approximately $23 billion (approximately $17 billion by the property and casualty associations since 1969, and over $6 billion by the life and health associations since the early 1980s).

When finding an insurer in poor financial condition, state insurance regulators can take various actions, including rehabilitation. However, when insolvencies do occur, state regulators must institute receivership and/or liquidation proceedings under state laws. In an effort to make good on the outstanding insurance obligations of insurers to their policyholders, all states have now instituted state guarantee funds to pay unearned premiums and the balance on outstanding claims often up to statutory limits, if any. Yet, these payments are not uniform and can vary by state, type of insurance, and net worth of the policyholder. The funding for those claim payments derives from the guarantee funds' assessments upon the remaining licensed insurers in those states. These assessments range from one to two percent of premium volume on a pro rata basis of each insurer's state market share in those lines of business written by the insolvent insurer. Each state has its own laws establishing separate guarantee funds for life and health insurance and for property and casualty insurance for specified lines of business written by licensed insurers. However, only one state, New Jersey, has a guarantee fund for surplus lines insurance (i.e., insurance written by unlicensed companies under special permissive provisions), and there are no guarantee funds covering captive insurers.

All states make post-event assessments on insurers to cover insolvent insurer claims except New York, which has historically pre-assessed its property and casualty guarantee fund up to $200 million. In most states, insurers can offset such assessments against premium taxes payable to the states (some industry critics point out that such offsets amount to a taxpayer subsidy). The insurers licensed in a particular state constitute the guarantee fund in that state under the supervision of a board of directors and, ultimately, the state's insurance regulator. The various state guarantee funds coordinate their work, especially with regard to multi-state insolvencies, through two private national organizations, the National Organization of Life and Health Insurance Guaranty Association and the National Conference of Insurance Guaranty Funds, of which all state guarantee funds are members.

Consumer Protection

Even though the NAIC's Accreditation Program has succeeded in making solvency regulation somewhat more uniform and effective, achieving uniformity in other state regulatory functions, such as in the areas of consumer protection or market regulation, has failed. These areas include regulation focusing on insurer practices, independent of solvency concerns, which might be detrimental to policyholders, such as deceptive advertising, unfair policy terms, or discriminatory or unfair treatment.

Licensing of Insurers
In the area of company licensing, insurers must receive a license from each state in which they plan to do business. The filing requirements for licenses vary significantly from state to state, and companies must ascertain and comply with each of those requirements.

Each state requires that in order to be licensed an insurer must possess a certain minimum level of capital and policyholder surplus, or net worth, which can be relatively small in some states and quite substantial in others. The insurance regulator also must review the fitness and competence of the insurer's management and board of directors, as well as its business plan, product lines, and market conduct practices and procedures. The NAIC has made some progress in its efforts to streamline the state licensing system, but much remains to be done.

Licensing of Producers

Licensing of sales personnel is also subject to divergent state requirements. All states require that those who wish to sell insurance within their borders must obtain a license. The licensing process typically requires passing an examination, background checks, and, in some states, fingerprinting. The GLB Act's provisions to establish a federal preemptive sales force licensing system, the NARAB, if at least a majority of the states failed to develop a more unified system within three years of the GLB Act's enactment, compelled the streamlining of the multi-state licensing of insurance sales personnel. To be more precise, at least a majority of the states had to enact either "uniform laws and regulations governing the licensure of individuals and entities authorized to sell and solicit the purchase of insurance" or "reciprocity laws and regulation governing the licensure of nonresident individuals and entities authorized to sell and solicit insurance."[19] Although unable to meet the "uniform" test, twenty-six states, a majority, adopted the necessary laws and reciprocity arrangements to meet the "reciprocity" test, and thus prevented the triggering of NARAB. Since successfully preventing the triggering of NARAB by meeting the reciprocity statutory requirement, states have failed to achieve uniformity in licensing standards.

Form Regulation

Form approval is the system or process by which state insurance regulators review and approve (or disapprove) policy forms (i.e., the terms and conditions of the contract of insurance) used by life insurers and property and casualty insurers for compliance with state laws and to protect consumers. Life insurers perceive that their financial institution competitors with similar financial products can market their new products in less than two months due to their federal-based or dual regulator, whereas it takes insurers up to two years or more to get their new products approved in enough states to mount a national product roll-out. Insurance policy form approval regulation varies widely from state to state. Most states require product approval prior to market introduction (as noted in the second and third listed categories below). Those states justify such prior approval requirements because of the complexity and technical nature of insurance contracts, which makes them difficult for the average consumer to understand. At least seven categories of state policy form systems exist in the various states:

- State-adopted forms - required to be used by insurers;
- Strict prior approval - cannot be used without affirmative approval;
- Prior approval - an express standard that the form is "deemed" approved after the elapse of a specified waiting period, unless specifically disapproved;
- File and use - must be filed on or before the proposed effective date;

- Use and file - may use prior to filing, but must be filed in required number of days from effective date;
- Form filing only - must be filed with no time period specified; and
- No form filing required.

The NAIC attempted to achieve a higher degree of uniformity and efficiency in form approval by creating the Coordinated Advertising, Rate and Form Review Authority ("Review Authority") to provide a centralized review of certain life insurance products based on a set of uniform standards. However, the states have not used the Review Authority due to the standards being riddled with deviations.

In 2002 the NAIC considered the possibility of using uniform national standards as a way to institute more "speed to market" by establishing an interstate compact to facilitate a single point of filing for certain insurance products such as life, disability, long-term care, and annuities. As a result, in 2003 the NAIC endorsed a draft Interstate Insurance Product Regulation Compact ("the Compact"). By 2006, the required twenty-six states had joined the Compact, allowing it to become operational through its Interstate Insurance Product Regulation Commission ("the Product Regulation Commission"). Thirty-one states now have adopted the Compact and, in July 2007, the Product Regulation Commission approved its first insurance product filings, all of which were life insurance products. Whether the Compact will ultimately succeed in providing the needed "speed to market" is still unclear.

Rate Regulation and Price Controls

The term "price controls" frequently describes state regulation of rates used by property and casualty insurers licensed or admitted in a state (the "licensed or admitted market"). The price controls issue is considered to be a property and casualty industry problem, as life insurance products are not subject to price controls. The licensed or admitted property and casualty market provides the bulk of commercial property and casualty insurance in the United States, focusing mostly on standard insurance policies in terms of types and sizes of covered risks. Some common types of property and casualty insurance provided by the licensed or admitted market include fire, burglary, theft, workers' compensation, and commercial automobile.

States generally do not formulate mandatory rates for their licensed insurers. Instead, insurers determine the rates they want to use in a particular state in which they are licensed, and then they must comply with the applicable rate regulation required in that state. Insurers must be able to justify their rates, either by the use of their own loss data and projections, or by the use of rating information and loss cost factors developed by national insurance advisory organizations accepted by the state regulators, such as the Insurance Services Organization ("ISO") or the American Association of Insurance Services ("AAIS"). The legal standard for rates in all states is that they not be "inadequate, excessive, or unfairly discriminatory." State insurance regulation initially emphasized the adequacy of rates so as to prevent solvency problems. However, today insurance regulators have used price controls to hold down prices for their constituents by denying proposed rate increases on the grounds that they are excessive.

States address rate regulation in a number of different ways. For example, there is wide variety regarding rates on most lines of commercial property and casualty insurance:

- Five states have no filing requirements and are said to have a deregulated open market for commercial lines ("No File");
- Two states require informational rate filings only ("Information Only");
- Two states provide for the automatic approval of rate changes within a specified band ("Flex Rating");
- Nine states allow rates to be used without pre-filing, but they must be subsequently filed ("Use and File");
- Thirteen states and the District of Columbia require rates to be filed before they are used ("File and Use");
- Nineteen states require rates to be filed and approved before they can be used, and generally allow rates to be "deemed" approved thirty days after they are filed if the state has not taken any action during that time ("Prior Approval with Express Deemer"); and
- Of the forty-three states with some degree of rate control, nineteen and the District of Columbia also provide for the exemption of rate approval requirements on large commercial property and casualty policies, based on policy premium "triggers" that vary in each state (from $10,000 to $500,000).

Surplus Lines: An Exception to Form and Price Controls

In contrast to the licensed or admitted market, there is also a non-admitted market in all states in which unlicensed insurers are allowed to transact business in a particular state without being subject to that state's form or rate regulation. This surplus lines market evolved historically due to the lack of capital of licensed insurers to meet the needs of a growing country and economy; property owners needed to turn to the unlicensed market to insure their "surplus" needs. This market allows the insurance buyer access to unlicensed or non-admitted insurers in a state, generally through a specially licensed insurance broker, when the insurance buyer is unable to find the desired coverage in the licensed and admitted market or when the insurance buyer is a large commercial policyholder. In theory, the prospective insurance purchaser must first perform due diligence in seeking to obtain insurance from one or more licensed companies as required by the state in which the insured risk is located. If such due diligence is unsuccessful, the purchaser may seek insurance from an unlicensed or non-admitted surplus lines insurer not subject to that state's rate or form regulatory requirements, but still meeting certain NAIC-developed minimum requirements. However, upon an insurer's insolvency, the state's guarantee fund does not cover the resulting surplus lines insurance policy.

The surplus lines market focuses on larger and more difficult insurance risks that cannot be placed in the licensed or admitted market. Surplus line insurers can include U.S.– based insurers not licensed in the particular state of the insured risk, as well as non-U.S. insurers granted surplus lines eligibility by the states. The NAIC is unable to provide complete data on the extent of the surplus lines market, but it encompasses a large percentage of the high-end and high-risk commercial property and casualty market. For example, the surplus lines market, without state or form regulation, covered much of the World Trade Center losses on September 11, 2001.

Market Conduct Examinations

Market conduct examinations of licensed insurers' practices affecting consumers in areas such as selling and underwriting vary among the states. Some states, such as California, perform in-depth, standardized examinations on a routine basis, while other states perform few, if any, such examinations. States frequently cooperate in multi-state examinations, appointing one state a lead examiner. Still, some insurers will undergo market conduct examinations from several different states in a given year, and others will receive none over an extended multi-year period.

International Dimensions

Insurance is truly a global business with an international marketplace subject to international exchanges and negotiations. However, under the current U.S. state-based insurance system, no regulatory official at the federal level can speak for the interests of U.S. regulators of insurers and reinsurers. Assuming that role by default, the NAIC has thus far failed in obtaining a satisfactory degree of state regulatory uniformity. Yet, currently the NAIC is the only U.S. regulatory voice on insurance matters, a fact emphasized by proponents of a federal insurance regulator who demand a role in international negotiations as well as on national insurance policy issues.

According to a statement on its website, the NAIC represents the views of U.S. regulators before the International Association of Insurance Supervisors ("IAIS"), the Organization for Economic Cooperation and Development ("OECD"), and other international bodies, and represents the views of state insurance regulators in negotiations with trading partners and the Office of the U.S. Trade Representative. The NAIC also assists officials from the Department of Commerce and other U.S. government agencies by engaging in implementation efforts under existing trade agreements.

A few state regulators, through the auspices of the NAIC, have also engaged in a dialogue with representatives of the European Commission and the Committee of European Insurance and Occupational Pensions Supervisors to provide input to the European Commission in the development and oversight of the implementation of European Union ("E.U.") directives on insurance regulation. A current contentious issue on the U.S.-E.U. insurance agenda relates to the state requirements for collateral posted by non-U.S. reinsurers. All states have adopted the NAIC model law on reinsurance collateral, a required step to be accredited under the Accreditation Program. Any change would require modification of the NAIC model law, revision of the Accreditation Program to reflect this modification, and state enactment of the modified model law, a process that is likely to take several years.

Chapter 4

SHORT-TERM RECOMMENDATIONS

This chapter describes recommendations designed to be implemented immediately to strengthen and enhance market stability and business conduct regulation in the wake of recent events in the credit and mortgage markets. These recommendations serve as a useful transition to the intermediate-term recommendations and the optimal regulatory structure. However, each short-term recommendation stands on its own merits, as well as on its merits as a transitional element.

PRESIDENT'S WORKING GROUP ON FINANCIAL MARKETS

Recommendation Overview

Treasury recommends a modernization of the current President's Working Group on Financial Markets Executive Order to reinforce the mission and purpose of the group as an ongoing mechanism for coordination and communication on financial policy matters including systemic risk, market integrity, investor and consumer protection, and capital markets competitiveness. Treasury also recommends an expansion of the President's Working Group on Financial Markets membership.

Background and Historical Context

Since 1988, the President's Working Group on Financial Markets ("PWG") has served as an effective and useful inter-agency coordination and communication mechanism regarding financial market regulatory and policy issues. While requiring important and fundamental changes in several areas, the optimal regulatory structure will also require time for reflection and consideration by all interested parties. As the debate regarding the merits of more rationalized regulation progresses, the need to manage the operations of how the regulatory community interacts with each other is ongoing. The PWG has the potential to serve as one of the most useful devices to this end.

In October 1987, a significant price decline occurred in U.S. and global equity markets. As a result of this steep decline, in March 1988 President Reagan issued Executive Order 12631 to establish and instruct the PWG to report on the major issues raised by that stock market decline and on actions to enhance market integrity and maintain investor confidence.

The heads of the Department of the Treasury ("Treasury"), the Federal Reserve, the Securities and Exchange Commission ("SEC"), and the Commodity Futures Trading Commission ("CFTC") comprise the PWG with the Secretary of the Treasury designated as the chairman. The Executive Order contemplated that the PWG would provide an initial report on the stock market decline, as well as subsequent periodic reports.

Evolution

Since its 1988 report to President Reagan, the PWG has continued to serve as an interagency mechanism to facilitate coordination and communication consistent with the mission to enhance market integrity and maintain investor confidence. In keeping with this broad mission, the PWG has considered many different issues not directly related to the 1987 events.

For example, the PWG has issued reports, principles, and draft legislative language on terrorism risk insurance, hedge funds and other private pools of capital, over-the-counter derivatives, the Commodity Exchange Act, and financial contract netting. Each of these publications provided valuable information to policymakers and market participants. In addition, members of Congress have periodically sought the views of PWG members. As such, the PWG's coordination and communication role itself, even absent formal reports, has enhanced the policy and legislative processes.

As referenced by the GAO,[20] in addition to producing reports, principles, and draft legislative language, the PWG has also served as an informal mechanism for member and non-member agencies to discuss policy initiatives extending across jurisdictional lines. The PWG is now a key tool for coordination and communication among U.S. financial regulatory policymakers, providing members and other agencies with an overarching market perspective, and facilitating the information-sharing process.

Recommendation

Treasury recommends modernizing the current Executive Order to augment the PWG's role as a coordination and communication mechanism for financial policy. The PWG has evolved to serve this role. The Executive Order should clarify the PWG's mission and purpose as a tool to achieve such coordination and communication, without altering in any way a participating agency's existing authorities and responsibilities.

As such, Treasury recommends replacing the current Executive Order with a new Executive Order differing in four respects. Each of these changes will permit the types of helpful policy coordination and communication that has occurred over the past two decades.

First, the new Executive Order should reinforce the PWG as an ongoing financial policy coordination and communication mechanism. The new Executive Order should also instruct the PWG to focus on the financial sector more broadly, rather than solely on financial markets.

Second, the new Executive Order should clarify that the PWG should strive to facilitate inter-agency coordination and communication in four distinct areas in a manner fully consistent with the distinct and separate role of each agency, and with no abridgment or diminution in those agencies' statutory roles.

- The PWG should work to facilitate inter-agency coordination and communication with respect to mitigating systemic risk to the financial system. The PWG should recommend regular meetings and information sharing among federal financial supervisory agencies.
- The PWG should work to facilitate inter-agency coordination and communication to enhance financial market integrity. For example, the PWG should encourage consistent and regular coordination and communication across all federal regulators to discuss financial market integrity.
- The PWG should work to facilitate inter-agency coordination and communication to promote investor and consumer protection.
- The PWG should work to facilitate inter-agency coordination and communication to promote capital markets efficiency and competitiveness, including the consideration of benefits and burdens arising from statutes, rules, regulations, or other means, as well as from the regulatory structure itself.

Third, the PWG's membership should be expanded to include the heads of the Office of the Comptroller of the Currency ("OCC"), the Federal Deposit Insurance Corporation ("FDIC"), and the Office of Thrift Supervision ("OTS"). The new Executive Order should also clarify that the PWG has the authority to engage in consultation efforts, as might be appropriate, with other entities such as the Federal Reserve Bank of New York, the National Credit Union Administration ("NCUA"), the Office of Federal Housing Enterprise Oversight, the Federal Housing Finance Board, the Farm Credit Administration, and international regulatory and supervisory bodies. The reason for this formalization is that financial regulatory policy coordination often requires a broad range of financial regulatory experience and knowledge. As such, the specific permission to garner individual perspectives of financial policymakers with varied responsibilities and expertise will result in continued comprehensive and informed PWG policy discussions.

Finally, the new Executive Order should clarify that the PWG should have the ability to issue reports or other documents to the President and others, as appropriate, through its role as the coordination and communication mechanism for financial policy.

Treasury believes that these enhancements to the PWG's current role should maintain and in no way detract from the PWG's existing benefits. Furthermore, the new Executive Order should in no way alter, limit, or in any way change any of the PWG members' or participating agencies' existing statutory roles and responsibilities.

MORTGAGE ORIGINATION

Recommendation Overview

Treasury's recommendation has three components. First, Treasury recommends the creation of a new federal commission, the Mortgage Origination Commission ("MOC"), to evaluate, rate, and report on the adequacy of each state's system for licensing and regulating participants in the mortgage origination process. Federal legislation should set forth (or provide authority for the MOC to develop) uniform minimum licensing qualification standards for state mortgage market participant licensing systems. Second, Treasury recommends that the Federal Reserve continue to write regulations implementing national mortgage lending laws. Third, Treasury recommends clarification and enhancement of the enforcement authority over these laws.

Background

Mortgage market participants (both brokers and lenders) with no federal supervision have been responsible for a substantial portion of the mortgages and over 50 percent of the subprime mortgages originated in the United States.[21] These mortgage market participants are subject to uneven degrees of state level oversight (and in some cases limited or no oversight).

The high levels of delinquencies, defaults, and foreclosures among subprime borrowers in 2007 and 2008 have highlighted gaps in the U.S. oversight system for mortgage origination. Brokers and lenders not subject to federal oversight have repeatedly been cited as the source of abusive subprime loans with adverse and profound consequences for consumers, the mortgage markets, and the financial system as a whole.

The problem was not, however, entirely at the state level. Federally insured depository institutions and their affiliates did originate, purchase, or distribute some problematic subprime loans. There has also been some debate as to whether the OTS, the Federal Reserve, the FTC, state regulators, or some combination of all four oversees the affiliates of federally insured depository institutions.[22] Treasury supports the enhancement of mortgage lending standards at the federal level, and the clarification and strengthening of federal supervisory authorities.

Federal Level Oversight of State Systems – The Mortgage Origination Commission

Participants involved in the mortgage origination process make essential contributions to the home-buying process, one of the most important financial transactions that individuals conduct in their lifetimes. These participants in the mortgage origination process include mortgage brokers who assist consumers in securing mortgage products and lenders who develop and fund mortgage products. However, no readily available source of information exists regarding the background, experience, or disciplinary history of participants in the mortgage origination process with whom a borrower is considering doing business. In addition, no uniform minimum qualification standards for participants in the mortgage origination process exist. Current standards are set by individual states, and these standards vary in terms of both types of institutions or individuals that are required to obtain a license and specific licensing requirements.

To address part of this issue, the Conference of State Bank Supervisors ("CSBS") and the American Association of Residential Mortgage Regulators ("AARMR") have developed a Nationwide Mortgage Licensing System and Registry ("NMLSR"). NMLSR is designed to increase and centralize information regarding participants in the mortgage origination process. As of January 2008, seven states are participating in the NMLSR and forty states have indicated a commitment to participate in the system. Ultimately the NMLSR will provide information to regulators, the mortgage industry, and the general public on mortgage market participants' background, experience, and disciplinary history. Treasury supports this effort.

While the NMLSR is an important step, it still does not put in place a set of minimum licensing standards for participants in the mortgage origination process. Therefore, Treasury recommends subjecting participants in the mortgage origination process that are not employees of federally regulated depository institutions (or their subsidiaries) to uniform minimum licensing qualification standards.[23] In order to ensure a baseline consistency across state criteria for determining qualification and competencies of state licensees, federal standards should set uniform minimum standards for a qualifying state licensing system. These should include personal conduct and disciplinary history, minimum educational requirements, testing criteria and procedures, and appropriate license revocation standards.

This is not the first time Congress has seen the need to create a federal-level authority to evaluate the adequacy of aspects of the mortgage origination process.[24] Believing this to be another appropriate time to create such a federal-level authority, Treasury recommends the MOC's creation. Treasury's recommendation builds on existing state regulatory and supervisory systems, rather than establishing a new federal entity preempting state law.[25] Treasury believes it imperative to measure and publicly validate how well the state system is performing given federal reliance on its efforts.

The President should appoint a Director of the MOC for a four- to six-year term. The Director should be required to be someone of independent stature from either the mortgage regulatory community or the private sector mortgage market. The Director also should have demonstrated expertise in the legal and regulatory requirements and private sector standards governing the U.S. primary and secondary mortgage markets. The Director would chair a seven-person board comprised of the principals (or their designees) of the Federal Reserve, the OCC, the OTS, the FDIC, the NCUA, and a representative from the CSBS. The MOC should be granted broad authority to ensure that states are effectively monitoring compliance with federal mortgage lending laws. The MOC should perform several key functions:

- First, federal legislation should set forth (or provide authority for the MOC to develop) uniform minimum licensing qualification standards for state mortgage market participant licensing systems.

- Second, the MOC should develop and apply criteria to evaluate and audit periodically the adequacy of state systems for regulating mortgage market participants, including licensing, supervision, and enforcement.[26]
- Third, to perform the above task, the MOC should have authority to hire an expert staff from the regulatory community and the private sector, supplemented by interagency staff derived from the participating members of the MOC's board on an "as-needed" basis.

The MOC's evaluations should grade the overall adequacy of a state system by descriptive categories indicative of a system's strength or weakness. The MOC should publicly issue and conduct the evaluations on a rolling cycle, but any state could request a new evaluation out of its regular cycle based on a material change in information significant to its rating.

The public nature of these evaluations should provide strong incentives for states to address weaknesses and strengthen their own systems. Once this system is in place, these evaluations could be used in a number of ways. For example, regulators of government-sponsored enterprises ("GSEs") could use these evaluations to make distinctions with regard to capital charges (e.g., a low evaluation would signal higher levels of risk). Similarly, private-label securitizers or GSEs could use these evaluations as part of their underwriting process and disclosure practices. Some underwriters may choose to exclude mortgages from poorly rated states in newly created mortgage-backed securities.

Treasury believes the MOC will provide more information to the market and will make a significant contribution to addressing the gaps between the federal and state regulatory systems. It is also necessary, however, to clarify the applicability of and enforcement regimes for federal mortgage lending standards.

Uniform Federal Mortgage Lending Standards

Federal mortgage lending laws should ensure adequate consumer protection for all types of mortgage originators.[27] Today, this is accomplished primarily through the Truth in Lending Act ("TILA"), including the Home Ownership and Equity Protection Act ("HOEPA"), a part of TILA dealing specifically with subprime loans and imposing additional disclosure requirements and substantive standards in connection with those loans. TILA standards apply to all "creditors," not just federally regulated depository institutions extending consumer credit, provided they are the party to whom the debt is initially payable. The Federal Reserve is the only agency vested with rulemaking authority under TILA (including HOEPA).

Treasury recommends that the Federal Reserve, given its existing role, experience, and expertise in implementing the TILA provisions affecting mortgage transactions, retain the authority to write regulations implementing TILA in this area. In developing rules associated with TILA, the Federal Reserve currently has a comprehensive process to take into account the balance between new requirements' costs and benefits. This should include existing TILA provisions and any additional provisions enacted to enhance consumer protections against abusive or predatory mortgage lending practices. In addition, however, it also may be necessary to amend TILA to ensure that it appropriately covers both mortgage lenders and mortgage brokers.[28] The Federal Reserve should be required to consult with the other federal banking regulators in developing its rules in this area.

Enforcement Authority

Enforcement authority over federal mortgage lending standards can be confusing and needs clarification. Currently, TILA enforcement authority for federally regulated depository institutions rests with the institution's primary federal banking regulator. A depository institution's federal regulator also supervises its subsidiaries, examining them as part of the parent institutions' required regular examination and subjecting them to enforcement by that regulator.[29] This aspect of the enforcement framework of federal mortgage lending law is satisfactory.

Oversight and enforcement with respect to other mortgage originators present concerns, however. These mortgage originators fall into two basic categories: affiliates of depository institutions within a federally regulated holding company, and independent participants in the mortgage origination process (i.e., those unaffiliated with depository institutions).[30] Enforcement authority needs to be clarified for these types of institutions.

For mortgage originators that are affiliates of depository institutions within a federally regulated holding company, mortgage lending compliance and enforcement must be clarified. Any lingering issues concerning the authority of the Federal Reserve (as bank holding company regulator), the OTS (as thrift holding company regulator), or state supervisory agencies in conjunction with the holding company regulator to examine and enforce federal mortgage laws with respect to those affiliates must be addressed.

The benefits of federal supervision must be applied to the mortgage origination activities of those affiliates. Treasury recommends that the appropriate state supervisory agency, in conjunction with the appropriate holding company regulator, examine the holding company affiliates' mortgage origination activities on a regular examination cycle.

Finally, for independent participants in the mortgage origination process, the sector of the industry responsible for the majority of subprime loan origination in recent years, it is essential that states have clear authority to enforce federal mortgage lending standards. State agencies responsible for licensing and regulating participants in the mortgage origination process need clear authority to enforce compliance with the TILA provisions governing mortgage transactions.[31] Treasury recommends that this authority be provided to state agencies for the non-federally regulated participants in the mortgage origination process subject to state jurisdiction. Although federal mortgage lending standards may, on their face, apply to all types of creditors, consistent oversight and enforcement of those standards are essential to ensure that those standards work in practice.

LIQUIDITY PROVISIONING BY THE FEDERAL RESERVE

Recommendation Overview

The Federal Reserve's March 2008 opening of the discount window to non-depository institutions was necessary to restore market stability. While the Federal Reserve used this authority for the first time since the 1930s, given the increased importance of non-depository institutions to overall market stability, there is a possibility that this decision might be revisited in future periods of instability. In that context, Treasury recommends the consideration of two issues. First, the Federal Reserve should consider the current process in terms of ensuring that the process is calibrated and transparent, appropriate conditions are attached to lending, and information flows are adequate. Second, the President's Working Group on Financial Markets should consider broader issues associated with providing discount window access to non-depository institutions.

Background

The disruptions in credit markets in 2007 and 2008 have caused the Federal Reserve to address some of the fundamental issues associated with the discount window and the overall provision of liquidity to the financial system. The Federal Reserve has considered alternative ways to provide liquidity to the financial system. In addition to the Term Auction Facility ("TAF") program for depository institutions, the Federal Reserve has had to think more broadly about overall liquidity issues associated with non-depository institutions. This process has resulted in the creation of additional sources of liquidity for non-depository institutions by providing access to the discount window and through the establishment of a Term Securities Lending Facility ("TSLF").

The Federal Reserve's recent actions reflect the fundamentally different nature of the market stability function in today's financial markets compared to those of the past. The Federal Reserve has balanced the difficult tradeoffs associated with preserving market stability and considering issues associated with expanding the safety net.

While the Federal Reserve used its authority for the first time since the 1930s to provide access to the discount window to non-depository institutions, given the increased importance of non-depository institutions to overall market stability, there is a possibility that this decision might be revisited in future periods of instability. However, these are important issues that deserve further consideration as described below. At a minimum, to reflect better the changing nature of financial instability associated with non-depository institutions, Treasury recommends a few enhancements to the current process. These recommendations would preserve the principle contained in the Federal Reserve's current authority that lending to non-depository institutions should only occur in rare circumstances, would improve the transparency of the process, and would allow the Federal Reserve to better protect its balance sheet and ultimately U.S. taxpayers.

Enhancements to the Current Discount Window Lending Process

The recent action to use the discount window to lend to non-depository institutions on the same terms and conditions as are available to insured depository institutions was an appropriate response to address potential market stability issues. It is important to note that such access contains a number of checks on the process, which makes it much different than the discount window access currently provided to insured depository institutions. First, Federal Reserve lending to non-depository institutions can only be provided after it has been approved by a sufficient number of members of the Board of Governors. That makes access to discount window lending much less certain for non- depository institutions. Second, the Federal Reserve's decision to extend discount window lending to non-depository institutions is conditioned on the existence of "unusual and exigent circumstances" related to the inability to "secure adequate credit." [32] Those conditions clarify that such authority will only be used in rare circumstances and this source of funds should not be relied upon as a general source of liquidity.

Under the Federal Reserve's current authority, some additional issues should be considered so that the Federal Reserve has an appropriate structure in place and possesses the necessary information if market events require the Federal Reserve to provide a liquidity backstop to non-depository institutions. These changes would be designed to prevent the blurring between bank regulation, which involves a taxpayer-funded backstop, and non-bank regulation, where taxpayers do not provide insurance.

A Calibrated and Transparent Lending Process

Providing access to the discount window for non-depository institutions on the same terms and conditions as are available for depository institutions does raise significant issues. To address that concern, the Federal Reserve should consider ways to calibrate better and make this type of lending more transparent if the need arises in the future. The TAF process provides a good model for such a structure.

Conditions Attached to Non-Depository Institution Lending

Opening the discount window to non-depository institutions raises obvious concerns about protecting the Federal Reserve's balance sheet, and ultimately the U.S. taxpayers. In particular, the regulatory structure that applies to non-depository institutions is different than what applies to depository institutions. The Federal Reserve typically has little or no direct supervisory role over non-depository institutions. Due to these differences, the Federal Reserve may have less confidence regarding the financial condition of non-depository institutions.

The Federal Reserve currently has authority to impose limitations and restrictions on discount window borrowing by non-depository institutions.[33] One key way that the Federal Reserve protects its balance sheet is through collateral requirements. However, this broad authority could be used in additional ways to protect the Federal Reserve's balance sheet. The Federal Reserve is already doing much of this today. Further consideration of what measures might be imposed on lending to non-depository institutions is important.

Greater Availability of Information

As noted above, the Federal Reserve may not have access to the same type of supervisory information over non-depository institutions that it has over depository institutions. This lack of supervisory information hinders not only the Federal Reserve's ability to make prudent discount window decisions, but also its ability to evaluate any potential need for providing discount window lending to non-depository institutions. Key to this information flow is a focus on liquidity and funding.

To address this gap in information, Treasury recommends that the Federal Reserve enter into a collaborative agreement with the CFTC and the SEC that would allow the Federal Reserve to access examination information and to accompany the SEC and the CFTC on financial examinations. While the Federal Reserve and the SEC have been working closely throughout the recent credit market events, a more formalized arrangement would contribute to the Federal Reserve's overall understanding of financial market conditions. Such an agreement would also provide useful information for the Federal Reserve's operation of the discount window should the need to invoke broader lending authority arise in the future.

Broader Regulatory Issues Associated with Expanded Access to Liquidity Facilities

What was described above are broader regulatory issues to consider under the Federal Reserve's current liquidity provisioning authority, under the basic assumption that such an action would be taken only in unusual circumstances.

Providing broader access to the discount window raises issues of expanding the government's safety net. Some might suggest that because the Federal Reserve has provided non-depository institutions access to the Federal Reserve's liquidity facilities these institutions should be supervised and regulated in the same way as insured depository institutions. Under this view the safety net has been irrevocably expanded, and doing anything less would create distortions, increase risk in the financial system, and expose the Federal Reserve's balance sheet to significant levels of risk.

These are difficult issues that we need to address. The optimal structure described in Chapter VI provides a framework to consider these issues. As we work through this period, we will surely gain important insight into the root financial causes that led to the need to provide broader access to the discount window. It is appropriate that we evaluate that experience in the coming months, and use the lessons of that experience to inform a path forward.

It is important to ask for the PWG's perspective on these events.

Chapter 5

INTERMEDIATE-TERM RECOMMENDATIONS

This chapter describes recommendations focused on eliminating some of the duplication in the U.S. regulatory system, but more importantly on modernizing the regulatory structure applicable to certain sectors in the financial services industry (i.e., banking, insurance, futures, and securities) within the current framework. These recommendations serve as a useful transition to the optimal regulatory structure. However, each intermediate-term recommendation stands on its own merits, as well as on its merits as a transitional element.

THRIFT CHARTER

Recommendation Overview

Treasury recommends phasing out the federal thrift charter over a two-year period and transitioning the federal thrift charter to the national bank charter. Treasury also recommends the merger of the Office of the Comptroller of the Currency and the Office of Thrift Supervision during this period.

Background and Historical Context

In the past, the thrift (or savings and loan) and banking industries had distinctly different missions, authorities, regulators, and deposit insurance entities. Now, however, the differences between the two industries have substantially diminished and their respective activities and authorities have converged. These developments raise the critical policy question of whether to retain the thrift charter and, if not, whether to eliminate and replace the federal thrift charter with a unified charter containing features of both existing federal charters.

The modern day regulatory structure for thrifts can be traced back to the Great Depression Era of the early 1 930s.[34] In the wake of the infamous stock market crash of 1929, a number of banks and thrifts failed. In response to the near collapse of the financial system, Congress passed a number of new statutes to strengthen financial institutions and the economy. The Federal Home Loan Bank Act of 1932 ("FHLB Act"), the

Home Owners' Loan Act of 1933 ("HOLA"), and the National Housing Act in 1934 laid much of the foundation for today's mortgage finance industry.

The FHLB Act established the Federal Home Loan Bank ("FHLB") System and the FHLB Board ("FHLBB") in order to improve conditions in the mortgage finance sector. Up and until that time, thrifts were state-based institutions, most operating under a mutual form of organization. These state-based thrifts were primarily in the business of making mortgage loans to their mutual depositors. The rising number of defaults and foreclosures resulting from the Great Depression put severe stress on the thrifts. During this time more than 1,700 thrifts failed, and their depositors lost $200 million, or about one-third of the value of their deposits.[35] The FHLB System, a network of twelve cooperative regional banks created to borrow funds on behalf of their thrift members, helped to restore liquidity to the thrift industry. Congress established the FHLBB to oversee the FHLB System.

The FHLB System's creation only represented the federal government's first step in support of the faltering housing market and troubled thrifts. In 1933 Congress passed HOLA, which among other things granted the FHLBB the authority to charter and regulate federal thrifts. These federally chartered thrifts were required to become members of one of the twelve regional FHLBs.

Despite the fact that the federal government had made significant efforts to reform and restructure the thrift industry, thrifts were not immune from competitive pressures resulting from recent legislative changes affecting the banking industry. The creation of federal deposit insurance for banks in the Banking Act 1933 afforded banking institutions a significant advantage over thrifts in retaining and attracting customer deposits. As a result, Congress passed the National Housing Act of 1934, creating the Federal Savings and Loan Insurance Corporation ("FSLIC"). Much like the Federal Deposit Insurance Corporation ("FDIC"), the FSLIC acted as deposit insurer, conservator, and receiver for federally chartered thrifts. The FSLIC insured deposits in these institutions. State-based thrifts were eligible for FSLIC insurance if they met certain minimum safety and soundness standards.

Evolution of the Thrift Charter

As noted in Chapter III, in 1967 Congress adopted the Savings and Loan Holding Company Amendments. These amendments to the National Housing Act emerged largely due to two concerns: thrifts were enjoying competitive advantages vis-à-vis banks as a result of the requirements contained in the Bank Holding Company Act of 1956 ("BHC Act")[36] and a diversified ownership structure could allow a parent company to use the depository institution in order to benefit affiliated businesses.

The Financial Institutions Regulatory and Interest Rate Control Act of 1978 created the interagency Federal Financial Institutions Examination Council ("FFIEC"). In large measure to harmonize certain aspects of depository institution regulation and supervision, Congress established the FFIEC to prescribe uniform standards and make recommendations in other areas of supervision.[37] Since the creation of FFIEC, depository institution regulators have used the FFIEC as a vehicle to implement consistent oversight standards across the federally regulated thrift and bank depository institutions.

Subsequent to the elimination of the restrictions on interest rates that thrifts could pay on deposits, many thrifts faced the challenge of procuring sufficient funding for their assets and a significant mismatch between their higher-rate assets and their low-rate deposit liabilities.[38] Congress responded to the thrifts' predicament by passing the Garn-St Germain Depository Institutions Act of 1982 ("Garn-St Germain Act"), which allowed the thrift industry significantly more lending and investment flexibility than it previously had possessed. More specifically, the Garn-St Germain Act raised the investment ceiling from 20 to 40 percent of their assets in non-residential real estate, from 20 to 30 percent of their assets in consumer loans, and from 20 to 30 percent of their assets in equity investments.[39] In order to generate returns sufficient to remain profitable and attract and retain depositors' funds, thrifts used their newly broadened authority to engage in more risky lending practices, ultimately resulting in significant losses and a government bailout of the thrift industry.

In 1987 the Competitive Equality Banking Act ("CEBA") closed the "nonbank bank" loophole in the BHC Act by broadening the definition of "bank" in the BHC Act to cover any institution that is either FDIC-insured or both accepts demand deposits and makes commercial loans. CEBA's relevance to the thrift industry is its establishment of the qualified thrift lender ("QTL") test in order to keep the thrift industry focused on the provision of residential mortgage loans to U.S. consumers. More specifically, in order to receive many of the special benefits available to a thrift at that time, a financial institution had to pass the QTL test, requiring that at least 65 percent of an institution's portfolio assets be qualified thrift investments, primarily residential mortgages and related investments. Among other things, a thrift's failure to meet the QTL test resulted in its parent unitary thrift holding company losing its exemption from HOLA's activities restrictions.[40]

As a response to the large number of thrift failures that occurred during the 1980s, in 1989 Congress passed the Financial Institutions Reform, Recovery and Enforcement Act ("FIRREA"). Many reasons caused the significant number of thrift failures in that decade. After the easing of investing restrictions, thrifts invested significantly in shopping centers, malls, office buildings, and other types of non-housing related investments, particularly in the Southwest. A number of particularly aggressive thrifts invested in highly speculative enterprises, including oil operations and windmill farms. Thrift institutions also heavily invested in high yield bonds that subsequently experienced significant declines in value. Additionally, regulators estimated that 40 percent of thrift failures were attributable to fraud or insider abuse.[41]

FIRREA's passage resulted in a number of important changes to the regulatory, chartering, and deposit insurance regime governing the thrift industry. Specifically, FIRREA terminated the FSLIC and the FHLBB; established the Office of Thrift Supervision ("OTS") as a new office in the Department of the Treasury ("Treasury") to charter and oversee thrift holding companies and thrifts; formed and capitalized the Savings Association Insurance Fund ("SAIF") within the FDIC to replace FSLIC's insurance fund; established the Federal Housing Finance Board to regulate the FHLB System; and incorporated and funded the Resolution Trust Corporation to manage failed bank and thrift assets. FIRREA also added two directorships to the FDIC Board of Directors, with one automatically held by the new OTS Director.

In the wake of FIRREA, the OTS, an office in Treasury modeled after the Office of the Comptroller of the Currency ("OCC"), now regulated thrifts. Furthermore, the FDIC, historically the insurer and back-up bank supervisor, was now performing those same functions for thrifts.[42] Thus, FIRREA represented another legislative action in which Congress determined it to be good public policy to continue to eliminate previously significant distinctions between banking and thrift institutions.

Additional Changes from the 1990s to the Present

In 1991 the Federal Deposit Insurance Corporation Improvements Act ("FDICIA") substantially changed the way in which depository institution regulators must supervise their regulated institutions. In large measure Congress enacted FDICIA as a response to the prevailing opinion that regulatory forbearance was one of the key policy underpinnings of the resulting bank and thrift failures of the late 1980s and early 1990s.[43] In FDICIA, Congress established a system of capital-based prompt corrective action ("PCA").[44] FDICIA also ordered federal regulators to implement risk-based capital measures. These changes, along with other provisions, led to greater convergence of federal bank and thrift charters. As a result, both charters were now subject to capital-based PCA and risk-based capital requirements. As capital is a major driver of financial institution operations, FDICIA eliminated any significant charter arbitrage opportunities in the areas of capital requirements or potential regulatory forbearance.

While thrifts had enjoyed liberalized interstate branching privileges since the passage of HOLA, federally regulated banks were strictly limited in their ability to branch across state lines.[45] In 1994, Congress passed the Riegle-Neal Interstate Banking and Branching Efficiency Act ("Riegle-Neal Act"), further eroding differences between bank and thrift branching flexibility.

The Gramm-Leach-Bliley Act of 1999 ("GLB Act") received a great deal of attention because of its repeal of provisions of the Glass-Steagall Act of 1933 which had mandated the separation of commercial and investment banking activities. One of the GLB Act's key provisions established a financial holding company ("FHC") structure as a vehicle to allow affiliations among banks, securities firms, and insurers.

More specific to thrifts, the GLB Act changed the landscape for thrift holding companies. Prior to the GLB Act, unitary thrift holding companies owning a single thrift institution were allowed to affiliate with commercial entities, despite the general overall policy framework prohibiting any linkages between banking and commerce. The GLB Act eliminated the ability of non-grandfathered unitary thrift holding companies[46] to affiliate with commercial entities, one of the major remaining distinctions between the bank and thrift charters. Prior to the GLB Act the non-bank affiliates of bank holding companies ("BHCs") could only engage in activities that the Federal Reserve deemed closely related to banking. After the passage of the GLB Act, no commercial entity could acquire a federally chartered depository institution.

The Federal Deposit Insurance Reform Act of 2005 ("FDIR Act") made significant changes to the deposit insurance regime for banks and thrifts. Arguably the most important change was the legislation's merging of the Bank Insurance Fund ("BIF") and the SAIF into one single fund, the Deposit Insurance Fund. As a result, both banks and thrifts, regardless of which type of institution is responsible for the loss, bear indirectly any losses triggering FDIC payments. In light of this change, the FDIR Act's joining of the deposit insurance mechanisms for banks and thrifts represents one more significant reduction in the differences between the bank and thrift charters. However, bifurcation of the safety and soundness oversight of the charters remains.

Remaining Comparative Advantage of the Thrift Charter

Historically, banking institutions have not generally been subject to either a forced orientation toward a particular area of lending, such as real estate financing, or to specific asset-type lending constraints. In contrast, thrifts are subject to several specific lending constraints, including asset concentration limits on nonresidential real estate loans, commercial loans, and unsecured residential construction loans. However, as long as thrift institutions continue to meet the QTL test,[47] thrifts continue to maintain some limited competitive advantages vis-à-vis their banking competitors.

Branching Rights
The federal thrift charter confers the broadest geographic expansion authority of any federally insured depository institution charter. Despite the fact that the Riegle-Neal Act reduced much of thrifts' historical branching advantages, some states still subject banks to a limited range of restrictions on their statewide branching authority.

Service Corporation Activities
Federally chartered thrifts may invest up to three percent of their assets in service corporations. Major activities permissible for service corporations, but not currently for national banks, include real estate development activities[48] and real estate management for third parties.

Thrift Holding Company Activities
The Savings and Loan Holding Company ("SLHC") Act, administered by the OTS, subjects thrift holding companies to regulation similar to that of BHCs but with several important distinctions. The OTS has authority to deal with any activity of a thrift holding company posing a serious risk to the safety, soundness, or stability of the holding company's subsidiary thrifts. Thrift holding companies with multiple thrifts are subject to strict limitations on activities, but there are no permissible activities or ownership structure restrictions on unitary thrift holding companies whose thrifts meet a housing- related QTL test. However, as noted above, the GLB Act mandated regulating new unitary thrift holding companies as multiple thrift holding companies and generally permitted new unitary thrift holding companies to engage in activities permissible for FHCs, with certain limited grandfathered exceptions.

Other Differences in Authority over Thrifts

There are a couple of other remaining benefits of the thrift charter, primarily related to OTS' broader legal authority over thrifts than the banking regulators have over their regulated institutions.

Stronger Federal Preemption Authority

Both the federal regulator and its regulated institutions view the regulator's ability to preempt a myriad of state laws, regulations, and oversight of its regulated entities as a powerful and significant authority. A regulator with strong preemptive authority may establish uniform rules for its regulated institutions, providing for consistent and fair oversight. Likewise, regulated entities can benefit from uniform oversight by not being subject to the potential inefficiency of having to deal with multiple state regulators, laws, regulations, and standards.

From a banking and thrift regulatory perspective, the legal system historically has viewed HOLA as granting the OTS stronger preemptive authority than the National Bank Act's granting to the OCC. While over time, and especially in recent years, the OCC has expanded and affirmed its preemptive authority regarding national bank regulation, there is widespread agreement that HOLA provides the OTS with stronger field preemption authority.[49] As a result, holders of thrift charters benefit from the uniformity and certainty of regulatory oversight that goes along with clear state law preemption.

Office of Thrift Supervision's Unfair and Deceptive Acts and Practices Authority

The Federal Trade Commission Act ("FTC Act") provides that OTS "shall prescribe regulations to prevent unfair or deceptive acts or practices by savings associations in or affecting commerce, including acts or practices that are unfair or deceptive to consumers." This section also states that OTS's regulations may take a variety of approaches "including" (but not limited to) regulations "defining with specificity" which acts or practices are unfair or deceptive, as well as principles-based regulations "containing requirements prescribed for the purposes of preventing such acts or practices." This provision of the FTC Act assigns the same rulemaking authority to the Federal Reserve with respect to banks and the National Credit Union Administration ("NCUA") with respect to federal credit unions. The OCC and the FDIC do not possess this independent authority.

The OTS recently issued an advance notice of proposed rulemaking to highlight the history of OTS's independent regulatory actions undertaken through the FTC Act and its own statutory authority under the HOLA to address unfair or deceptive acts or practices or other consumer protection issues.

Reasons for the Unification of Thrift and Bank Charters Background

Treasury concludes that the thrift charter is no longer necessary to ensure sufficient residential mortgage loans are made available to U.S. consumers. This position is supported by four developments: asset securitization, bank versus thrift volume and market share of residential mortgage loans, changes to the FHLB System's composition and asset allocation, and remaining charter differences' hindering the ability of thrifts to diversify their portfolios effectively.

Asset Securitization

A critical financial innovation rendering depository institutions, in general, and thrifts, in particular, less relevant in the context of residential mortgage lending is asset securitization. This process involves the collection or pooling of loans and the sale of securities backed by those loans. Asset securitization has had a major impact on the traditional financial institution methods of funding mortgages and holding them in portfolio. There are four steps to the asset securitization process: originate a mortgage loan, pool the loan with other mortgage loans in a portfolio of assets, service the loan by collecting payments and providing tax or other information to the borrower, and selling securities backed by the pool of mortgage loans to obtain funding from the public with which to originate new mortgage loans.

Issuers of securitized assets receive several benefits: a lower cost of funds, more efficient use of capital, ease in managing rapid portfolio growth, enhanced financial performance, and diversification of funding sources. From the investor perspective, securitization converts illiquid loans into securities usually having greater liquidity and reduced credit risk. The diversified pools of loans backing the security and the credit enhancements attached to the security generally reduce credit risk.

The advent of the residential mortgage securitization market and the large growth of both government-sponsored enterprises ("GSEs"), such as the Federal National Mortgage Association ("Fannie Mae") and the Federal Home Loan Mortgage Corporation ("Freddie Mac"), and other asset-backed securities markets have shrunk traditional depository institutions' share of the overall residential mortgage market. For example, at the end of 2005, Fannie Mae's and Freddie Mac's combined book of business (mortgage-backed securities ("MBS") held by other investors and each GSE's mortgages and MBS not guaranteed by other GSEs) represented 40 percent of the total residential mortgage debt outstanding, slightly down from the 43 percent share at the end of 2004.

At the end of 2006, non-GSE asset-backed securities issuers' share of the market was approximately 20 percent of the $10.4 trillion residential mortgage debt outstanding. Thus, the GSEs and non-GSE securitizers control approximately 60 to 65 percent of the total residential mortgage market. Despite recent stress in the securities market, there is still a robust level of GSE securitization.

Thrift and Bank Amount and Shares of the
Overall U.S. Residential Mortgage Market

As highlighted throughout this analysis, thrifts, distinct from banks, focus mainly on the provision of residential mortgage credit. Since the 1930s national policy has encouraged home ownership, the special focus of the thrift industry since that time.

However, thrifts' and banks' relative shares and volumes of residential mortgage portfolios have shifted significantly over the past few decades, resulting in commercial banks being a far more significant player in the residential mortgage market than thrifts. With other institutions providing availability to the U.S. residential mortgage markets, thrifts are no longer necessary to this market's effective functioning.

Several key statistics support this position. For example, while the thrift industry held a 50 percent share of the total residential mortgage market in 1980, that percentage had slipped to only 10 percent by the end of 2005. Meanwhile, the commercial banking industry had achieved almost a 20 percent share of the overall residential mortgage market by the end of 2005. In 1993, the commercial banking industry passed the thrift industry in total dollar volume of residential mortgage assets ($532 billion versus $470 billion) and has surpassed the thrift industry every year since with increasingly higher residential mortgage volume levels than thrifts. As a result, the commercial banking industry held more than twice the dollar volume of residential mortgage assets than the thrift industry ($2.1 trillion versus $870 billion) at the end of 2006. These statistics clearly demonstrate thrifts diminished role and commercial banks' increasing role in the overall residential mortgage market.

Federal Home Loan Bank System Membership and Asset Allocation

Over the past number of years, Congress has opened up the FHLB System to financial institutions other than the thrift industry. This has eliminated the thrift industry's historical advantage in being able to tap the FHLB System's alternative funding source in times of financial system illiquidity, including during the latter months of 2007.

For example, as of the end of the third quarter of 2007, OTS-regulated thrift institutions constituted only about 10 percent of the FHLB System's total membership (805 out of 8,080 members). Commercial banks and FDIC-examined savings banks totaled 6,230 out of 8,080 members, or approximately 77 percent of the FHLB System's total membership. Furthermore, thrifts held less in total advances outstanding than commercial banks.[50] Commercial banks held $422 billion in advances, or 53 percent of the total advances outstanding, while thrifts held only $328 billion, or 41 percent of the total advances outstanding.[51] Credit unions and insurers held the remaining advances.

Remaining Asset Constraints on the Thrift Industry

The thrift industry remains subject to serious lending constraints that limit portfolio diversification on a product basis. This limitation leaves thrifts more susceptible to earnings and capital problems in the face of a decline in the single-family housing market such as the United States experienced in 2007 and 2008.

In general, for thrifts, nonresidential real estate secured loans may not exceed 400 percent of capital. Commercial loans may not exceed 20 percent of total assets, and amounts in excess of 10 percent of total assets may only be used for small business loans. Unsecured residential construction loans may not exceed the greater of 5 percent of assets or 100 percent of capital. Finally, the combination of consumer loans, commercial paper, and corporate debt securities may not exceed 35 percent of total assets.

Recommendation

Treasury recommends transitioning the federal thrift charter to the national bank charter, removing the need for separate federal regulation of thrifts. Unitary thrift holding companies should fall under the same regulatory structure as BHCs.[52] This combination of the thrift industry with the banking industry should transition over a two-year period. Treasury believes in the need for such a transition period to allow thrifts to prepare to become banks and also to permit an orderly merger of the OTS and the OCC.

At the end of the two-year conversion period, all federally chartered thrifts should convert to national banks by operation of law. (These thrifts should have the right to elect an earlier conversion date, and should retain their current rights to convert to any other available charter prior to the end of the two-year period.) All state-chartered thrifts should be treated as state-chartered banks for all federal bank regulatory purposes.

As a result of the conversion of federally chartered thrifts to banks and the treatment of state-chartered thrifts as banks, thrift holding companies should become BHCs under the BHC Act. Unitary thrift holding companies grandfathered under the GLB Act should be exempted from the activity limitations under the BHC Act, provided they continued to meet nontransferability, QTL tests, enhanced firewall and other conditions of existing thrift law on the conversion date.

To facilitate the conversion of the thrift industry to bank regulation, each banking agency should institute a program to accommodate voluntary specialization in housing finance and the conversion of thrift institutions to bank charters. A mutual national bank charter should be made available to accommodate thrifts presently operating in mutual form, and mutual holding companies should be authorized.

The OTS and the OCC should be merged, pursuant to plans developed by the Secretary of the Treasury, effective two years after enactment. With the merger of the OTS and OCC, the size of the FDIC Board should be restored to three members, as it was for the fifty-six years before the OTS's creation. As part of the plan, Congress should transfer supervision and regulation of approximately eighty-four state-chartered thrifts[53] to the FDIC, which already supervises over 400 state-chartered savings banks.[54]

STATE BANK REGULATION

Recommendation Overview

Treasury recommends the rationalization of direct federal supervision of state-chartered banks. Treasury recommends a study be conducted to rationalize the Federal Reserve's and the Federal Deposit Insurance Corporation's regulation of state-chartered banks with a federal guarantee.

Background

As noted above, federal depository institution regulation and supervision are quite complicated, with five different federal agencies performing this role, each for a statutorily assigned portion of depository institutions. In banking, the federal supervisory responsibilities are divided by charter (i.e., federal or state) and membership in the Federal Reserve System.

National banks are both chartered and regulated by the OCC. The fact that the chartering agency is also the supervisory agency generally lowers the need for coordination with other banking agencies in any specific banking examination.

State-chartered banks with deposit insurance are supervised at the federal level by the Federal Reserve if they are members of the Federal Reserve System, and by the FDIC, if they are not members of the Federal Reserve System. In the case of these state-chartered banks, whether the supervisory agency is the Federal Reserve or the FDIC, the need for coordination with another agency is generally significant, because the state banking agency that chartered the bank has strong and continuing responsibilities for the bank. Moreover, state laws provide a very wide and diverse range of bank charters, from mutual banks, to commercial banks to others. Thus, in the context of these state- chartered institutions, federal examinations must take into account the powers authorized by the state charter, and thus both federal law and state law influence those examinations.

Rationalization of Federal Supervision over State-Chartered Banks

A more efficient, and thus competitive, system for federal banking supervision of state chartered-banks should effectively focus examination resources and avoid duplication.

One approach would be to place all such banking supervisory responsibilities for state-chartered banks with the Federal Reserve. A central bank generally focuses on monetary policy and the operation of the payment system, both linked to central bank responsibilities for promoting liquidity and financial stability. The Federal Reserve has argued that having a role in bank supervision is important for its role in formulating monetary policy. However, state-chartered banks are mostly smaller institutions with limited impact on overall financial stability. In addition, while discount window access is available to insured depository institutions the Federal Reserve does not supervise, the Federal Reserve also argues that having a staff of bank examiners is still useful in making discount window lending decisions.

Another approach would be to place all such banking supervisory responsibilities for state-chartered banks with the FDIC. The FDIC currently has banking supervisory responsibilities for what are typically the smallest banks in the United States and for banks that reflect a wide range of charters. The FDIC has extensive experience in the examination of small community banks, such as many of those that have a state charter. In addition, the FDIC's mission of insuring deposits, examining and supervising financial institutions, and managing receiverships, is directly related to the supervision of smaller state-chartered banks.

Recommendation

Treasury recommends a study, one that fully and fairly examines the roles of the Federal Reserve System and the FDIC in state-bank supervision. Any such shift of supervisory authority for state-chartered banks with federal deposit insurance from the Federal Reserve to the FDIC or vice versa raises a number of issues regarding the overall structure of the Federal Reserve System. In particular, this study should also examine the evolving role of Federal Reserve Banks as part of developing a recommendation for the appropriate federal supervisory regime for state-chartered banks.

Payment and Settlement Systems

Recommendation Overview

Treasury recommends the creation of a federal charter for systemically important payment and settlement systems. The Federal Reserve should have primary oversight responsibilities for such systems.

Background

Payment and settlement systems are the mechanisms used to transfer funds and financial instruments between financial institutions and between financial institutions and their customers in order to discharge obligations arising from financial market and economic activity. For example, large-value payment and settlement systems supporting important financial markets typically make fund transfers for the purchase of securities and other financial instruments. These systems are a critical underpinning of the financial services sector, and of the economy as a whole. For example, U.S. payment and settlement systems on a typical business day settle transactions valued at over $13 trillion. In other words, a sum roughly of the magnitude of the entire U.S. annual gross domestic product is typically transacted every single business day. These transactions settle among financial intermediaries, such as banks and dealers, with the bulk of value settling among the largest financial institutions. Payment and settlement systems play a fundamental and extremely important role in the U.S. economy by providing the set of institutional, procedural, and technical mechanisms through which financial institutions can easily settle transactions.

Payment and settlement systems, especially the most important systems, have the ability to contribute to financial system risk, if either the system or the rules governing the system are not well-designed and well-run. As a result, a poorly designed or poorly run system or series of rules governing such systems can contribute to financial crises, rather than reduce them, thereby imperiling the stability of U.S. and foreign financial markets. It is important that all participants in a payment or settlement system have a clear understanding of the system's impact on the financial risks they incur. Moreover, participants must have confidence that the system is highly reliable, without detracting from its convenience or price. As a result, the establishment of high degrees of safety and efficiency of systemically important systems is an important element of U.S. financial policy.

In the United States, and in most of the world, almost all economic transactions involve some form of payment. The U.S. financial system also involves substantial trade in financial instruments such as futures, securities, and derivatives. Payment and settlement systems enable these transactions and trades to settle through the transfer of bank deposits and financial instruments. The United States has various payment and settlement systems, including large-value funds transfers, settlement systems for securities and other financial instruments, central counterparty systems, and retail payment systems. Depository institutions often play important roles in the functioning of these systems, including the provision of credit and contingent liquidity, custody or deposit services, or operational support.

International Best Practices

International best practices, as described by the Bank for International Settlements, recommend that central banks have general oversight authority for payment and settlement systems, and that such authority be clear and tailored to the nature of such systems. This responsibility is given to central banks because of the role that central banks generally play in developed countries:

- Central banks act as the monetary authority, and are charged with supplying money that meets the purpose of serving as a liquid means of exchange of value. Payment systems functionally provide the mechanism for transferring money and discharging economic claims among economic actors.
- Central banks are charged with ensuring liquidity for an economy, and are authorized to supply emergency liquidity when necessary to encourage the orderly settlement of transactions in the overall financial system. Safe and efficient payment and settlement systems facilitate the provision of such support should it prove necessary.
- Central banks are generally charged with ensuring price stability. The Federal Reserve implements monetary policy by influencing short-term interest rates primarily through the purchase and sale of government securities or through collateralized lending to depository institutions. It is important that safe and efficient payment and settlement systems are available to allow a reliable transfer of funds and securities among the central bank, its counterparties, and the other participants in the financial system so that the effect of these transactions, and thus the impact of monetary policy, is spread throughout the economy.

U.S. Regulatory Structure for Payment and Settlement Systems

In the United States, major payment and settlement systems are generally not subject to any uniform, specifically designed, and overarching regulatory system. Payment and settlement systems have sought organizational forms within the existing regulatory structure best meeting their needs. Some systems are clearinghouses or banking associations subject to the Bank Service Company Act. Others have various state or federal banking charters or are registered as securities clearing agencies or clearing organizations under the securities or commodities laws and regulations. Still others are organized as general corporations.[55] As a result, regulation of major payment and settlement systems is idiosyncratic, reflecting choices made by such systems based on their business models and available charters and regulatory schemes at the time of their formation. These systems are generally not subject to an overall, specifically designed regulatory system for oversight from a prudential safety and soundness perspective.

Moreover, the ideal regulatory structure for payment and settlement systems may be quite different than that for other types of financial services providers. This is because payment and settlement systems exist to provide services within short time-frames and with minimal financial risk to the funds and instruments transferred. Thus, risk-based capital standards and similar criteria may not provide the same degree of protection for payment and settlement systems as for traditional financial institutions.

This idiosyncratic approach may detract from the overall efficiency of U.S. payment and settlement systems. It has the potential effect to over-regulate payment and settlement systems with respect to provisions of law intended for a very different type of financial services firm. It also has the potential to under-regulate payment and settlement systems with respect to the financial and operational risks relevant to the safeguarding of the value (funds and financial instruments) being transferred and the integrity of the mechanisms used to make such transfers.

It also should be noted that in the case of payment and settlement systems owned and operated by the Federal Reserve Banks, policy questions also arise. Simply put, a question tends to arise when the payment systems are viewed as being operated by institutions within the same organization as the regulator of such systems as to whether all systems are held to comparable and objective standards. However, notwithstanding any such questions, it remains important to consider the finality and scope of benefits that access to central bank funds and transfer mechanisms bring to the nation's payment and settlement infrastructure.

Appendix D provides a listing and description of select U.S. payment and settlement systems.

U.S. Payment and Settlement Systems and International Standards

Regulation and oversight of payment and settlement systems are tightly linked to the core responsibilities of central banks, including the Federal Reserve: issuing money, providing a trusted means of exchange, and safeguarding financial and monetary stability. The aim of such regulation and oversight should be to promote these existing responsibilities.

It is extremely important that large-scale payment and settlement systems manage their financial and operational risks in a sound and prudent manner commensurate with their important role in the financial system. This means that such systems must be capable of mitigating and managing the credit and liquidity risks arising during the payment and settlement process as well as be operationally sound and resilient. Interruptions in the movement of the funds and financial instruments, whether due to credit, liquidity, or operational problems, can rapidly cause contractions in financial system liquidity. As such, the Federal Reserve needs to be in the position to identify and address any potentially serious risk to the key payment and settlement systems. Given the implications of such risks for various financial markets and among various financial institutions, the need to coordinate views and understandings of underlying facts and desired regulatory outcomes between the Federal Reserve and other appropriate regulators may be significant.

Safe and efficient payment and settlement systems are important to the U.S. role as a leading economic and financial power. As a result, a charter tailored to the unique roles and responsibilities of payment and settlement systems would have clear benefits. For example, payment and settlement systems, unlike risk-taking financial institutions, are not in the business of putting capital at risk to achieve returns for investors. Instead, payment and settlement systems strive to process and settle funds and financial instruments in a manner minimizing financial and operational risks to their participants and the markets generally. As such, capital, collateral, permissible asset holdings requirements, and risk management arrangements for a payment or settlement system provider would be quite different than those for a bank or other financial institution.

Recommendation

Treasury recommends the creation of a mandatory federal charter for certain payment and settlement systems. The purpose of these regulatory and oversight reforms of payment and settlement systems is to reduce risks, improve efficiency, and ultimately improve the well-being of the American public through more robust stability of the financial system. The necessary features of a federal charter are described below.

First, the charter should be limited to payment and settlement systems having systemic importance to the U.S. financial system and economy. The type of regulation under discussion should extend only to those systems that, because of the values they settle or markets they support, have the potential to create systemic disruptions to the financial system or economy more broadly should they fail to perform as expected or to manage risks prudently. Systems not posing any potential for systemic disruption to the financial system or the economy more broadly, such as some "retail" payment systems, should not be subject to the type of regulation under discussion.

Second, the Federal Reserve should be required to charter, regulate, and supervise any payment or settlement system it determines to be systemically important.[56] The Federal Reserve should have broad discretion to designate payment and settlement systems as systemically important.

Third, the charter should incorporate federal preemption. Systemically important payment and settlement systems are inherently interstate in nature. Moreover, such systems deal exclusively with financial institutions or institutional investors, and not with individuals or businesses. As such, it is appropriate that there be federal preemption for such inherently interstate activity.

Fourth, provided that the Federal Reserve has not required a federal charter for a particular system, existing state charters would continue to remain an option. The U.S. financial system has benefited in many instances from the ability of financial firms to elect between federal and state licensing and chartering. As such, a federal charter for systems need not undermine any existing state chartering arrangements. However, the Federal Reserve should have the authority to require systemically important systems to convert to the charter specifically designed for such entities.

Fifth, the charter should provide lead authority to the Federal Reserve, with a responsibility to coordinate, as may be appropriate, with other federal or state agencies. The Federal Reserve's statutory role encompasses responsibilities regarding the U.S. payment and settlement systems. As such, the Federal Reserve should be the primary regulator for federally chartered payment and settlement systems. However, depending on the nature of the specific system, there may be an important role for other federal agencies (e.g., the Securities and Exchange Commission ("SEC") or others). The Federal Reserve's role should encompass the ability and responsibility to coordinate and consult with other relevant federal and state agencies.

Sixth, the Federal Reserve should have authority to establish regulatory standards to ensure the safety and efficiency of systemically important payment and settlement systems. Those standards, which may include, for example, standards governing finality of settlement, mitigation of credit and liquidity risks, certainty of settlement, segregation of funds, permissible investments for such funds, and operational safeguards, are best set by the regulator, rather than by statute, so as to preserve flexibility.

Seventh, the Federal Reserve, as the lead regulatory agency, should have the authority to conduct examinations of and obtain reports from systemically important payment and settlement systems. It also should have the authority to require such systems to adhere to applicable law, regulations, and standards through, for example, the ability to impose cease and desist orders, civil monetary penalties, and to bar individuals from service in federally chartered payment and settlement systems organizations.

Eighth, federally chartered payment and settlement systems should bear a portion of the costs associated with their supervision and regulation. However, these systemically important payment and settlement systems play an important role in containing financial crises, and their role is not limited to the parties with which they directly and immediately interact, but rather has an impact on the entire economy. As such, it is appropriate that these systems not be necessarily required to pay the full share of regulatory programs that pertain to them. Moreover, too high a level of costs could impair or retard the development or use of technological means that have been so important to the enhancement of payment systems. Therefore, it is appropriate that the Federal Reserve be able to utilize existing funds from other sources, in addition to fees charged to the regulated entity, in order to fund such regulatory efforts.

Ninth, analogous licensing statutory authority should be developed for U.S. operations of a systemically important payment or settlement system based abroad. The Federal Reserve should be authorized to license and to require such a federal license of foreign-based payment and settlement systems with U.S. operations so as to ensure that effective risk mitigation and containment procedures exist between the U.S. and foreign regulators.

A systemically important system may be headquartered abroad, yet nevertheless have important U.S. operations.

Finally, a study should be performed of whether all systemically important payment and settlement systems, including those the Federal Reserve Banks currently operate, are subject to comparable risk management and efficiency standards, taking into account the finality, customer base, and other attributes associated with each system.

FUTURES AND SECURITIES

Recommendation Overview

Treasury recognizes the convergence of the futures and securities markets and the greater need for unified oversight and regulation of the futures and securities industries. Treasury recommends the following changes to modernize the Securities and Exchange Commission's oversight of the securities market: the adoption of "core principles" for exchanges and clearing agencies, an expedited rule approval process for self-regulatory organizations, a general exemption under the Investment Company Act for certain products already actively trading in the United States or in foreign jurisdictions, and new congressional legislation to expand the Investment Company Act to permit a new "global" investment company. Treasury recommends a merger of the Commodity Futures Trading Commission and the Securities and Exchange Commission. Treasury also recommends statutory changes to harmonize the regulation and oversight of broker-dealers and investment advisers offering similar services to retail investors. To that end, Treasury recommends that investment advisers be subject to a self-regulatory regime similar to that of broker-dealers.

Market Developments

Product and market participant convergence, market linkages, and globalization have rendered regulatory bifurcation of the futures and securities markets untenable, potentially harmful, and inefficient. The realities of the current marketplace have significantly diminished, if not entirely eliminated, the original rationale for the regulatory bifurcation between the futures and securities markets. These markets were truly distinct markets in the 1930s at the time of the enactment of the federal securities laws and the Commodity Exchange Act ("CEA"). This bifurcation operated effectively until the 1970s when futures trading began to expand beyond agricultural commodities to encompass the rise and eventual dominance of the trading of futures on non-agricultural commodities.[57]

Two events occurring in the early 1970s have contributed to the current tension between futures and securities regulation. First, the Securities and Exchange Commission ("SEC") assumed jurisdiction over a new exchange-traded product, the stock option, whose underlying economics closely resemble a futures product.[58] Second, Congress amended the CEA to transfer exclusive oversight of the futures markets from the Department of Agriculture to the newly created Commodity Futures Trading Commission ("CFTC").

Jurisdictional disputes have ensued as the increasing complexity and hybridization of financial products have made the "definitional" determination of agency jurisdiction (i.e., whether a product is appropriately regulated as a security under the federal securities laws or as a futures contract under the CEA) increasingly problematic.[59] This ambiguity has spawned a history of jurisdictional disputes, which critics claim have hindered innovation, limited investor choice, harmed investor protection, and encouraged product innovators and their consumers to seek out other, more integrated international markets, engage in regulatory arbitrage, or evade regulatory oversight altogether.

For example, in 1975 the CFTC approved the trading of futures contracts on Government National Mortgage Association ("GNMA") certificates, a government security subject to the securities laws. The SEC objected to the CFTC's claim of jurisdiction over the GNMA futures contracts, but to no avail; the CFTC, having determined that GNMA certificates were "commodities" under the CEA, had exclusive jurisdiction over the contracts. In 1981, however, the SEC approved the trading of GNMA options on the Chicago Board Options Exchange ("CBOE"). This time, the futures industry challenged the SEC, reasoning that because the CFTC had determined GNMA certificates to be "commodities" the CFTC had exclusive jurisdiction over options on such commodities. The Seventh Circuit Court of Appeals ("Seventh Circuit") agreed and determined that the GNMA options could not trade on the CBOE or on any other exchange due to the CFTC's ban on commodity options that was then in place.[60]

Moreover, the Seventh Circuit's decision effectively expanded the CFTC's exclusive jurisdiction over commodity options, in part by vesting the CFTC with exclusive jurisdiction over any options referencing commodities underlying CFTC-designated futures contracts (which at the time already included U.S. Treasury bonds and bills), and limiting the SEC's jurisdiction to options on single traditional stocks.

Attempts to ameliorate these jurisdictional disputes have for the most part failed.[61] That is, while jurisdictional boundaries may have been clarified, such clarification came at the cost of hindering or entirely prohibiting the development of certain products. For example, in 1981 the SEC and the CFTC signed the Shad-Johnson Accord ("Accord") to delineate jurisdiction over securities-based derivatives. Under the Accord, the CFTC retained exclusive jurisdiction over futures on securities, while the SEC had jurisdiction over all securities and options on securities. Perhaps most significantly, the Accord prohibited the trading of futures on individual stocks (i.e., single stock futures) and narrow-based indexes of securities. Meanwhile, certain foreign jurisdictions (e.g., the United Kingdom) permitted the trading of single stock futures, including futures contracts on individual U.S. stocks.

Despite the Futures Trading Act of 1982's codification of the Accord, conflict arose again when several securities exchanges developed index participations ("IPs"), contracts based on the value of an index of securities, usually cash-settled, and designed to trade as securities on securities exchanges. The futures industry again challenged the new products arguing that because IPs possessed elements of futures contracts, including daily settlement, expiration dates, and cash payments, they were in fact futures contracts subject to the CFTC's exclusive jurisdiction. The Seventh Circuit found that IPs were both futures and securities and stated that "if an instrument is both a security and a futures contract, then the CFTC's jurisdiction is exclusive."[62] As a result, IPs were now subject to CFTC regulation and could not trade on securities exchanges. No futures or securities exchange ever successfully traded IPs.

The prohibition on the trading of single stock futures was not lifted until the enactment of the Commodity Futures Modernization Act ("CFMA"), which mandated joint CFTC-SEC oversight of single stock futures and futures on narrow-based security indexes. However, joint agency cooperation has not proceeded smoothly. The agencies have been unable, for example, to agree on margin requirements, and critics claim that this has hindered the growth of the U.S. market for these products.

In addition to product convergence and the resulting inefficiencies of a functional approach to futures and securities regulation, the increasing convergence of market participants calls for a merger of the agencies. Investors, intermediaries, and trading platforms are converging. Institutions dominate the trading in both markets. Trading volume in futures is now concentrated among sophisticated market participants in non-agricultural commodities. Financial intermediaries, such as broker-dealers and futures commission merchants, are often affiliated. Finally, stock, options, and futures exchanges are merging.[63] A unified agency would better promote regulatory efficiency and effectiveness.

The 1988 *Report of the Presidential Task Force on Market Mechanisms* noted that the securities, options, and futures markets are linked markets and recommended the coordination by one agency of clearing and settlement processes, margin requirements, circuit breaker mechanisms, and trading surveillance programs. Even though intermarket trading continues to increase, this coordination, except for circuit breaker mechanisms, remains unfulfilled. There is no general surveillance and enforcement of this inter-market trading, leading to gaps in investor protection and unnecessary market volatility. There is also a lack of unified knowledge in the regulatory sector over risk concentration in these markets. As the then U.S. General Accounting Office noted over a decade ago, a unified agency would have the ability to better monitor overall financial system risk and police the inter-linked markets.[64]

The lack of coordination between the futures and securities markets over clearance and settlement of transactions may contribute to increased market volatility and may impair market participants' ability to accurately estimate their risk exposure. Further, if unable to assess the total risk exposure of potential customers, institutions might unnecessarily constrain lending.

Globalization and the increasing need to present a unified regulatory front on futures and securities regulation in the international policy arena also encourage a merger. Two separate agencies handling futures and securities inhibit the ability of the United States to negotiate with foreign regulators and harmonize international regulatory standards. Perhaps the most significant difference in approach is with respect to the concept of mutual recognition, whereby financial intermediaries registered or supervised in a foreign jurisdiction are permitted access to U.S. markets without registering in the United States, a concept embraced by the CFTC in the 1980s and a concept currently being considered by the SEC.

Steps to Improve and Modernize the Process of the Securities and Exchange Commission

An oft-cited argument against combined oversight is the potential loss of some of the merits of the CFTC's principles-based regulatory philosophy. Treasury recommends that the SEC undertake specific actions within its current regulatory structure and under its current authority to address these concerns. These recommendations should modernize and update the SEC's process to reflect rapidly evolving market dynamics.

Core Principles

In addition to mandating joint agency oversight over single stock futures, the CFMA also established "core principles" for derivative clearing organizations and contract markets (i.e., futures exchanges).[65] In 2000 a CFTC task force had developed and issued the major reforms that would form the basis of the CFMA, including the replacement of "design-based rules with core regulatory principles that are sufficiently broad to encompass all technologies and business organizations."[66]

In effectuating this process transition, the CFMA codified core principles for certain sophisticated market participants, including futures exchanges and clearing organizations.[67] These principles were "tailored to match the degree and manner of regulation to a variety of market structures, to the varying nature of the commodities traded and to the sophistication of customers."[68]

The CFMA generally required derivatives clearing organizations to register for the first time and to demonstrate to the CFTC their compliance with fourteen core principles:[69] relating to having reasonable discretion in establishing their compliance with the core principles; financial, operational, and managerial resources; member and product eligibility; risk management procedures and tools; adequate settlement procedures; treatment of customer funds; member default procedures; rule monitoring and enforcement system; clearing system safeguards; reporting; recordkeeping; public information; information sharing; and antitrust considerations.

The CFMA required contract markets to comply with eighteen core principles[70] relating to: having reasonable discretion in establishing their compliance with the core principles; rule compliance and enforcement; listing of contracts not readily susceptible to market manipulation; trade monitoring system; position limits; emergency authority; information availability; daily publication of trading information; contract execution; procedures for recording and safe storage of trade information; financial integrity; market participant protections; dispute resolution; fitness standards; conflict of interest management; governing board composition; recordkeeping; and antitrust considerations.

· Market participants have also noted the benefits of such an approach: flexibility to adapt to market changes, outcome-focused, acknowledgement of the possibility of more than one path of regulatory compliance, allowing for creativity and innovation, and facilitation of global regulatory cooperation.

Treasury recommends that the SEC use its exemptive authority to adopt core principles applicable to securities clearing agencies and exchanges. Embracing such an approach for these sophisticated market participants will not only be more conducive to the modern marketplace, but it will also facilitate a smoother merger of the CFTC and the SEC.

Treasury also believes that the same principles adopted for derivative clearing organizations under the CFMA can be adopted for securities clearing organizations.[71] In June 1980, the SEC issued standards for clearing organizations, *Regulation of Clearing Agencies,* that remain effective today over a quarter century later.[72] These standards resemble many of the principles promulgated for derivative clearing organizations under the CFMA, such as financial, operational, and managerial resources and member eligibility. Yet, many of these SEC standards are prescriptive and some are outdated in that they prohibit the same sort of flexibility as the CFMA's core principles, and limit the way clearing organizations can both conduct their operational and risk management systems in a modern environment and ensure a more effective external and internal governance and internal control system reflective of marketplace evolution. Treasury believes updating these standards will allow the securities clearing agencies to function more effectively from an operational, internal controls, and risk management perspective, enhancing investor protection and market integrity.

Treasury believes that the core principles adopted for contract markets under the CFMA should also be adopted for securities exchanges, with appropriate modifications. The core principles relating to the listing of contracts not readily susceptible to market manipulation and position limits should not apply in the securities context, but the other core principles are compatible with the operations of securities exchanges.[73] Again, these principles should allow exchanges to adapt their operations, internal control system, and risk management practices to the dynamic market environment, thus enhancing investor protection and market integrity.

Self-Regulatory Organization Rule Changes

Section 19 of the Securities Exchange Act ("Exchange Act") governs the procedures for approving self-regulatory organization ("SRO") rulemakings, including those for the approval of new products. Each SRO must file a proposed rule change with the SEC and the SEC publishes notice of the rule change, permitting public comment.[74] Within thirty-five days of the publication of the notice, the SEC must approve the rule change or institute proceedings to determine whether to disapprove the rule change.[75] The SEC must approve most rule changes before they become effective, although rule changes related to the interpretation of current rules, fees, or administrative matters, or others not significantly affecting investor protection or burdening competition are deemed effective upon filing.[76]

The effective and efficient functioning of the SRO rule change process is critical to the integrity and competitiveness and integrity of the markets in the United States. The SRO rule change process is key to developments in market structure. Market participants have criticized the SEC for its delay in approving SRO rule changes, in particular those relating to trading systems and operations and new products.

Markets and financial products have evolved and continue to evolve at a pace that the SEC's current procedural practices fail to accommodate. Competitive pressures from technological innovation and globalization have rendered these delays problematic. Stock and options exchanges are competing both domestically and globally and must be able to make technical adjustments to their trading systems through rulemaking in a more rapid fashion. These adjustments typically relate to market and operational integrity. New securities products are often introduced and begin trading in other jurisdictions before appearing in the United States because of delays in regulatory approval. This limits investor choice and hinders the competitiveness of financial institutions.

Treasury notes that the SEC has historically updated the SRO rulemaking process to adapt to evolving market circumstances, including two updates in the 1990s. In 1994, the SEC streamlined and expedited the review process for non-controversial rule filings.[77] In 1998, the SEC allowed SROs to list and trade new derivative securities products without filing a proposed rule change ("1998 Rule").[78] The SEC reasoned then that "SROs need to bring new derivative securities products to market quickly to provide investors with tailored products that directly meet their evolving investment needs...the listing and trading of certain new derivatives securities products will significantly speed the introduction of new derivative securities products and enable SROs to maintain their competitive balance with overseas and over-the-counter derivative markets."[79]

Most recently, in January 2001, the SEC issued *Proposed Rule: Proposed Rule Changes of Self-Regulatory Organizations* ("2001 Proposed Rule"),[80] which would have expedited the SEC's responsiveness to proposed SRO rule changes, including requiring the SEC to issue a release within ten days of receiving an SRO rule change proposal. The 2001 Proposed Rule would have greatly expanded and clarified the ability of SROs to file immediately effective trading rules. The SEC noted that the impetus for the 2001 Proposed Rule was the "competitive landscape" the U.S. markets face vis-à-vis their domestic competitors, such as alternative trading systems which are not subject to the SRO rulemaking process, and their foreign counterparts, which can typically make more rapid rule amendments.[81] The SEC explained that "[e]nhancing the SROs' ability to implement and to respond quickly to changes in the marketplace should encourage innovation and better services to investors... Investors should also benefit from a competitive environment in which SROs may easily adapt their trading rules to respond to market opportunities."[82]

Although the 2001 Proposed Rule was never finalized, the concerns behind the proposal's impetus still exist today and perhaps are even greater. The competitive landscape has shifted considerably since 2001 with exchanges moving away from floor-based trading to electronic trading systems. In June 2005, the SEC finalized Regulation NMS, which altered trading systems and has warranted SRO rule amendments.[83]

In light of the foregoing and in the spirit of the 2001 Proposed Rule, Treasury recommends that the SEC issue a rule expediting the SRO rule approval process and clearly delineating and expanding the type of SRO rule filings that should be deemed effective upon filing, including those rules "concerned solely with the administration of the self-regulatory organization."[84]

The SEC should consider including a firm time limit for the SEC to publish SRO filings and more clearly defining and expanding the type of rules deemed effective upon filing, including trading rules and "administrative" rules[85] The SEC should also consider the streamlining of approval for any securities products common to the marketplace as it did in the 1998 Rule vis-à-vis certain derivatives securities products. An updated, streamlined, and expedited approval process will allow U.S. securities firms to remain competitive with the over-the-counter markets and international institutions and increase product innovation and investor choice.

Investment Company Act Exemptions and Expansion

The Investment Company Act governs three types of investment companies, the shares of which are offered widely to investors today: open-end funds ("mutual funds"), closed-end funds, and unit investment trusts.[86] Since the passage of the Investment Company Act, investment companies and their products have developed in ways that were not anticipated at the time of the Investment Company Act's enactment and do not fit squarely into traditional investment company categories. The SEC has often responded by using its broad exemptive authority under the Investment Company Act to exempt from registration innovative investment companies.

For example, exchange-traded funds ("ETFs") are not authorized under the Investment Company Act and ETF sponsors must seek exemptive relief from the SEC under the

Investment Company Act. The SEC granted the first ETF exemptive relief in 1992 and since then has issued approximately fifty exemptive orders, some of which permit multiple ETFs. Currently over 300 ETFs are permitted to trade in the United States. Even with the issuance of several exemptions and the robust ETF market, ETF sponsors must still go through an extensive exemptive relief process. The SEC recently proposed a rule to codify its exemptive orders issued to ETFs from certain provisions of the Investment Company Act and its rules over fifteen years after the product was first granted relief. [87]

A former SEC official has recently recommended that the SEC use its exemptive authority, consistent with investor protection, to modernize the Investment Company Act as the SEC recently did in relation to the Securities Act to allow the introduction into the United States of certain products currently trading successfully in other jurisdictions.[88]

The SEC itself has recognized the Investment Company Act's limits. In its 1992 report, *Protecting Investors: A Half Century of Investment Company Regulation*, the SEC's Division of Investment Management conceded these limits and recommended the creation of a new registered investment company, a unified fee investment company.[89] In addition, the SEC noted in that same report the limits on the ability of U.S. investment companies to market their shares on a global basis. One of the more significant impediments is the tax treatment of investments in funds. For example, U.S. federal tax law imposes distribution and withholding requirements on income and gain on shareholder investments in investment companies' shares. This is not the case for foreign-registered investment companies which do not impose a tax until redemption of the shares.[90] In this report, the SEC did recommend eliminating the tax disadvantages for U.S. registered investment companies being offered overseas.[91]

Treasury is concerned with the fact that the limitations in the Investment Company Act and the registration processes may be compelling U.S.-based sponsors of investment vehicles to introduce their products offshore. This limits investor choice and industry competition. Treasury recommends that the SEC undertake a general exemptive rulemaking under the Investment Company Act, consistent with investor protection, to permit the trading of those products already actively trading in the United States or foreign jurisdictions, such as ETFs: This means that sponsors can introduce new funds that meet the same terms and conditions of previously exempted funds without registering as an investment company. Treasury also notes the inability of the U.S. fund industry to market successfully on a global basis shares of U.S. registered investment companies because of a variety of issues, including the tax implications outlined above. This limits investor choice and the growth and competitiveness of the U.S. fund industry. Thus, Treasury also recommends that the SEC, in consultation with retail and institutional investors, other domestic and international regulators, the asset management industry, academics, tax professionals, and other market participants, propose to Congress legislation to expand the Investment Company Act to provide for the registration of a new "global" investment company. This global investment company should provide investor protections equivalent to the current U.S. investment company regulatory framework, such as a robust governance system, fee disclosures, and other disclosures.

Effectuation of Merger between the Commodity Futures Trading Commission and the Securities and Exchange Commission

These steps should prepare for a potential merger of the CFTC and the SEC. This merger, of course, will require congressional action. Legislation should not only call for a structural merger, but also a process to merge regulatory philosophies, in a sense, to continue and enhance the modernization in the aforementioned pre-merger steps, and to harmonize futures and securities statutes and regulations. We believe a merger will enhance investor protection, market integrity, market and product innovation, industry competitiveness, and international regulatory dialogue.

Overarching Principles

Treasury recommends that concurrent with the merger the new agency should adopt overarching regulatory principles focusing on investor protection, market integrity, and overall financial system risk reduction. The new principles, therefore, will help build a common regulatory philosophy (incorporating the best from each) among the staff transferring from the two predecessor agencies. Treasury recommends that congressional legislation calling for a merger of the two agencies task the PWG to draft a set of principles for the merged agency.

Self-Certification of SRO Rule Changes

The CFMA permitted self-certification for *all* futures exchanges' and clearing organizations' rule filings and rule changes. Under this provision the SROs file self-certified rule proposals and these rules are deemed effective upon filing. This provision also covers the listing and trading of new products. The CFTC retains the authority to abrogate any rulemaking. Many futures market participants claim this self-certification provision has substantially contributed to the growth in the futures markets.

Treasury noted above the detrimental impact of an outdated and inefficient SRO rulemaking process and recommended that the SEC update, expedite, and streamline its SRO rulemaking approval process under its existing authority. Treasury also recommends that all clearing agency and market SROs, and other SROs as the SEC deems appropriate, be permitted by statute to self-certify all rulemakings (except those involving corporate listing and market conduct standards), which then become effective upon filing. The SEC should retain its right to abrogate the rulemakings at any time.

Treasury believes by limiting self-certified SRO rule changes to non-retail investor related rules, investor protection will be preserved. Treasury believes market participants will be reluctant to self-certify rules harmful to the marketplace.

Harmonization of Futures and Securities Statutes and Regulations

Aside from codification of overarching principles and a reformed SRO rulemaking process, several other differences between federal securities regulation and futures regulation should be harmonized. These include rules involving margin, segregation, insider trading, insurance coverage for broker-dealer insolvency, customer suitability, short sales, SRO mergers, implied private rights of action, the SRO rulemaking approval process, and the new agency's funding mechanism.

In general, margin is a very different concept in the futures and securities worlds. In the securities context, margin means a minimum amount of equity that must be put down to purchase securities on credit, while in the futures context margin means a risk-based performance bond system which acts much like a security deposit. With respect to portfolio margining, the CFTC and the SEC are in agreement in principle, but have been unable to overcome certain legal impediments and philosophical differences to agree on a single approach.

The securities and the futures laws generally take different approaches to the protection and management of customer funds. Under the CEA and the CFTC's regulations, futures commission merchants ("FCMs") must keep customers' funds apart from the FCM's own funds. FCMs may commingle the funds of their customers in a single account, but they may not use customer funds for their own activities or to margin or guarantee the transactions of other customers. Some customers may be eligible to "opt-out" of the CFTC's segregation requirements. Under the SEC's customer protection rule (Exchange Act Rule 1 5c3-3), broker-dealers must keep customers' funds separate from their own, but the amounts they must hold are determined according to a reserve requirement that permits some netting of broker-dealers' liabilities to and claims on customers. Like FCMs, broker-dealers may not use customer funds to fund their own business or trading activities, but they may loan out customers' margin deposits to other customers.

Securities customers' funds have the added protection of being insured against broker-dealer insolvency by the Securities Investor Protection Corporation ("SIPC"). Futures customers' funds, so long as properly segregated, have bankruptcy preference in the event of insolvency of a FCM, but they generally are not otherwise insured. With the permission to market security futures products ("SFPs") under the CFMA, the CFTC and the SEC had to reconcile how customer funds should be protected without requiring market participants to comply with both agencies' requirements. The solution in that case was to allow certain broker-dealers and FCMs to hold customer SFPs in either a securities account under Exchange Act Rule 1 5c3 -3 or in a futures account under the CFTC's segregation rules.

While both the securities laws and the CEA contain provisions prohibiting insider trading, the prohibitions under the securities laws, and the penalties applied, are generally considered to be much more stringent and extensive.

SIPC provides limited insurance coverage for securities holders in the event of broker-dealer default or insolvency. There is no equivalent coverage for futures customers in the event of the insolvency of a FCM or other futures intermediary.

The securities laws and SEC regulations require that brokers determine the suitability of investments for customers before making recommendations or effecting transactions. Neither the CEA nor the CFTC's regulations have such requirements. However, the National Futures Association ("NFA") has adopted a customer suitability rule for its members. The NFA adopted this rule mainly to comply with the CFMA and to permit its members to trade security futures products.

A short sale in the securities context is usually depicted as a risky bet that stock prices will decline. Moreover, some observers contend that heavy short-selling deliberately to drive down the price of a stock may constitute manipulation. In contrast, short selling in the futures context is generally viewed as a necessary and critical component of liquidity in the futures markets. Although the risk profile of short selling is similar in both the futures and securities contexts (price declines mean profitability for the short, while price increases mean unlimited potential losses), the SEC imposes extensive restrictions on the practice while the CFTC imposes few.

The securities laws and the CEA provide for self-regulatory organizations in their respective industries. A merger of a futures SRO and a securities SRO should require the consolidation and harmonization of their rulebooks.

Implied private rights of action may generally be more available under the securities laws than under the CEA, but this is essentially a question for the courts to determine.

As previously discussed, the SRO rulemaking approval process for the futures industry is more streamlined than is the process for the securities industry.

The SEC is funded through congressional appropriations and the collection of certain regulatory (e.g., registration) fees, whereas the CFTC is funded by congressional appropriations. In addition, the CFTC must be "reauthorized" by Congress every five years (the agency is currently operating under a continuing resolution), whereas the SEC has a permanent mandate.

Due to the complexities and nuances of the differences in futures and securities regulation, Treasury believes that the vehicle best equipped to harmonize these differences would be a joint CFTC-SEC staff task force with equal agency representation. Congress must provide the necessary funding for such a task force. The model for such a task force is the CFTC's staff task force that modernized the regulatory approach to futures regulation and developed the framework codified under the CFMA. In addition, the task force should be charged with recommending structural aspects of the merged agency, including its offices and divisions.

- **Broker-Dealer and Investment Adviser Recommendation**

As discussed above, convergence of financial services providers across industries has occurred. This convergence is also occurring in the securities industry and is demonstrated by the ongoing debate regarding broker-dealer regulation and investment adviser regulation.

Broker-Dealer and Investment Adviser Regulation

The two principal categories of securities professionals addressed by the securities laws are broker-dealers and investment advisers. Though broker-dealers generally may engage in a wider range of securities-related activities than investment advisers (e.g., broker-dealers may act as underwriters in registered public offerings of securities), both broker-dealers and investment advisers serve as intermediaries between investors and securities markets. Despite this fundamental similarity, these financial intermediaries are regulated under different securities laws: broker-dealers are subject to the Exchange Act; while investment advisers are subject to the Investment Advisers Act ("Advisers Act"). Both broker-dealers and investment advisers are subject to the SEC's rules and regulations implementing various provisions of the Exchange Act and the Advisers Act, respectively.

Definitions

Sections 3(a)(4) and 3(a)(5) of the Exchange Act define, respectively, "broker" and "dealer."[92] A broker is essentially any person who acts as an intermediary or agent and effects transactions between buyers and sellers of securities, usually charging a commission for its services. A dealer is generally any person who is in the business of buying and selling its securities for its own account, either directly (i.e., acting as principal) or through a broker. Many firms operate as both brokers and dealers.

Section 202(a)(11) of the Advisers Act defines an "investment adviser" as any person who is in the business of receiving compensation for providing advice to clients as to the value of, or whether to purchase or sell, securities.[93] The definition explicitly excludes several types of persons as being investment advisers, including: banks and bank holding companies, savings associations, nationally recognized statistical rating organizations, government securities dealers, certain professional persons (such as lawyers, accountants, and teachers) whose advisory services are solely incidental to their job, and publishers. The definition also gives the SEC authority to designate "other persons" as being excluded from the term investment adviser. Moreover, broker-dealers who only perform advisory services that are "solely incidental" to their main line of business and do not receive any "special compensation" for such services are not investment advisers. The exclusion of broker-dealers is intended to preclude such persons from being unnecessarily covered by two regulatory statutes. However, as discussed below, the line between broker-dealers and investment advisers is sometimes unclear.

Registration

The Exchange Act prohibits any person from acting as a broker or dealer unless registered with the SEC or unless an exemption applies. The Exchange Act also generally requires broker-dealers to be members of a registered national securities exchange or national securities association. Today, nearly all broker-dealers in the United States are members of the Financial Industry Regulatory Authority ("FINRA"), a SRO formed in 2007 by the merger of the National Association of Securities Dealers ("NASD") and the regulatory and enforcement units of the New York Stock Exchange. Thus, in addition to the Exchange Act and SEC rules and regulations, broker-dealers are subject to the rules and oversight of a SRO, either the exchange or the securities association (or both) of which they are members. Further, registered broker-dealers are generally required to be members of and pay an annual assessment to SIPC.

Section 203 of the Advisers Act requires investment advisers, unless exempt or subject to limited state regulation, to register with the SEC and file periodic reports which are made publicly available.[94] Registered investment advisers, unlike broker-dealers, are not required to be members of a SRO. There is no SRO for investment advisers, so investment advisers are subject to the Advisers Act, other securities laws as applicable, SEC rules and regulations, and state laws and regulations, as applicable.

Section 203A of the Advisers Act prohibits certain investment advisers from registering with the SEC.[95] Following the adoption of the National Securities Markets Improvement Act of 1996, investment advisers with less than $25 million under management are subject to registration with state securities regulators.

The main registration form for broker-dealers is Form BD, which the SEC has developed to be as similar as possible to Form ADV, the registration form for investment advisers. In addition, many firms operate both as broker-dealers and investment advisers, or as broker-dealers with investment advisory divisions separate from their broker-dealer business. Broker-dealers that are also investment advisers are generally dually registered under the Exchange Act and the Advisers Act.

Under the Exchange Act, the SEC inspects and, if appropriate, initiates disciplinary proceedings against broker-dealers who violate the securities laws, SEC rules, or SRO rules. Broker-dealers are also subject to examination and disciplinary proceedings by FINRA. Similarly, the Advisers Act provides the SEC with inspection and enforcement authority over investment advisers. Such investigations and disciplinary proceedings of broker-dealers and investment advisers can result in censure, suspension, or revocation of registrations, or civil or criminal penalties and fines.

Conduct and Other Basic Requirements

Registered broker-dealers and their salespeople (i.e., "associated persons") are subject to a broad range of SEC and FINRA regulatory requirements, including standards of operational conduct and financial capability, training, experience, and competence in their line of business. Associated persons of broker-dealers must pass examinations (administered by FINRA) related to the securities business.

Broker-dealers are subject to various antifraud and reporting provisions of the securities laws and regulations. Exchange Act Rule 10b-5 prohibits misstatements or misleading omissions of material facts, and other types of fraudulent or deceptive practices in connection with a purchase or sale of a security. Other SEC rules specifically apply to fraud, manipulation, and deceptive practices in brokerage transactions. Broker-dealers face restrictions and rules on specific activities as well, including short sales, offerings of securities, and their interactions with research analysts. Broker-dealers must also disclose certain conflicts, such as when they recommend securities in which they own a position or when they sell securities from their own inventory. They must also have written policies and procedures designed to prevent insider trading.

A substantial part of the requirements applicable to broker-dealers relates to their interactions with and responsibilities toward their customers, many of which are SRO rules. FINRA Rule 2110, for example, requires that "[a] member, in the conduct of his business, shall observe high standards of commercial honor and just and equitable principles of trade."[96] Broker-dealers owe their customers a duty of fair dealing and a duty of best execution. They must also provide customers with certain information relating to securities transactions (customer confirmation rule, Exchange Act Rule 10b-10), and disclose the terms of credit and other information to customers who (even prospectively) purchase securities on credit (Exchange Act Rule 10b-16). Broker-dealers' standards of conduct are intended to address the inherent conflicts of interests in their roles as intermediaries between the markets and investors and include rules relating to the "suitability" of the securities they recommend to their customers. This means that brokers must "know their customer," "know the security," and have reasonable grounds for believing a particular transaction is appropriate for the customer. In addition, broker- dealers have a duty to comply with customers' instructions, to avoid excessive trading ("churning") in customers' accounts, and not to charge unreasonable markups.

Investment advisers, whether or not required to be registered with the SEC, are subject to the antifraud provisions of Section 206 of the Advisers Act. In general, investment advisers are prohibited from making willful misstatements or misleading omissions of material facts or engaging in other fraudulent or deceptive practices. The Advisers Act contains additional provisions that address disclosure requirements, advertising by investment advisers, excessive trading, bookkeeping and recordkeeping requirements, assignment of advisory contracts, performance fees, and restrictions on payment of referral fees.

One critical factor that distinguishes investment advisers from broker-dealers is that investment advisers are fiduciaries, which means that they owe undivided loyalty to their customers and may not engage in any practices that conflict with their clients' interests (unless their clients have consented). Investment advisers, therefore, are generally required to take into account clients' financial resources, investment objectives, risk tolerance, and experience so as to provide their clients only with investment advice that is "suitable" for their particular needs and circumstances. Broker-dealers, while subject to strong standards of conduct and "suitability" requirements, generally are not fiduciaries of their clients and thus are perceived by some as having weaker obligations to customers.

Financial Responsibility

Rules specifying and safeguarding the financial responsibilities of broker-dealers and investment advisers are central to their roles as financial markets intermediaries. For broker-dealers, such rules are more extensive due to the fact that broker-dealers commonly hold client funds in brokerage accounts. The financial responsibilities of broker-dealers include: maintaining a minimum amount of liquid financial assets, as specified in the net capital rule (Exchange Act Rule 15c3-1); providing certain information to customers whenever broker-dealers use customers' free credit balances in their businesses (Exchange Act Rule 15c3-2); complying with segregation and reserve requirements for customer funds as specified in the customer protection rule (Exchange Act Rule 15c3-3); and recordkeeping and reporting requirements. In addition, broker-dealers' extension of credit (i.e., margin) to customers for use in the purchase of securities is covered by Section 7 of the Exchange Act.[97]

The financial responsibilities of investment advisers turn principally on their roles as fiduciaries to their clients. As noted above, investment advisers are subject to a variety of statutory and SEC standards of conduct, but, in contrast to broker-dealers, they are subject to relatively few statutory provisions and rules specifically addressing their financial responsibilities. For example, investment advisers are not subject to a net-capital rule. However, Rule 206(4)-2 under the Advisers Act specifies how client funds and securities in custody of an investment adviser must be held and requires specified information to be provided by the investment adviser to the client. Additionally, investment advisers are subject to various disclosure obligations and books and recordkeeping requirements.

Self-Regulation

As discussed above, self-regulation is another important factor that distinguishes the broker-dealer and investment adviser industries. As previously noted, the federal securities laws require registered broker-dealers to be members of an industry SRO. Today, nearly all broker-dealers are members of FINRA. Registered investment advisers, in contrast, have no corresponding statutory requirement to join an SRO and, as noted above, there is no SRO for the investment adviser industry.

Self-regulation in financial markets and services is often characterized as the first line of defense in preserving market integrity and protecting against fraud and abuse. A self-regulatory system can help to cover any gaps in federal regulation and can typically respond to market developments more quickly than can government oversight. Whereas government regulators are mainly focused on antifraud enforcement, SROs can adopt and amend industry rules that address a wider range of activity and professional conduct. As private bodies, SROs may adopt rules and aspire to standards that extend beyond statutory or regulatory requirements while at the same time maintaining a flexibility that can help to better protect investors and encourage innovation in the offering of financial services and products.

In general, SROs can impose governance standards, set rules, and undertake enforcement and disciplinary proceedings with respect to their members: SROs carry out continuing education and training of professionals at member firms in technical competence as well as ethics; administer professional tests and issue certifications; conduct examinations of professionals for compliance with both SRO and federal rules; and sanction firms that fail to comply (including barring firms and individuals from the industry). SROs also arbitrate disputes and provide additional sources for investor education and information. These and other functions are typically enhanced through the direct market knowledge and expertise that SROs possess, which can help lead to rules that better address specific issues, or identify solutions to emerging issues before they become widespread.

A self-regulatory system can also lead to more cost-efficient regulation. Although a federal regulator typically oversees SROs and SRO rulemaking, the industry directly bears the costs of regulation, which results in significant savings to taxpayers. An SRO can raise revenues through registration, membership, and other fees paid by its members, which the SRO can then use to support its monitoring, enforcement, and training programs. This private source of funding for SROs may even be more flexible than that for government regulators, which typically depend upon Congress and an annual appropriations process.

Self-regulation is not free of criticism. First and foremost is the potential for redundant or duplicative regulatory burdens, whether with respect to the industry's federal regulator or one or more additional SROs. Self-regulation is also susceptible to a wide range of conflicts of interest, including the potential that the SRO may have a financial interest in its members or their business activities. Many of these potential problems, however, may be practically dealt with by structuring SROs as not-for-profit entities and requiring that a majority of an SRO's board members or policymakers are from outside the industry (i.e., independent) and that consumer and investor interests are well represented.

Broker-Dealer or Investment Adviser?

The Advisers Act exempts a broker-dealer from registering as an investment adviser if the broker-dealer offers advisory services "solely incidental to the conduct of his business as a broker or dealer and who receives no special compensation therefore."[98] In one of its initial interpretative releases relating to the Advisers Act, the SEC reasoned in 1940 that the broker-dealer exemption "amounts to a recognition that brokers and dealers commonly give a certain amount of advice to their customers in the course of their regular business and that it would be inappropriate to bring them within the scope of the Advisers Act merely because of this aspect of their business."[99]

Convergence and Recent Regulatory Debate

Upon passage of the federal securities laws in the 1930s and 1940s, there was a clear difference between a broker-dealer and an investment adviser based primarily on how they were compensated. These differences have largely disappeared.

In 1994, SEC Chairman Arthur Levitt, Jr. formed the Committee on Compensation Practices, known now as the "Tully Committee," after its Chairman, former Merrill Lynch Chairman Daniel P. Tully. The Committee's mandate was three-fold: review the retail brokerage industry's compensation practices, identify potential conflicts of interest of brokerage industry employees, and identify the industry's best practices eliminating or reducing these conflicts of interest.[100]

In 1995, the Tully Committee released its report, delineating best practices, including firms' awarding compensation based on account assets rather than on trading activity.[101] The Tully Committee reasoned that these "fee-based" accounts would reduce churning of account assets for the benefit of commissions and better align the interests of broker-dealers with their clients.

Broker-dealers had traditionally operated on a commission basis, earning fees or commissions based on the securities transactions (purchases and sales) they performed for clients. In recent years, however, encouraged by the Tully Committee's explicit endorsement, more and more brokers began to offer fee-based brokerage accounts, whereby clients are assessed a percentage (commonly one or two percent) of the assets held with the broker-dealer, as well as discounts and other packages of brokerage services that carry different levels of fees. The differentiation in brokerage fees has raised questions regarding whether broker-dealers are receiving "special compensation" and thus whether they are properly excluded from the Advisers Act. The SEC has struggled in attempting to bifurcate the regulation of these financial intermediaries.

As discussed above, the Advisers Act exempts broker-dealers from registering as investment advisers as long as they are offering investment advice "solely incidental" to brokerage services and not receiving "special compensation." The question arose whether the fee-based compensation the broker-dealer received was "special compensation," because it was not the traditional commissions-based compensation.

The growth in the retail brokerage industry's offering of these accounts prompted the SEC to propose a rule in 1999 to provide clarification that broker-dealers were exempt from Advisers Act registration if they were merely "re-pricing" their traditional brokerage services, rather than altering the nature of the services provided (the "1999 Proposed Rule").[102]

The 1999 Proposed Rule would have exempted a broker-dealer from registering as an investment adviser if the broker-dealer was not exercising investment discretion over the account, the investment advice was solely incidental to the brokerage services, and the broker-dealer disclosed to its clients the accounts were brokerage accounts. The SEC reasoned that Congress would not have intended for these fee-based accounts, "not substantially different" from traditional brokerage accounts, to be subject to the Advisers Act and clearly not have intended to subject these accounts to both the Advisers Act and the Exchange Act.[103]

Having not finalized the 1999 Proposed Rule, the SEC reopened the comment period on the 1999 Proposed Rule in 2004 and issued another Proposed Rule in 2005, before issuing a final rule in April 2005 (the "2005 Final Rule"). The 2005 Final Rule resembled the prior rule proposals, exempting broker-dealers from Advisers Act registration if the services provided were solely incidental to the brokerage services (investment discretion over an account would be deemed not to be solely incidental) and the broker-dealer disclosed that the accounts were brokerage accounts. The Financial Planning Association successfully challenged the 2005 Final Rule: specifically, the U.S. Court of Appeals for the D.C. Circuit vacated the rule in March 2007, holding that the SEC had exceeded its authority by, among other things, attempting to establish broader exemptions than textually warranted under the Advisers Act.

In connection with the release of the 2005 Final Rule, appreciating the difficulties in distinguishing between broker-dealers and investment advisers, the SEC commissioned the RAND Corporation to undertake a study regarding the current business practices of broker-dealers and investment advisers and investor perception of the differences between broker-dealers and investment advisers ("RAND Study"). Released by the SEC in January 2008, the RAND Study concluded that investors commonly do not understand the differences between the two financial services providers. Firms represent a range of business models: while the majority of firms are providing strictly either investment advisory or brokerage services, many firms provide one service, but are affiliated with firms providing complementary services. A minority of firms are offering both services. The various business models contribute to investors' failure to distinguish between broker-dealers and investment advisers. In addition, investors fail to understand the differences in the standards of care of broker-dealers and investment advisers and question whether those standards are actually different in practice. The SEC is currently considering the RAND Study's conclusions in an effort to update the regulatory scheme over broker-dealers and investment advisers.

Recommendation

Treasury notes the rapid and continued convergence of the services provided by broker-dealers and investment advisers and the resulting regulatory confusion due to a statutory regime reflecting the brokerage and investment advisory industries of decades ago. An objective of this report is to identify regulatory coverage gaps and inefficiencies. This is one such situation in which the U.S. regulatory system has failed to adjust to market developments, leading to investor confusion. Accordingly, Treasury recommends statutory changes to harmonize the regulation and oversight of broker-dealers and investment advisers offering similar services to retail investors. In that vein, Treasury also believes that self-regulation of the investment advisory industry should enhance investor protection and be more cost-effective than direct SEC regulation. Thus, in effectuating this statutory harmonization, Treasury recommends that investment advisers be subject to a self-regulatory regime similar to that of broker-dealers.

INSURANCE

Recommendation Overview

Treasury recommends the establishment of a federal insurance regulatory structure to provide for the creation of an optional federal charter. This structure is similar to the current dual-chartering system for banking. An Office of National Insurance within Treasury should oversee this federal regulatory structure. Treasury also recommends that, as an intermediate step, Congress establish a Federal Office of Insurance Oversight within Treasury to establish a federal presence in insurance for international and regulatory issues.

Background

For over 135 years states have primarily regulated insurance.[104] However, insurance constitutes a large part of the U.S. financial sector. According to the Federal Reserve, at the end of 2006 U.S. insurers held assets totaling $6 trillion, as compared with U.S. banking sector assets of $12.6 trillion and U.S. securities sector assets of $12.4 trillion.[105]

Like other financial services, the substance and structure of the regulatory system impact the insurance industry's cost, safety, and ability to innovate and compete. The lack of uniformity across state insurance regulation can lead to inefficiencies and undue regulatory burden, and can directly limit insurers' ability to compete across state boundaries and international borders. This ultimately diminishes the quality of services and consumer choice, and can result in higher prices for insurance consumers. Treasury has previously expressed concerns as to several issues associated with the current state-based insurance regulatory system (in which each state regulates the insurance products sold in it), including the potential inefficiencies, the undue regulatory burden, price controls, possible international impediments, and the need for federal authorities to be able to monitor the impact of the insurance sector on financial system soundness.

Insurance performs an essential function in the overall economy by providing a mechanism for consumers and businesses to safeguard their assets from a wide variety of risks. Consumers benefit from being able to purchase protection for various types of losses that would be difficult for individuals to absorb on their own. The ability of businesses to insure against risk adds a degree of certainty to their planning and thus contributes to greater economic activity and enhanced economic growth. Insurers are in the business of managing these risks. They specialize in evaluating the potential for losses and perform an important function by spreading that risk widely across various segments of the U.S. economy and population.

As a result of both the sector's importance as a separate line of economic activity, as well as its influence upon commerce and economic growth more broadly, it is important that the insurance regulatory system be consistent with the efficient and cost-effective provision of the industry's services, as well as with the continuing evolution and innovation in insurance products. In addition, the insurance regulatory system must be prepared to meet the challenges of today's evolving and increasingly global insurance market. Therefore, Treasury concludes that a fundamental restructuring of insurance regulation is needed.

Today, state insurance regulators continue to be solely responsible for regulating most aspects of insurance, including the licensing of insurance producers and insurers, overseeing and approving insurance products, setting financial standards aimed at preventing insurer insolvencies, and monitoring consumer protection and market activities. Generally speaking, in order to do business in a particular state an insurer must first receive a license and become subject to some degree of regulatory supervision. State insurance regulatory standards vary from state to state, and are sometimes conflicting. Having the functional regulation of a major national financial services industry such as insurance rest in a fragmented and non-uniform state-by-state regulatory system is unique to the United States. Other developed countries have consolidated insurance regulatory regimes and some have moved to a single consolidated regulator for all financial institutions.[106]

The lack of regulatory uniformity in the United States in a time of increasing convergence and globalization has caused many insurers to question the effectiveness and efficacy of state insurance regulation. This has led some to express concerns that the breakdown of barriers between banks and insurers as a result of the Gramm-Leach-Bliley Act ("GLB Act") combined with significant and varying state regulations, will slow insurers' competitive innovations and responses to bank incursions on their insurance business.

On the other hand, there has been some progress in modernizing state regulation as exemplified by the development of uniform solvency standards through the National Association of Insurance Commissioners ("NAIC") Accreditation Program initiated in the early 1990s (currently the insurance departments of all states except New York have been accredited).[107] Thirty-one states now have adopted an interstate compact on standards for life insurance, annuities, disability income, and long-term care insurance. Despite some progress, significant differences remain in insurance regulation across the states in terms of the required approvals of policy forms, filing procedures, and allowable premium charges. The regulation of insurance needs to be modernized in order to keep the insurance sector competitive with other financial institutions.

Some insurers have increasingly pointed to the rising costs of compliance with the laws and regulations of fifty states and the District of Columbia, and have supported recent academic studies that have analyzed the projected cost savings and efficiencies of having one federal insurance regulator.[108]

Creation of a Federal Regulatory Structure and Optional Federal Charter for Insurance

Any modern and comprehensive insurance regulatory structure should enhance competition among insurers in national and international markets, increase efficiency, promote more rapid technological change, encourage product innovation, reduce regulatory costs, and, above all, provide the highest quality of consumer protection. Treasury believes that congressional authorization of a federal regulatory structure allowing insurers the choice of being regulated at the national level pursuant to an optional federal charter ("OFC") issued by a newly established Office of National Insurance ("ONI"), or continuing to be regulated by the states, may offer the best opportunity for the establishment of a modern and comprehensive system of insurance regulation.[109] Such a dual federal-state regulatory structure would allow the new ONI time to integrate current portions of the state-designed body of regulation into the new national system without causing major disruptions to the marketplace.[110]

Legislation creating a federal regulatory structure would reestablish the federal government's role in regulating the insurance industry by reclaiming a portion of its delegation of insurance regulation to the states, thereby creating a dual federal-state regulatory structure. Such federal regulatory structure legislation should provide for a system of federal chartering, licensing, regulation, and supervision for insurers, reinsurers, and insurance producers (i.e., agents and brokers). It would also provide that the current state-based regulation of insurance (authorized by the McCarran-Ferguson Act) would continue over those not electing to be regulated at the national level. States would not have jurisdiction over those electing to be federally regulated. However, insurers holding an OFC could still be subject to some continued compliance with other state laws, such as state tax laws, compulsory coverage for workers' compensation and individual auto insurance, as well as requirements to participate in state mandatory residual risk mechanisms and guarantee funds.

An OFC should be issued specifying the lines of insurance that each national insurer would be permitted to sell, solicit, negotiate, and underwrite. For example, an OFC for life insurance could also include annuities, disability income insurance, long-term care insurance, and funding agreements. On the other hand, an OFC for property and casualty insurance could include liability insurance, surety bonds, automobile insurance, homeowners, and other specified lines of business.

Under the current state-based regulatory structure some lines of property and casualty insurance, such as automobile and homeowners, are frequently subject to some form of rate regulation. While numerous arguments have been made to justify such rate regulation, they are unpersuasive, especially since several states leave insurers largely free to set their own rates and Illinois does not have any rate regulation.[111] In those states there is vigorous price competition and there has been no evidence of excessive profits, and the insurers competing in those states have remained financially sound. States that do not impose onerous rate controls generally do not have large residual markets (markets of last resort) and they have more competing insurers and overall lower rates. As a substitute for price controls, a federal regulatory structure should ensure that insurers are financially sound and that consumers are protected from misconduct by competing market participants.

Basic Guidelines for Establishing a Federal Regulatory Structure

Overview

In considering the core concepts that should be incorporated into the establishment of a federal regulatory structure, Treasury believes that the legislation authorizing an OFC should address some fundamental regulatory concepts. For example, legislation should ensure safety and soundness, enhance competition among insurers in national and international markets, increase efficiency, promote more rapid technological change, encourage product innovation, reduce regulatory costs, and provide consumer protection.

Legislation also should provide for the protection of the interests of policyholders by establishing a separate Division of Consumer Affairs, as well as a Division of Insurance Fraud. Finally, in governing federally chartered insurers, legislation should meet the basic objectives of solvency regulation, market competition, and consumer protection.

Solvency Regulation

Solvency regulation aims at preventing insurer insolvencies and mitigating consumer losses should insolvencies occur. The legislation authorizing a federal regulatory structure and an OFC should grant the newly established federal regulator the powers to regulate and supervise the operations, practices, and solvency of federally chartered insurers and reinsurers and their producers (i.e., agents and brokers). It should also provide for a system of capital-based prompt corrective action ("PCA") under the ONI similar to that granted to depository institution regulators under the Federal Deposit Insurance Corporation Improvements Act. PCA requires regulatory action when regulated entities fail to meet certain prescribed tests. It is also important that legislation authorizing an OFC provides for a comprehensive scheme for the receivership for federally chartered insurers. This approach should require federally chartered insurers to participate in qualified state guarantee funds to protect state citizens without having to create duplicative insurer-funded federally managed guarantee systems.[112] There are benefits to retaining these funds at the state level: The state system has been tested by several previous insolvencies; reliance on the tested system eliminates the need to create an additional federal entity; and the system appears to be adaptable to companies electing a federal charter.

Market Competition

In the area of market competition it is imperative that the legislation authorizing a federal regulatory structure and an OFC provide the necessary framework for well-functioning markets. It should be designed so as to establish an even playing field for federally chartered insurers with other financial institutions such as banks, securities firms, and foreign insurers and reinsurers; it should also promote competition among financial institutions. It should provide for uniformity and consistency in order to remove barriers to consumer choice and offer consumers the same products and protections nationwide.

So long as they conform to minimum coverage guarantees, insurers should be allowed, under a national insurance regulatory structure, to introduce products to the marketplace more quickly than the current state-by-state process for approvals. In addition, insurers should neither be subject to rate regulation nor be required to use any particular rate, rating element, or price.

Consumer Protection

Insurance is a unique consumer product since customers purchase a promise to pay if an insured event occurs, rather than the immediate delivery of consumer goods and financial products. Insurance contracts are complex, and thus readily susceptible to abuse. According to the latest figures, in 2006 state insurance departments received over 394,000 official complaints from policyholders.[113] Thus, there is a real need for strong consumer protection and any legislation authorizing a federal regulatory structure and an OFC should address anti-consumer practices such as deceptive advertising, unfair policy terms, and discriminatory or unfair treatment of policyholders. Legislation should grant the authority necessary to supervise the operations, practices, and conduct of federally chartered insurers and producers. Such authority should be broad enough to engender the highest level of consumer protection by ensuring safety and soundness and requiring suitable forms and disclosures. It should also allow the national regulator to work in tandem with the states in some areas of market conduct, such as unfair claims practices and fraud.

Basic Guidelines for Creating an Office of National Insurance

Overview

Treasury recommends the creation of an ONI to regulate those engaged in the business of insurance pursuant to an OFC. The ONI should be established within Treasury and be modeled on the OCC. It should be headed by a Commissioner of National Insurance ("CNI"), should be self-funded by assessments imposed upon federally chartered insurers, and should be subject to oversight by the appropriate congressional committees. Treasury believes that such an ONI should be in a position to promote regulatory cooperation and consistency between federal and state regulatory structures. The CNI should be empowered to address international issues with other national regulators, both in terms of comity (e.g., facilitating international firms' operations in the United States) and competitiveness (e.g., facilitating U.S. firms' operations abroad), a role currently beyond the scope of the state-based system. The CNI should also be qualified to provide true national regulatory expertise and guidance on the insurance sector and how it relates to the overall economy, as well as provide expertise and guidance on other insurance and financial sector legislative issues pending before Congress. Additionally, the CNI should be able to understand and respond to the insurance sector's evolving contribution to risks affecting the financial system as a whole.

Powers of the Commissioner of National Insurance

Treasury recommends that the federal regulatory powers of the CNI should be comparable in scope and force to those of other world-class financial supervisors, fully sufficient to carry out the legislative mandate. The CNI should have specified regulatory, supervisory, enforcement, and rehabilitative powers to oversee the organization, incorporation, operation, regulation, and supervision of national insurers and national agencies. These powers should include the authority to issue charters and licenses for all national insurers and producers and to provide for their examination. They should also include the authority to license and oversee insurers which are state chartered or a U.S. branch of a non-U.S. insurer providing reinsurance.

In the corporate transaction area, the CNI should have the power to oversee acquisitions, mergers, and bulk transfers (i.e., sales of blocks of business), as well as transactions within an insurance holding company system to which a licensed national insurer is a party. In the enforcement area, the CNI should have the power to revoke or restrict a national insurer's federal charter for conduct that is hazardous and represents an undue risk to policyholders, violates any law, regulation, or written agreement, or that is inconsistent with the continuation of existing operations. The CNI should also have the power to establish a receivership for a national insurer for the purpose of rehabilitation or liquidation, as deemed to be appropriate.

Other regulatory powers granted to the CNI should include those to issue such rules, regulations, orders, and interpretations as deemed necessary to carry out the purposes of the legislation establishing the ONI; to sue and be sued, defend, and otherwise litigate in any federal or state court (other than the Supreme Court of the United States in which the CNI shall be represented by the U.S. Solicitor General); and to provide for the registration and oversight of an insurance self-regulatory organization(s) to carry out a specific limited purpose authorized under the legislation establishing the ONI.

In the international area, the CNI should have the power to engage in international efforts to secure bilateral and multilateral cooperation and agreements, as appropriate, with respect to insurance regulation in global markets; to provide appropriate technical assistance to, and cooperation with, individual foreign insurance regulators and regulatory organizations in insurance matters affecting international commerce; and to consult and coordinate with the Executive Office of the President and the U.S. Trade Representative.

Creation of an Office of Insurance Oversight

Acknowledging that the OFC debate in Congress is difficult and ongoing, Treasury believes that some aspects of the insurance sector and its regulatory regime require immediate attention. Treasury recommends that Congress create a national Office of Insurance Oversight ("OIO") within Treasury, which could be rolled into the ONI/OFC federal regulatory regime once Congress passes significant insurance regulatory reform. The OIO, through its insurance oversight, should be able to focus immediately on key areas of federal interest in the insurance sector and should not require the creation of a federal regulatory structure. The Secretary of the Treasury should appoint a director to lead the OIO.

The OIO should be established to accomplish two main purposes. First, the OIO should exercise newly granted statutory authority to deal with international regulatory issues, such as reinsurance collateral. Second, it should advise the Secretary of the Treasury on major domestic and international policy issues.

With regard to international regulatory issues, the OIO should be granted the authority to recognize international regulatory bodies for specific insurance purposes. The OIO should become the lead negotiator in the promotion of international insurance policy for the United States, and should have the benefit of consulting with the NAIC and state insurance regulators, who should still be primarily responsible for implementing international regulatory agreements. However, if the NAIC and state insurance regulators were unable to achieve the needed uniformity in implementing the declared U.S. international insurance policy goals, the OIO should have authority to preempt inconsistent laws or regulatory actions of any state and assume an implementation role as to those matters. This model of preemption was used successfully in the GLB Act when Congress authorized the creation of a new non-profit entity to adopt uniform licensing standards for insurance agents or brokers if a prescribed number of states failed to adopt a uniform approach on their own.[114]

In its policy function, the OIO should advise the Secretary of the Treasury on various domestic and international insurance policy matters. For example, the OIO could develop expertise on issues such as financial guarantee insurance (i.e., bond insurers), private mortgage insurance, and natural catastrophe insurance. This should enable the federal government to have a repository of experts to respond to legislative and regulatory matters affecting consumers and insurers. While the OIO's statutory powers related to international regulation should be transferred to the ONI once it becomes operational, the general policy apparatus should remain in Treasury to serve in an advisory capacity to the Secretary of the Treasury.

Chapter 6

THE OPTIMAL REGULATORY STRUCTURE

This chapter presents a conceptual model for an optimal regulatory structure. This model is intended to begin a discussion about rethinking the current regulatory structure and its goals. It is not intended to be viewed as altering regulatory authorities within the current regulatory framework.

RECOMMENDATION OVERVIEW

Treasury recommends a regulatory structure that recognizes the differences between business models centered on transactions with consumers (i.e., retail transactions) and those focused on transactions with other businesses (i.e., wholesale transactions). Strong arguments exist for distinguishing the regulation of businesses (or the portions of businesses) with explicit guarantees from the federal government (e.g., deposit insurance) from the regulation of those entities with no explicit guarantee from the federal government.

Treasury proposes a modernized regulatory structure that recognizes the convergence of the financial services industry. The proposed structure will be more efficient and strengthen our capital markets. Treasury proposes the creation of three regulators focused exclusively on financial institutions and two other key authorities, a federal insurance guarantee corporation and a corporate finance regulator. Each of these authorities is described below.

The market stability regulator should be responsible for overall conditions of financial market stability that could impact the real economy. Given its traditional central bank role of promoting overall macroeconomic stability, the Federal Reserve should assume this role. A primary function of the Federal Reserve's market stability role should continue through traditional channels of implementing monetary policy and providing liquidity to the financial system. In addition, the Federal Reserve should be provided with a different, yet critically important regulatory role and broad powers focusing on the overall financial system. In terms of its recast regulatory role, the Federal Reserve should have specific authority regarding the collection of appropriate information from financial institutions, disclosing information, collaborating with other regulators on rulemaking, and taking corrective actions when necessary in the interest of overall financial market stability.

The prudential financial regulator should focus on financial institutions with some type of explicit government guarantees associated with their business operations. Although protecting consumers and helping to maintain confidence in the financial system, explicit government guarantees often erode market discipline, creating the potential for moral hazard and a clear need for prudential regulation. Prudential regulation in this context should be applied to individual firms, and should operate like the current regulation of insured depository institutions, with capital adequacy requirements, investment limits, activity limits, and direct on-site risk management supervision. To perform this function, a new regulator, the Prudential Financial Regulatory Agency, should be established.

The business conduct regulator should be responsible for business conduct regulation across all types of financial firms. Business conduct regulation in this context includes key aspects of consumer protection such as disclosures, business practices, and chartering or licensing of certain types of financial firms. One agency responsible for all financial products should bring greater consistency to areas of business conduct regulation where overlapping requirements currently exist. The business conduct regulator's chartering and licensing function focuses on providing standards for firms to be able to enter the financial services industry and market and sell their products and services to customers. To perform this function, a new regulator, the Conduct of Business Regulatory Agency, should be established.

The Federal Insurance Guarantee Corporation should function as an insurer for institutions regulated by the prudential financial regulator. The Federal Insurance Guarantee Corporation should possess the authority to set risk-based premiums, charge ex-post assessments, and act as a receiver for failed prudentially regulated institutions.

The corporate finance regulator should be responsible for general issues related to corporate oversight in public securities markets. These responsibilities should include corporate disclosures, corporate governance, accounting and auditing oversight, and other similar issues. These responsibilities are not unique to financial institutions, but are broadly applicable across all publicly traded companies and publicly traded securities. The Securities and Exchange Commission would continue to perform this function in the optimal structure.

GENERAL CHOICES FOR REFORM

While there are many possible options to reform and strengthen the regulation of financial institutions in the United States, the Department of the Treasury ("Treasury") considered four broad conceptual options in this review. First, the United States could maintain the current approach of the Gramm-Leach-Bliley Act ("GLB Act"), broadly based on "functional" regulation keyed off historical industry segments of banking, insurance, and securities. Second, the U.S. regulatory structure could move to a more activities-based functional system regulating the activities of financial services firms as opposed to industry segments. Third, the country could move to a single regulator for all financial services as, for example, in the United Kingdom. Finally, the United States could move to an objectives-based regulatory approach (often associated with a "twin-peaks" approach) as in Australia and elsewhere.[115]

Institutionally Based Functional Regulation

The current U.S. regulatory system, while often characterized as functional regulation, could more appropriately be characterized as an institutionally based functional system. The GLB Act made important changes to our financial regulatory structure by allowing broader affiliations of financial services firms. At the same time, it maintained separate regulatory agencies (or multiple agencies for insured depository institutions) broadly responsible for all aspects of regulatory oversight across segregated "functional" lines of banking, insurance, securities, and futures. The GLB Act also established the Federal Reserve as the umbrella regulator of financial services holding companies and maintained a role for the Federal Reserve in bank regulation.

An institutionally based functional system allows for specialization of regulation, its most significant benefit. Such a system can work reasonably well as long as the institutionally based functions remain distinct. These differences have eroded in the United States for many activities and products.

As financial institutions and markets evolve, an institutionally based functional system exhibits several inadequacies, the two most significant being the fact that no single regulator possesses all of the information and authority necessary to monitor systemic risk, and the potential that events associated with financial institutions may trigger broad dislocation or a series of defaults that affect the financial system so significantly that the real economy is adversely affected. Greater coordination among regulators can improve the information and knowledge within the system, and Chapter IV contains a recommendation along these lines. However, the inability of any regulator to take coordinated action throughout the financial system makes it more difficult to address problems related to financial market stability.

In the face of increasing convergence of financial services providers and their products, disputes among regulators regarding appropriate jurisdiction often arise. For example, until Congress finally forced a resolution, nearly a decade of inter-agency disputes delayed the Federal Reserve's and the Securities and Exchange Commission's ("SEC") recently completed Regulation R defining permissible securities activities for banks. Other examples of inter-agency disputes include: the prolonged process surrounding the development of U.S. Basel II capital rules in banking, the characterization of a financial product as a future or a security, and the scope of banks' insurance sales.

An institutionally based functional system also results in duplication of certain common activities across regulators. While some degree of specialization might be important for the regulation of financial firms, many aspects of financial regulation and consumer protection regulation have common themes. For example, while key measures of financial health have different terminology in banking and insurance (i.e., capital and surplus, respectively) they both serve a similar function of better ensuring the financial strength and ability of financial institutions to meet their obligations. Similarly, while there are specific differences across institutions, the goal of most consumer protection regulation is to ensure consumers receive adequate information regarding the terms of financial transactions and industry complies with appropriate sales practices.

Pure Functional Regulation

In a system of pure functional regulation, that is, activities-based functional regulation, regulatory structure is based on activities instead of institutions. The key advantage to this approach is that the same set of rules would apply to all institutions performing a particular activity. The implementation of such an approach would eliminate regulatory arbitrage and allow for specialization in regulation. In general, in a pure functional regulatory structure, a separate regulator would oversee each of the functions performed by financial institutions.

Conceptually elegant, pure functional regulation presents a number of operational difficulties. At the outset, the key functions of the financial system must be defined. These might include clearing and settlement, lending, investment offerings, investment management, and risk management. Next, individual regulatory authorities should be established to oversee these clearly defined functions. However, like the institutionally based functional system described above, disputes among regulatory authorities regarding various jurisdictional issues would likely arise.

Finally, a system of pure functional regulation presents, perhaps, its greatest disadvantage in terms of financial oversight of individual firms. In a system of pure functional regulation multiple regulators responsible for certain activities would regulate financial institutions. However, due to links to a particular government guarantee or risk to the overall financial system, regulators must consider financial condition and risk exposures of the institution itself, as opposed to the activity. With multiple regulators responsible for various activities in a system of pure functional regulation, the oversight of overall financial condition at an individual financial institution would be more difficult, as would the ability to evaluate overall risk to the financial system.

Single Consolidated Regulator

Under a single consolidated regulator approach, one regulator responsible for both financial and consumer protection regulation would regulate all financial institutions. The United Kingdom's consolidation of regulation within the Financial Services Authority exemplifies this approach, although other countries such as Japan have also moved in this direction. The general consolidated regulator approach eliminates the role of the central bank from financial institution regulation, but preserves its role of determining monetary policy and performing some functions related to overall financial market stability.

A key advantage of the consolidated regulator approach is enhanced efficiency from combining common functions undertaken by individual regulators into one entity. This should reduce staffing needs and lead to a more consistent approach to overall regulation across different types of financial products and institutions. A consolidated regulator approach also allows for a clearer view of overall risks to the financial system as one entity would regulate all financial institutions. This last benefit increases in importance as the size and significance of diversified financial conglomerates rises. Finally, a consolidated regulator approach avoids issues associated with overlapping jurisdictions of individual regulators.

While the consolidated regulator approach can deliver a number of benefits, several potential problems also arise. First, housing all regulatory functions related to financial and consumer regulation in one entity may lead to varying degrees of focus on these key functions. Limited synergies in terms of regulation associated with financial and consumer protection may lead the regulator to focus more on one over the other. There may also be difficulties in allocating resources to these functions. Second, a consolidated regulatory approach to financial oversight might also lead to less market discipline as the same regulator would regulate all financial institutions, whether or not they have explicit government guarantees. This would seem to be particularly important in the United States where a number of financial institutions have access to explicit government guarantees of varying degrees. Third, since regulatory reform must consider the role of the central bank, the consolidated regulatory approach must maintain some degree of close coordination with the central bank if the central bank is going to be ultimately responsible for some aspect of market stability. The United Kingdom's recent experience with Northern Rock highlights the importance of this function in the consolidated regulator approach. Finally, the scale of operations necessary to establish a single consolidated regulator in the United States could make the model more difficult to implement in comparison to other jurisdictions.

Objectives-Based Regulation

In a system of objectives-based regulation, key objectives would guide the regulatory functions: market stability regulation, prudential financial regulation, and business conduct regulation (linked to consumer protection regulation). Market stability regulation generally remains the key responsibility of the central bank. As a result, market stability regulation focuses on the financial system and the economy as a whole as opposed to individual institutions' financial conditions. Individual countries generally implement market stability regulation through monetary policy and other macro- regulatory functions. Prudential financial regulation in this context focuses on individual institutions' financial and risk management characteristics. Business conduct regulation focuses on ensuring consumers possess appropriate information regarding financial transactions and industry complies with appropriate sales practices. A number of countries, including Australia and the Netherlands, have moved toward this model.

A major advantage of objectives-based regulation is the focus on key types of market failures and the consolidation of regulatory responsibilities in areas where natural synergies take place. For example, prudential financial regulation housed within one regulatory body can focus on common elements of risk management across financial institutions, with ample opportunity to develop specialization for particular types of activities such as lending or the provision of insurance. In addition, prudential financial regulation can focus on areas and institutions with the greatest potential for market failures in terms of limited market discipline (e.g., explicit deposit insurance or other types of financial promises made directly to retail consumers). Establishing clear criteria for prudential financial regulation helps to harness and preserve market discipline in these areas and for these financial institutions.

In terms of business conduct regulation, the business conduct regulator would generally be responsible for setting standards for business practices broadly across all financial firms, products, and activities. Such a structure should lead to greater consistency in regulation and supervision.

An objectives-based regulatory structure does pose a key problem in ensuring that effective lines of communication exist among the various objectives-focused regulators. Effective communication among regulators is important for coordinating examinations and other activities impacting the operations of financial institutions. Effective communication throughout the system is also critically important to ensure that the market stability regulator possesses the information necessary to perform its functions. Even with enhanced information from other regulators, determining when the market stability regulator has authority to take corrective actions or when the conditions triggering corrective actions are present poses challenges. This could raise similar concerns as other potential structures do in terms of the market stability regulator's ability to take appropriate actions related to overall stability.

OPTIMAL STRUCTURE: AN OBJECTIVES-BASED REGULATORY STRUCTURE

A key goal of this report is to set forth an optimal long-term regulatory structure for the United States. The current regulatory structure for financial institutions in the United States developed in a piecemeal fashion over time, often in response to various financial and economic conditions existing in the past.

Considering the evolution of financial institutions and markets, the optimal structure is a way to think about improving the effectiveness of regulation in the future. The changes suggested in the optimal structure are difficult to implement due to the structure being a considerably different approach than the current framework. Moving towards the optimal structure will require much debate and a series of incremental or transitional changes. In that regard, Treasury offers a series of short-term and intermediate-term recommendations in Chapters IV and V that can be viewed as transitioning our regulatory structure to achieve some of the goals set forth in this chapter.

After evaluating the four conceptual options presented above, Treasury believes that a regulatory structure centered on an objectives-based regulatory framework should represent the optimal structure. In particular, an objectives-based framework should improve regulatory effectiveness by more closely linking the regulatory objectives of market stability regulation, prudential financial regulation, and business conduct regulation to regulatory structure.

While some of the other conceptual options approach this goal, the clear dividing lines of the objectives-based framework appear to have the most potential for targeting regulation to the most relevant types of market failures or institutional structures. Clear regulatory dividing lines also have the most potential for establishing the greatest levels of market discipline because financial regulation can be more clearly targeted at the types of institutions for which prudential regulation is most appropriate. Finally, a dedicated business conduct regulator leads to greater consistency in the treatment of products and activities, minimizes disputes among regulatory agencies, and reduces gaps in consumer protection regulation and supervision.

The optimal objectives-based regulatory structure described below somewhat resembles the model adopted in Australia. In this optimal objectives-based structure there will be three regulators: a market stability regulator, a prudential financial regulator, and a business conduct regulator. The following figure is a graphical representation of the optimal structure.

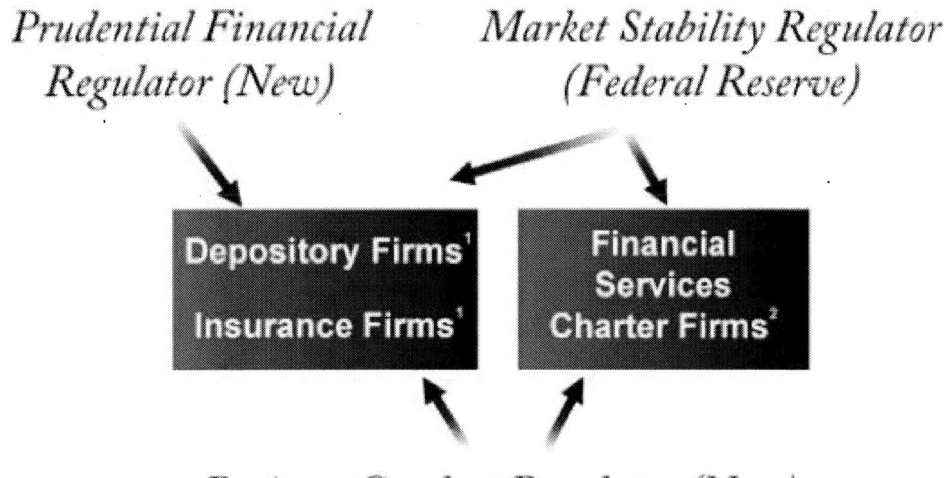

[1] Includes depository firms with access to federal deposit insurance and insurance firms with access to an insurance guaranty fund.
[2] Includes securities firms, futures firms, exchanges, investment advisors, private pools of capital, and surplus lines insurers.

The market stability regulator should be responsible for overall conditions of financial market stability that could impact the real economy. The Federal Reserve should assume this role in the optimal framework given its traditional central bank role of promoting overall macroeconomic stability. A primary function of the Federal Reserve's market stability role should continue through traditional channels of implementing monetary policy and providing liquidity to the financial system. In addition, the Federal Reserve should be provided with a different, yet critically important regulatory role and broad powers focusing on the overall financial system. In terms of its recast regulatory role, the Federal Reserve should have specific authority regarding: gathering appropriate information, disclosing information, collaborating with the other regulators on rulemaking, and taking corrective actions when necessary in the interest of overall financial market stability.

The new prudential financial regulator should focus on financial institutions with some type of explicit government guarantee associated with their business operations. Although protecting consumers and helping to maintain confidence in the financial system, explicit government guarantees often erode market discipline, creating the potential for moral hazard and a clear need for prudential regulation. Prudential regulation in this context should be applied to individual firms, and it should operate like the current regulation of insured depository institutions, with capital adequacy requirements, investment limits, activity limits, and direct on-site risk management supervision.

The new business conduct regulator should be responsible for business conduct regulation across all types of financial firms. Business conduct regulation in this context includes key aspects of consumer protection such as disclosures, business practices, and chartering and licensing of certain types of financial firms. One agency responsible for all financial products should bring greater consistency to areas of business conduct regulation where overlapping requirements currently exist. Differing from the prudential regulator's financial oversight responsibilities, the business conduct regulator's chartering and licensing function should focus on providing minimum standards for firms to be able to enter the financial services industry and sell their products and services to customers.

The optimal structure also sets forth a structure for rationalizing the chartering of financial institutions. The optimal structure would establish a federal insured depository institution ("FIDI") charter for all depository institutions with federal deposit insurance; a federal insurance institution ("FII") charter for insurers offering retail products where some type of government guarantee is present; and a federal financial services provider ("FFSP") charter for all other financial services providers. The Federal Reserve as the market stability regulator would have various authorities over all three types of federally chartered institutions. The new prudential regulator, the Prudential Financial Regulatory Agency ("PFRA"), would be responsible for the financial regulation of FIDIs and FIIs. The new business conduct regulator, Conduct of Business Regulatory Agency ("CBRA"), would be responsible for business conduct regulation, including consumer protection issues, across all types of firms, including the three types of federally chartered institutions. CBRA would also be responsible for chartering FFSPs.

The focus of these regulators in the optimal structure should be on issues unique to financial institutions. Other aspects of regulation associated with financial institutions common across other types of commercial firms should not be the responsibility of these regulators. Two such broad areas should be overall requirements associated with various aspects of corporate finance and antitrust regulation.

In terms of corporate finance, a corporate finance regulator should have the responsibility for general issues related to corporate oversight in public securities markets. These responsibilities should include the SEC's current responsibilities over corporate disclosures, corporate governance, accounting and auditing oversight, and other similar issues. These responsibilities are not unique to financial institutions, but are broadly applicable across all publicly traded companies and publicly traded securities. These same corporate standards should apply to financial institutions, however regulated in the optimal structure, if they offer securities in public markets. The regulators in the optimal structure could also impose additional requirements on corporate disclosures or corporate governance depending on the circumstances described below.

In terms of antitrust regulation, one of the key overarching objectives of the optimal framework is to enhance competition. By providing for an open and transparent way to conduct business in financial services, the optimal structure as described below will enhance competitiveness. Nonetheless, as in other sectors of the economy, concerns will likely continue to arise regarding competition and excessive market power. The Department of Justice ("DOJ") and the Federal Trade Commission ("FTC") broadly address those concerns for all sectors. Under today's regulatory system, individual financial institution regulators also share in those responsibilities in evaluating mergers of financial institutions. In the optimal structure, the DOJ's and FTC's antitrust regulation should generally govern financial institutions like any other firm in the United States. Still there likely will be a need to have some special consideration for certain financial institution mergers in terms of maintaining service levels in certain communities, allowing for the acquisition of troubled institutions, and not overly delaying reviews. Thus, financial institution regulators may have a continued role in some aspects of antitrust regulation in the optimal structure. In addition, to the extent that financial institutions have unique aspects of data sharing or other business relationships, special considerations may be necessary to accommodate those circumstances.

A number of overarching issues would have to be addressed in the optimal regulatory structure. First, while the optimal structure is designed to provide clarity to the focus of each regulator, for the structure to work properly there must be a high degree of coordination. To ensure that regulators are properly focused on their defined tasks and an appropriate amount of coordination takes place, there should be an overall coordinating body. Such a coordinating body could be headed by the Secretary of the Treasury, who would have the authority to settle disputes and ensure that appropriate amounts of coordination were taking place. Second, the funding for the prudential financial regulator and the business conduct regulator should derive from equitably distributed fees imposed on the regulated entities, with oversight by a third party to ensure discipline. Finally, all regulators in the optimal structure should be subject to guiding principles of regulation. Such principles should include: guidelines for regulatory process (e.g., public comment), analysis (e.g., cost-benefit analysis and alternative analysis), and review (e.g., monitoring compliance with the principles and reports to Congress).

The following sections describe the respective authorities of the market stability regulator, the prudential financial regulator, and the business conduct regulator. The following sections also describe key long-term issues that should be addressed in transforming the current regulatory structure in the United States into the optimal structure. Addressing all of the specific issues associated with transforming the current regulatory structure into the optimal structure is beyond the scope of this report.

MARKET STABILITY REGULATOR

Key Functions of the Market Stability Regulator

The primary function of the market stability regulator in the optimal framework is to focus on the stability of the overall financial sector in an effort to limit spillover effects to the overall economy. Typically, the market stability role is associated with the central bank. Most central banks have a general responsibility to achieve macroeconomic stability through the formation of monetary policy. The Federal Reserve plays this role in undertaking monetary policy with the goal of promoting overall macroeconomic stability in terms of output and prices.

In the optimal structure, key components of the market stability regulator's authority should include responsibility for formulating monetary policy, a lender of last resort function, and payment and settlement system oversight. Prudent use of a lender of last resort authority can help to preserve market stability in certain cases, and oversight of the payment and settlement system is necessary to promote confidence and limit potential spillovers.

In addition to these key components of the market stability regulator's authority, this regulator requires additional tools and authorities. Achieving financial market stability also requires the market stability regulator to have an understanding of potential risks to the financial system.

This broader concept relates somewhat to what has become known as macro-prudential regulation.[116] As opposed to PFRA's micro-prudential focus on the health of individual financial institutions in the optimal structure, a more macro-prudential approach should look at risks present in the overall financial system, including correlations and common exposures across financial institutions. In many ways, micro-prudential regulation is bottom-up, while macro-prudential regulation is top-down.

To perform its role effectively, the market stability regulator should have the ability to undertake macro-prudential regulation. In order to perform this role, the market stability regulator must have access to detailed financial information from PFRA- and CBRA-regulated institutions. Such detailed information would also be vital to the market stability regulator's role as a lender of last resort. In addition, the market stability regulator should have the authority to require disclosure by financial institutions of additional information so that market participants can better evaluate their risk profiles. The market stability regulator should also have the ability to consult and provide input into certain regulatory requirements developed by PFRA and CBRA so that a broader perspective associated with market stability issues could be considered. Finally, in addition to these authorities, the market stability regulator should have the ability to require financial institutions to undertake corrective actions to address financial stability problems.

In summary, given the traditional role of the central bank in promoting overall macroeconomic stability, in the optimal framework the market stability regulator should continue to be the Federal Reserve. A primary function of the Federal Reserve's market stability role should continue through traditional channels of implementing monetary policy and providing liquidity to the financial system. In addition, the Federal Reserve's financial institution regulation and supervision should not generally focus on the financial health or failure of an individual financial institution, but rather on the overall risk exposure of the entire financial system. To achieve this objective, the Federal Reserve should be provided with a different, yet critically important regulatory role and broad powers focusing on the overall financial system described below.

As the market stability regulator, the Federal Reserve should have a vitally important role in overall U.S. economic stability. The Federal Reserve's new role as the market stability regulator should complement its role for pursuing stability through monetary policy.

The Federal Reserve's broad and important authorities described below cut across all types of financial institutions, not just insured depository institutions, and involve the consideration of issues fundamental to the stability of the U.S. financial system. Treasury notes that the President's Working Group on Financial Markets ("PWG"), the Federal

Reserve Bank of New York, and the Office of the Comptroller of the Currency ("OCC") have previously stated that market discipline is the most effective tool to limit systemic risk.[117] Treasury recognizes the need for enhanced regulatory authority to deal with this risk. The Federal Reserve's responsibilities would be broad, important, and difficult to undertake. In a dynamic market economy it is impossible to eliminate fully instability through regulation. At a fundamental level, the root causes of market instability are difficult to predict, and past history may be a poor predictor of future episodes of instability. However, the Federal Reserve's enhanced regulatory authority along with clear regulatory responsibility would complement and attempt to focus market discipline to limit systemic risk. This important function should make the Federal Reserve even more competitive than it is currently in attracting qualified staff with economic backgrounds and financial market experience.

Key long-term issues associated with the market stability regulatory framework are presented below.

Key Long-Term Issues

The Federal Reserve currently plays an important role in financial system stability. The optimal structure, however, imposes a different and arguably broader responsibility on the Federal Reserve. The Federal Reserve's regulatory role should no longer be solely linked to insured depository institutions. In order to perform this important task, the Federal Reserve must have a robust set of authorities.

Authority over Information Access, Disclosure, and Standards
To perform its various functions, the Federal Reserve should have detailed information about the business operation of PFRA- and CBRA-regulated financial institutions. Such information will be important in evaluating overall issues in the financial system, potentially impacting overall financial market stability. In addition, releasing some portion of this information to the public should also increase market discipline.

Some of the key features of the Federal Reserve's authority in this regard are outlined below.

Information Sharing with PFRA and Reporting Requirements for PFRA-Regulated Institutions
A key method for the Federal Reserve to obtain information would be to enter into an information-sharing agreement with PFRA. PFRA should be required to share all financial reports and examination reports (as requested) with the Federal Reserve. Access to this type of information is important for the Federal Reserve's assessment of overall conditions in financial markets, and for the operation of the discount window.

The Federal Reserve should also have the ability to develop additional financial institution reporting requirements on issues important to overall stability. The Federal Reserve and PFRA should jointly develop this additional reporting requirement. Alternatively, the Federal Reserve could individually develop such information-reporting requirements through a rulemaking process. In addition to these regular reporting requirements, the Federal Reserve should be able to work closely with PFRA in obtaining any necessary information during times of financial instability.

Information from FFSPs and Holding Companies with Federally Chartered Financial Entities

The Federal Reserve should also have the authority to develop information-reporting requirements for FFSPs and for holding companies with federally chartered financial institution affiliates. In terms of holding company information-reporting requirements, such information could include a requirement to consolidate financial institutions onto the balance sheet of the overall holding company and at the segmented level of combined federally chartered financial institutions (e.g., similar to the consolidated reporting requirements currently contained in the Federal Reserve's Regulation Y). Such information-reporting requirements could also include detailed reports on overall risk management practices.

The Federal Reserve should subject such information-reporting requirements to a rulemaking process so that the reasons for firms' providing information are clearly articulated (i.e., the information is necessary for market stability purposes). In addition to these regular reporting requirements, the Federal Reserve should also have extended authority to obtain any necessary information during times of financial instability.

Examination of PFRA- and CBRA-Regulated Institutions

Another important information-gathering tool is the examination function. While PFRA and CBRA are charged with examination authority, the Federal Reserve should have the ability to engage jointly with PFRA and CBRA in examinations and to initiate such examinations targeted on practices important to market stability. Regular communication with PFRA and CBRA should also allow for information sharing on potential examinations' scope. As the Federal Reserve becomes aware of issues potentially impacting overall stability, regular or special PFRA and CBRA examinations could incorporate those issues. Targeted examinations of a PFRA- or CBRA-supervised entity should occur only if the information the Federal Reserve needs is not available from PFRA or CBRA and should be coordinated with PFRA and CBRA.

Aggregate Reports on Overall Risk in the Financial Sector

Based on the information tools described above, the Federal Reserve should publish broad aggregates or peer group information about financial exposures important to overall market stability. Disseminating such information to the public should provide additional information potentially highlighting areas of risk exposure that market participants should be monitoring. Publication of such material should be on an aggregate level to avoid influencing market interactions with particular financial institutions. The publication of such information could be provided through a mandated regular reporting requirement, and through special notices as needed.

Additional Public Disclosures for Publicly Traded Companies

The Federal Reserve should be able to mandate additional public disclosures for federally chartered financial institutions that are publicly traded or part of a publicly traded company. A corporate finance regulator will be responsible for corporate disclosure requirements for all publicly traded companies as the SEC is currently. However, given the significance of financial institutions to overall financial market stability and the importance of market discipline, enhanced public disclosures over and above the requirements applicable to other publicly traded companies would be important. Such public disclosures could be included as a separate section of standard corporate disclosures, or embedded within an existing section such as the public company annual report's *Management's Discussion and Analysis*. Similar to the Federal Reserve's authority to develop general information-reporting requirements for PFRA-regulated institutions, the Federal Reserve should develop this new public disclosure in consultation with the corporate finance regulator.

Standards for PFRA and CBRA Institutions

The Federal Reserve should have the authority to consult and provide input into the development of certain regulations for PFRA- and CBRA-regulated institutions. Such an arrangement allows the Federal Reserve to provide broader perspective to the development of certain regulatory requirements associated with market stability issues. PFRA and CBRA should be required to consult with the Federal Reserve prior to adopting or modifying regulations affecting market stability. Some areas where this perspective would be necessary include capital requirements for PFRA-regulated institutions, chartering requirements developed by CBRA and supervisory guidance regarding areas important to market stability (e.g., liquidity risk management, contingency funding plans, and counterparty risk management).

Authority to Require Corrective Actions

As described above, the Federal Reserve will have access to considerable amounts of information regarding all federally chartered financial institutions' financial condition and risk exposures. This type of information will be vitally important in performing the market stability role. However, if after analyzing this information the Federal Reserve determines that certain risk exposures pose a potential to create an overall risk to the financial system or the broader economy, the Federal Reserve should have authority to require corrective actions. For example, the Federal Reserve could be authorized to require that financial institutions limit or more carefully monitor risk exposures to certain asset classes or counterparties. Such a corrective action could require that exposures to certain asset classes (e.g., subprime mortgages) be constrained by either limiting future increases in exposure or limiting exposure to a certain percentage of capital. Similarly, the Federal Reserve could require that certain actions be taken to address liquidity and funding issues. Such a corrective action could require that financial institutions maintain or bolster their liquidity positions to ensure that short-term funding needs can be met. The potential scope of these actions would be broad, and could involve issues ranging from exposure to credit default swaps and the proper functioning of the repurchase market.

As with the Federal Reserve's redefined lender of last resort authority described below, such regulatory authority should be limited to instances threatening overall financial stability. Other actions such as public announcements regarding market stability concerns should normally precede the process envisioned for taking corrective actions. If those types of public announcements fail to lead to changes in behavior addressing potential stability issues, then the Federal Reserve should consider taking more formal corrective actions. Some key features of the Federal Reserve's corrective action authority are outlined below.

Scope of Corrective Actions

The Federal Reserve's authority to impose corrective actions should be broad, and by design would be focused on issues of overall market stability that could impact the real economy. The ability to gather information across a wide range of financial institutions should provide the Federal Reserve with the ability to evaluate instances where corrective actions are necessary. Key areas that would likely inform the Federal Reserve's decision making process would include the size, interconnectiveness, and concentrations across particular market segments. Having the power to initiate the corrective actions would also influence market behavior, which likely (and hopefully) would limit the need to take formal corrective actions. If corrective actions are necessary, they should, wherever possible, be focused broadly across particular types of institutions or asset classes. Such actions should generally not focus on specific individual institutions.

Process for Initiating Corrective Actions

Certain process steps should govern the Federal Reserve's authority to initiate a corrective action. At the internal level, similar to the process described below for invoking market stability discount window lending, a super majority vote of the Board of Governors should be required to initiate a corrective action. In making such a determination, the Board of Governors should clearly define the scope of the corrective action: the specific focus of the corrective action, the duration of the action, and the types of institutions covered.

This type of corrective authority provides a significant amount of authority to the Federal Reserve. Such authority should extend to all federally chartered financial institutions, including those regulated by PFRA and CBRA. But, this clearly could impact and potentially undercut PFRA's authority and to some extent CBRA's authority. To provide an additional check on the Federal Reserve's authority, a Market Stability Council ("Council") could be established. The Secretary of the Treasury, the Chairman of the Federal Reserve, and the head of PFRA should comprise the council. If the Federal Reserve, through its own internal process, decided that corrective actions were necessary for PFRA-regulated entities, a majority of the Council should have to approve such actions. If corrective actions are needed for CBRA-regulated entities only the Secretary of the Treasury's concurrence is needed.

Process for Implementing Corrective Actions

To the fullest extent possible, the Federal Reserve and the appropriate regulatory agency should jointly coordinate and implement the Federal Reserve's corrective actions. PFRA should implement corrective actions for FIDIs and FIIs. CBRA, or more likely an appropriate self-regulatory organization ("SRO"), should implement the corrective actions for FFSPs. But the Federal Reserve would have residual authority to enforce compliance with its requirements under this authority.

Overall Evaluation of Authority and Illustrative Examples

The authority described above provides the Federal Reserve with a broad set of tools to achieve its purpose. The Federal Reserve should have broad access to information, the ability to disseminate certain aspects of information, and the ability to require public disclosures of information. In terms of information, the Federal Reserve should also have the authority to be part of the examination function. In addition, as noted above, the Federal Reserve should have the ability to consult and provide input into the development of PFRA regulations (including capital requirements) and CBRA regulations (including chartering requirements). Finally, the Federal Reserve should have the ability to undertake certain corrective actions.

The Federal Reserve's responsibilities are broad, important, and difficult to undertake. Attempting to understand better the interactions that cause market instability and taking actions to address these issues should be part of the U.S. regulatory framework of the future.

The recent episode of instability in credit markets provides a few examples of where the Federal Reserve could have used this new authority. For example, issues associated with collateralized debt obligations ("CDOs") and other structured investment vehicles have created a number of problems. In particular, for whatever reason, investors may not have fully evaluated the credit and liquidity risk exposure with certain CDO obligations. With this new authority the Federal Reserve could access information on CDO exposure across a wide range of institutions and evaluate the potential risk exposure associated with those exposures. As a first step, the Federal Reserve could publish information about CDO exposure, and highlight issues associated with potential risk exposure. The publication of that type of information should have some impact on market behavior. Some adjustment could come through market forces, or the regulators could use this information as part of their regulatory process. If these initial steps do not address the potential problems, then the Federal Reserve would have the ability to take further actions. In this case, further actions could include limiting exposure to CDOs or requiring the adoption of more robust management or liquidity measures to constrain further activity.

Another area where the Federal Reserve could use this new authority is evaluating overall risk management practices. Again, the Federal Reserve's broad access to information (including through examinations) would give it a unique window on risk management issues across a wide range of financial firms. Considering the current problems in credit markets, risk management practices across financial institutions seem to have varied considerably. The Federal Reserve could start with publishing guidance on risk management issues and requiring particular disclosures about risk management practices. Similar corrective actions could follow if these efforts were unsuccessful.

This new structure is designed to provide an effective system of consolidated oversight by focusing the Federal Reserve on overall financial market issues, while at the same time better harnessing market forces. Consolidated supervision of financial conglomerates will likely remain an important feature of global financial regulation in the long-run. How that process will develop over the long-term is difficult to predict, but this new structure should be given consideration as an appropriate approach to deal with the objectives supporting the trend towards consolidated supervision. To the extent that other requirements become necessary, the structure is flexible enough to provide additional authorities to the Federal Reserve.

Lender of Last Resort Function

The Federal Reserve's current lender of last resort function is conducted through the discount window. A primary function of the discount window is to serve as a complementary tool of monetary policy by making short-term credit available to insured depository institutions to address liquidity issues. The Federal Reserve also has authority to provide emergency credit to non-insured depository institutions (individuals, partnerships, and corporations). Depending on the collateral pledged, discount window loans made through the emergency credit authority may require an affirmative vote of at least five members of the Board of Governors.[118] Until its March 2008 actions extending discount window access to primary dealers, the Federal Reserve had not extended emergency credit loans since the mid-1930s.[119]

The historic focus of Federal Reserve discount window lending within the banking system reflects the relative importance of banks as financial intermediaries and a desire to limit the spread of the federal safety net. However, banks' reduced role in overall financial intermediation may have diminished the effectiveness of this traditional tool in achieving market stability.

The experience in the credit markets throughout 2007 and 2008 highlights some of the limitations of the current discount window lending framework. As credit markets began to experience problems in August 2007, the Federal Reserve approved temporary changes to its main discount window lending program (i.e., reducing the primary credit rate by fifty basis points as well as changing the financing term to as long as thirty days instead of overnight) in an effort to encourage greater use.[120] While there was an increase in discount window borrowing after this announcement (reaching a peak of $7.2 billion on September 12, 2007), that amount soon fell off sharply in the following weeks.[121]

Much of banks' reluctance to use the discount window has often been attributed to a "stigma" that discount window borrowing appears to be a signal of fundamental weakness or could lead to additional Federal Reserve regulatory scrutiny. To address those issues, in December 2007 the Federal Reserve established a temporary Term Auction Facility ("TAF") program. Under the TAF program, the Federal Reserve can auction term funds to depository institutions against the wide variety of collateral used to secure loans at the discount window. All depository institutions judged to be in generally sound financial condition and eligible to borrow under the primary credit discount window program are eligible to participate in TAF auctions. By allowing the Federal Reserve to inject term funds through a broader range of counterparties and against a broader range of collateral than open market operations, this facility helped to promote the efficient dissemination of liquidity.[122]

Each TAF auction is for a fixed amount, with the rate determined by the auction process subject to a minimum bid rate. The minimum bid rate is set to approximate the expected average federal funds rate over the maturity of the auction. The TAF auction process seems to have been successful in encouraging greater use of the discount window. The first TAF auction of $20 billion on December 17, 2007 attracted ninety-three bids worth $61.6 billion. The most recent TAF auction of $50 billion on March 24, 2008 generated eighty-eight bids worth $88.9 billion.

The disruptions in credit markets in 2007 and 2008 have required the Federal Reserve to rethink some of the fundamental issues associated with the discount window and the overall provision of liquidity to the financial system. The Federal Reserve has considered alternative ways to provide liquidity to the financial system. In addition to the TAF program, the Federal Reserve has had to think more broadly about overall liquidity issues associated with non-depository institutions. This process has resulted in the creation of additional sources of liquidity for primary dealers by providing access to the discount window and through the establishment of a term securities lending facility.

The actions taken by the Federal Reserve in 2008 reflect the fundamentally different nature of the market stability function in today's financial markets compared to those of the past. The Federal Reserve has sought solutions within its current authority and balanced the difficult tradeoffs associated with preserving market stability while taking into consideration issues associated with expanding the safety net. However, in the optimal structure, if the Federal Reserve is to perform effectively its role as an emergency liquidity provider or lender of last resort, some additional changes should be considered. In particular, in the optimal structure the operation of the discount window should be segregated into two components: normal discount window lending and market stability discount window lending.

Normal Discount Window Lending

Access to "normal" discount window funding for FIDIs, including borrowing under the primary, secondary, and seasonal credit programs, could continue to operate much as it does today. All FIDIs should have access to normal discount window funding. Normal discount window funding for FIDIs should continue to serve as a complementary tool of monetary policy by providing a mechanism to smooth out short-term volatility in reserves and some degree of liquidity to FIDIs. Current Federal Reserve discount window policies regarding collateral, above market pricing, and maturity should remain in place. With such policies in place, FIDIs should likely use normal discount window funding infrequently.

Market Stability Discount Window Lending

The concept of market stability discount window lending is broadly embedded in the framework of the Federal Reserve's TAF auctions. Under the TAF auctions, maturities were extended, and an auction process determined loan pricing (which could fall between the pricing of the normal discount window funding rate and the target federal funds rate).

For market stability discount window lending to be more effective in addressing short-term liquidity issues in financial markets, consideration should be given to broadening access to this funding source. As noted above, the Federal Reserve currently has the ability to extend emergency credit to non-depository institutions: individuals, partnerships, and corporations. This authority is quite broad and could be viewed from a number of perspectives. One particular issue often associated with the ability to lend to individual non-depository institutions is that such lending is effectively bailing out specific institutions. While there certainly have been occasions in the past where an individual institution can cause broader market disruptions, a key goal of the optimal structure and this approach is to make such circumstances much less common. In that context, market stability discount window lending should be focused on overall market stability issues that cut across a range of institutions.

A clearer articulation of the Federal Reserve's lender of last resort function to include more types of financial institutions might be viewed as an expansion of the federal safety net. To avoid that outcome, a sufficiently high threshold for invoking market stability discount window lending (i.e., overall threat to financial system stability) should be established, and it should include significant checks on the process (e.g., maintaining the current super majority vote of the Board of Governors). Market stability window discount window lending should be focused wherever possible on broad types of institutions as opposed to individual institutions. In addition, market stability discount window lending would have to be supported by Federal Reserve authority to collect information and conduct examinations of borrowing firms in order to protect the Federal Reserve (and thereby the taxpayer).

Payment and Settlement System Oversight

Payment and settlement systems are the mechanisms used to transfer funds between financial institutions and their customers. Payment and settlement systems play a fundamental and extremely important role in the economy by providing a range of mechanisms to facilitate settlement of transactions. The United States has various payment systems, including large-value and retail payment and settlement systems as well as securities payment and settlement systems.

In the United States, major payment and settlement systems are generally not subject to any specifically designed or overarching regulatory system. Moreover, there is no defined category within financial regulation focused on, or intended for, payment and settlement systems. As a result, regulation of major payment and settlement systems is idiosyncratic, reflecting choices made by payment and settlement systems based on options available at some previous time. Consistent with the Federal Reserve's role as a market stability regulator and the importance of payment and settlement systems to that function, a specific recommendation is described in Chapter V to enhance the Federal Reserve's oversight of large-value and other systemically important payment and settlement systems.

PRUDENTIAL FINANCIAL REGULATOR

Key Functions of the Prudential Financial Regulator

In the broadest sense, financial regulation refers to regulatory oversight over financial institutions' financial condition and risk management practices. Financial regulation generally involves the establishment of certain standards for the safe and sound operations of various types of monitoring over financial institutions.

In the United States, standards for financial regulation often take the form of specific capital adequacy requirements, activity limits, or other types of limits to reduce risk exposure. In addition to these specific requirements, many financial institutions in the United States are subject to extensive on-site supervision to monitor both compliance with these specific requirements and to monitor overall risk management practices. Often, this type of financial regulation is referred to as prudential regulation.[123] In general, prudential regulation in the United States has focused on individual institutions' financial health or what has become known as micro-prudential regulation.

Historically, the prudential regulatory function has served many purposes. Its consumer protection element ensures that less sophisticated consumers (with the greatest problems of asymmetric information) have some degree of protection for certain financial transactions. Prudential regulation also helps to mitigate potential moral hazard problems in situations with an explicit government guarantee. Prudential regulation, although generally focused on the health of individual institutions, also helps to preserve overall financial stability by limiting the potential for individual institutions' failure, which could be transmitted more broadly throughout the economy.

In considering the role of the prudential financial regulator in the optimal framework, a key question about the scope of its responsibilities develops: What financial institutions should prudential regulation govern? Prudential regulation can play an important and, under certain conditions, necessary role in the optimal structure. However, prudential regulation also lessens market discipline as market participants rely to some degree on government monitoring and safeguards. In the optimal structure, there should be a clear determination of when and where the need for prudential regulation arises.

Financial institutions using some type of government guarantee as part of their business model possess the clearest need for prudential regulation. The most prominent examples of government guarantees in the United States are federal deposit insurance and state-established insurance guarantee funds. In both of these cases the degree of market discipline is limited, creating the potential for moral hazard.

Another aspect that is often associated with the need for prudential regulation across a wider range of financial institutions is the increasing complexity of financial transactions and structure of financial institutions. While complexity might seem like a logical reason for enhanced prudential regulation, greater complexity has not developed in a vacuum and does not serve as a reason for prudential regulation in its own right. Even as information technology and information flows have improved in recent decades, financial institutions have generally become more opaque and more difficult to understand. While the development of new financial products and complex risk-hedging strategies can have an overall benefit to the economy in terms of wider risk dispersion, if market participants are unable to fully evaluate the risk profiles of the financial institutions creating and using these products, then it remains unclear that innovation has reduced risk in the financial system. Greater prudential regulation of a wider range of complex firms can at times provide a false sense of security to market participants, potentially leading to less market discipline and even greater complexity and opacity in the future.

In summary, in the optimal structure a new prudential financial regulator, PFRA, should be created. PFRA should focus on financial institutions with some type of explicit government guarantee associated with their business operations. Prudential regulation in this context should resemble the current regulation of insured depository institutions, with capital adequacy requirements, investment limits, activity limits, and direct on-site risk management supervision. While the presence of explicit government guarantees limits market discipline, efforts to reverse this trend within the prudential regulatory framework should continue as a way to impact behavior and provide useful market information to supervisors. For example, the Pillar 3 portion of the Basel Accord requires enhanced public disclosures in an effort to increase market discipline. Also, over time a number of proposals have been put forth to mandate the issuance of subordinated debt or other types of market sensitive securities. Further consideration of these efforts is worthwhile, and research should continue into ways to enhance market discipline within the prudential regulatory framework.

Key Long-Term Issues

In considering the transformation of the current regulatory structure into the prudential financial regulatory framework of the optimal structure, it is necessary to make some minimum assumptions regarding the financial system of the future. In regard to the scope of the prudential financial regulator's responsibilities, a key minimum assumption is the future of government guarantees. While there have been long-standing issues surrounding the structure, scope, and need for federal deposit insurance coverage, a system of deposit insurance does provide a safe investment vehicle for retail consumers. Similarly, guarantees of insurance products also provide a benefit of some certainty to retail consumers. Both types of government guarantees create potential moral hazard problems. However, given the focus on retail consumers and potential market failures associated with retail transactions, these types of government guarantees contribute to a degree of overall economic efficiency and stability. So, in the long-run, it is assumed that the current system of federal deposit insurance and a type of insurance guarantee system will remain in place.

Chartering and Regulation of Insured Depository Institutions

Well over seventy years ago, Congress established the federal chartering structure for insured depository institutions.[124] Today three federal charters exist for insured depository institutions: the national bank, the federal savings association, and the federal credit union. A separate regulatory regime and regulatory oversight body governs each of these charters. Each of these charters was also established for a particular reason, and over time their historic distinctions have diminished and the activities of federally chartered insured depositories have converged.

Congress established the national bank charter in 1863 in response to the financial conditions of the United States during the Civil War period. The national bank charter has evolved over the years to reflect the dynamic nature of the business of banking. As of December 2007 there were 1,632 national banks with total assets of $7.8 trillion. Like other insured depository institutions the number of national banks has decreased, falling from 4,903 in 1984 to 1,632 as of December 2007. However, the share of total assets of national banks among insured depository institutions has increased, going from 40 percent in 1984 to 56 percent by December 2007.

Congress established the federal savings association charter (often referred to as the federal thrift charter) in 1933 as part of the federal government's response to the Great Depression. The federal thrift charter originally focused on providing a stable source of funding for residential mortgage lending. Over time federal thrifts' lending authority has expanded beyond residential mortgages. For example, Congress broadened thrifts' investment authority in the 1980s and permitted a broader inclusion of non-mortgage assets to meet the qualified-thrift lender test in 1996. In addition, federal thrifts' role as a dominant source of mortgage funding has diminished greatly in recent years as a result of increased residential mortgage activity of the government-sponsored enterprises ("GSEs") and commercial banks, and the general development of the mortgage-backed securities market. For example, the thrift industry's share of the residential mortgage market declined from 50 percent in 1980 to 10 percent in 2005. The commercial banking industry passed the thrift industry in total dollar volume of residential mortgage assets ($532 billion versus $470 billion) in 1993, and held more than twice the residential mortgage assets of the thrift industry ($2.1 trillion versus $870 billion) at the end of 2006.

Congress established the federal credit union charter in 1934 to make credit available to people of small means through a national system of cooperative credit. Federal credit unions are subject to a number of limitations on their activities: field of membership is generally limited to a single group (or multiple groups) of individuals sharing a common bond or a geographical community and lending limitations include usury ceilings, commercial lending restrictions, and more stringent investment limitations as compared to those of other insured depository institutions. Federal credit unions also have an important benefit in comparison to other insured depository institutions in being exempt from federal income taxation. Over time, a key aspect of the credit union system, the field of membership, has become less meaningful. For example, relatives (not just immediate family members) of credit union members are allowed to join the member's credit union, multiple-common bond credit unions can add "select employee groups" fairly easily, and community charters where members share a geographic bond (i.e., they all live, work, worship, or attend school in a "well-defined local" geographic area) have expanded rapidly in recent years. Some credit unions have arguably moved away from their original mission of making credit available to people of small means, and in many cases they provide services which are difficult to distinguish from other depository institutions. While credit union size is not a perfect proxy for this trend, the increasing share of credit union assets held by larger credit unions indicates movement toward a broader focus. In 2000, credit unions with less than $100 million in assets accounted for 39 percent of total credit union assets. Today, credit unions with less than $100 million in assets account for 17 percent of total credit union assets while the top 100 credit unions account for 37 percent of total credit union assets.

In addition to the existence of multiple federal charters for insured depository institutions, the dual banking system of joint federal and state oversight has also played an important historic regulatory role although a number of factors have served to lessen its importance. First, credit markets have become increasingly national as legal and technological barriers to operating throughout the United States have decreased. While some local knowledge is useful in evaluating the condition of financial institutions, a federal regulator with regional offices can replicate that function. Second, historically, states serving as a laboratory for experiment justified the preservation of a state banking system. However, over time, the permissible activities for state-chartered banks have converged to the standards set for national banks. For example, Federal Deposit Insurance Corporation ("FDIC")-insured state banks are generally limited to the activities permissible for national banks unless the FDIC makes certain determinations. In addition, other laws designed to improve the competitiveness of state-chartered banks (e.g., provisions of the Riegle-Neal Interstate Banking and Branching Efficiency Act dealing with the applicability of host state laws to out-of-state state banks) have eroded individual states' ability to regulate the activities of state-chartered banks from other states. Finally, funding a robust state oversight system has become more difficult as insured depository institutions have migrated to federal charters in recent years.

To address the issue of federal charter convergence and the diminished role of the dual banking system, a new federal insured depository institution charter, the FIDI charter, should be established. The FIDI charter should replace the national bank, federal savings association, and federal credit union charters. In addition, to obtain federal deposit insurance a financial institution should have to obtain a FIDI charter. The provision of federal prudential regulation and oversight should accompany the provision of federal deposit insurance. PFRA should be responsible for the financial regulation of FIDIs.

The goal of establishing a FIDI charter is to create a level playing field where competition among financial institutions can take place on an economic basis, rather than on the basis of regulatory differences. While numerous structural and technical issues associated with the establishment of a FIDI charter exist, some key issues to consider are presented below.

Corporate Form

The FIDI charter should be available to all corporate forms, including stock, mutual, and cooperative ownership structures. By opening up the charter to all corporate forms, there should be flexibility to structure a FIDI as a for-profit corporate entity or as a non-profit cooperative entity. In this way, benefits of cooperative or mutual ownership structures could exist, and customers could decide which structure offers the best value. The framework should not permit or necessitate the ownership of multiple FIDI charters.

Addressing the Needs of Local Communities

Community-based financial institutions serve a public purpose by offering financial services to areas of the country that are less affluent, less populated, or have other unique characteristics. In many cases these types of markets may be less profitable to serve. Even though technology has eliminated many geographic and other barriers in the provision of financial services, areas of the country still exist where financial institutions are unwilling to operate because of the prohibitively high cost of researching the local market conditions. By understanding the specific risks and opportunities of individuals, businesses, and governments in local areas, community-based financial institutions can offer localized financial services options that nationwide banks may be unwilling to provide.

To address the community-based purposes described above, a FIDI charter should provide an option of electing community status. The election of community status should provide an additional benefit in the form of a corporate tax exemption. A number of factors could be used to determine eligibility for community-based status. One factor could be an unconditional maximum asset size test, which presumes that small institutions below a certain size are necessarily community based. Above the unconditional asset size test other criteria could be imposed: a geographic focus test (e.g., maintaining branches in three or less contiguous states), a meaningful field of membership restriction (e.g., such as only employees and retirees of a certain company), a lending focus test (e.g., some percentage of lending in a geographic area), and/or maintaining branches in areas designated as underserved.

Applicability of State Law

A FIDI charter should provide field preemption over state laws in line with the preemptive authority currently held by federal savings associations related to a FIDI's specific operations (e.g., deposit taking, lending). Other state laws associated with general business practices (e.g., contracts, torts, taxation, or zoning) should continue to apply. Preemption in this context reflects the national nature of financial services and is broadly consistent with the current scope of federal preemption for federally chartered insured depository institutions and the diminished role of host state authority over state-chartered insured depository institutions. It is also reflective of the new structure of business conduct regulation for all types of financial services, whether such services are conducted by entities chartered at the federal or state level. In the optimal structure, states should have authority to charter financial institutions, and state authorities should continue to have a role in the development and enforcement of business conduct regulation.

Permissible Activities

Limiting the permissible activities of FIDIs serves the traditional prudential function of limiting risk to the deposit insurance fund. Activity limits, either at the institution level or the holding company level, also prevent federal subsidies associated with a FIDI charter from being expanded to a broader set of financial or non-financial activities.

In terms of activity limits on a FIDI, a number of approaches could be considered. One approach would be to move toward a more restrictive banking-like approach limiting FIDI's activities to traditional aspects of financial intermediation where FIDIs serve a unique public purpose. However, the restrictive nature of such an approach could involve substantial disruptions to depository institutions' current activities and could also lead to increased risk through less diversification.

A preferable approach could limit FIDIs to activities currently defined as permissible for national banks. The OCC provides a cumulative list of permissible national bank activities falling into a number of categories: general banking (e.g., consulting and financial advice, correspondent services, leasing, lending), fiduciary, insurance/annuities, securities, and technology/electronic.[125] Permissible FIDI activities could follow this framework; or, given other changes proposed in the optimal framework, such as the ability for broader affiliations and the establishment of other federal chartering options, some refinements to this framework could be appropriate. Finally, given the flexible nature of the optimal structure in terms of conducting activities outside of the FIDI, an approval process for conducing new activities within the FIDI should be more limited than the current process.

Permissible Affiliations and Regulatory Oversight

As described above, prudential regulation in the optimal framework should focus on financial institutions' making use of explicit government guarantees as part of their business model. Thus, prudential regulation should govern FIDIs, and as described below, FIIs. A key foundation of the optimal framework is that the same type of prudential regulation should not govern other types of financial institutions.

As it relates to permissible affiliations, the current regulatory system for commercial banks (and some other insured depository institutions) is based on the principle that affiliates should not pose significant risks to a commercial bank. Two common types of regulation are available under the current regulatory structure to implement this principle: regulations imposed at the individual bank level and regulations imposed at the holding company level.

At the individual bank level, Sections 23A and 23B of the Federal Reserve Act provide the primary protections for limiting the risk a commercial bank can face from its affiliates.[126] Section 23A limits the amount of capital a commercial bank can expose to an affiliate, and Section 23B requires that such transactions be done on market terms. The

23A/23B firewalls recognize the potential conflicts of interest present in affiliate relationships by limiting exposure and requiring transactions be conducted on a market basis. Other aspects of current banking law applicable at the individual bank level are also designed to provide protection from affiliate relationships and limit the transfer of the safety net. These registrations include restrictions on loans to insiders (i.e., Regulation O), anti-tying restrictions, the ability to examine affiliate relationships, and the ability to prohibit activities potentially harming an insured bank.

In addition to monitoring some of the same individual bank provisions described above, regulators impose other provisions at the holding company level to protect the commercial bank, including activity restrictions (e.g., approving financially related activities, new financial activities, and complementary activities) and consolidated capital requirements. Part of the motivation for this added level of protection is to provide a backstop in case the 23A/23B firewalls and other individual bank protection provisions prove ineffective. The current system of having individual bank level supervision that operates alongside holding company supervision results in a considerable amount of duplication in the oversight process, and unclear lines of jurisdiction in some instances.

To implement the key goals of the optimal framework, PFRA's regulation regarding affiliates should be based primarily at the individual FIDI level. Extending PFRA's direct oversight authority to the holding company should be limited as long as PFRA has an appropriate set of tools to protect a FIDI from affiliate relationships. At a minimum, PFRA should be provided the same set of tools that exist today at the individual bank level to protect a FIDI from potential risks associated with affiliate relationships. In addition, consideration should be given to strengthening further PFRA's authority in terms of limiting transactions with affiliates or requiring financial support from affiliates. For example, 23A firewalls could be strengthened to prohibit all loans to affiliates and more definitive authority could be established to ensure that a parent has an obligation to provide support to a FIDI (e.g., requiring the parent to maintain capital levels of a FIDI). To the extent necessary, PFRA should be able to monitor and examine the holding company and the FIDI's affiliates in order to ensure the effective implementation of these protections.

With these added protections in place, from the perspective of protecting a FIDI, activity restrictions on affiliate relationships are much less important. Therefore, in the optimal structure, a FIDI should be able to affiliate with a broad range of firms, including other federally chartered financial firms and commercial firms. Such affiliations should have to take place in a holding company structure, with all federally chartered financial companies forming a segregated part of the holding company.

Allowing a FIDI to affiliate with commercial firms raises the long-standing debate in the United States about allowing for a broader mix of banking and commerce.[127] Proponents of allowing FIDIs to affiliate with commercial firms generally point to several reasons: the potential for increased competition and innovation, safety and soundness benefits of diversification, adequate protection of a FIDI through separation and firewalls, and antitrust protections against improper exercise of economic power. Opponents raise several other concerns: increased safety and soundness risks (related to the ineffectiveness of firewalls), undue concentration of economic power, conflicts of interest in credit allocation, misallocation of resources in the economy, and inappropriate extension of the federal safety net.

In evaluating the issue of commercial affiliations with FIDIs, it is important to note that the GLB Act has already permitted broader affiliations between insured depository institutions and other financial firms though a financial services holding company framework. Concerns regarding the transfer of the safety net should not differ for financial or commercial firms. One key difference is that, in general, financial affiliates are subject to some degree of financial regulation while commercial firms are not. That might provide some comfort in terms of risks an affiliate may pose to a FIDI, but the history of commercial firms affiliating with insured depository institutions has not supported the view of greater risks present in such structures.[128] The enhanced individual bank oversight authority provided to PFRA is designed to address the range of concerns existing across all types of affiliations with FIDIs.

Holding company regulation was designed to protect the assets of the insured depository institution and to prevent the affiliate structure from threatening the assets of the insured institution. However, some market participants view holding company supervision as intended to protect non-bank entities within a holding company structure. In the optimal structure, PFRA will focus on the original intent of holding company supervision, protecting the assets of the insured depository institution; and a new market stability regulator will focus on broader systemic risk issues. Treasury believes that a combination of increased oversight of affiliate relationships by the prudential regulator and a market stability regulator with the appropriate expertise and authority to harness market forces provides the most effective and efficient method of supervision.

Access to Lender of Last Resort Funding and Other Funding

As described above, FIDIs should continue to have access to discount window funding for normal funding needs. Other access to discount window funding could also be available for market stability purposes. Issues related to another important funding source for FIDIs, the Federal Home Loan Bank ("FHLB") System, are described later in this chapter.

Federal Role in Prudential Insurance Regulation

States have conducted the regulation of insurance in the United States for over 135 years with limited direct federal involvement. While a state-based regulatory system for insurance may have been appropriate over some portion of U.S. history, developments in the insurance marketplace have increasingly put strains on this system.

The insurance sector clearly constitutes a large part of the U.S. financial sector and plays an important role in fostering overall economic activity. According to the Federal Reserve, at the end of 2006, U.S. insurers held assets totaling $6 trillion, compared with $12.6 trillion held by the U.S. banking sector and $12.4 trillion held by the U.S. securities sector. The provision of insurance performs an essential function in our overall economy by providing a mechanism for businesses and the general population to safeguard their assets from a wide variety of risks. The insurance industry's overall importance in the financial sector, as well as its role in promoting commerce and economic growth more broadly, provides a clear interest for the federal government to ensure that the regulatory structure surrounding insurance is efficient and effective.

Much like other financial services, over time the business of providing insurance has moved to a more national focus even within the state-based regulatory structure. While locally based insurers still play a role in the provision of some types of insurance, the growing trend is to develop products for a national market. Insurers with a national presence can spread product development costs over a broader customer base, and in many cases providing national products allows insurers to diversify better their risk exposure. The inherent nature of a regulatory system in which each state regulates the insurance products sold within its borders (i.e., a state-based regulatory system) makes the process of developing national products cumbersome and more costly, directly impacting the competitiveness of U.S. insurers.

In addition to a more national focus, the insurance industry today operates in a global marketplace with many significant foreign participants. This is especially the case for some types of insurance such as reinsurance, where over 2000 offshore reinsurers accounted for 53 percent of the ceded U.S. reinsurance premiums in 2006.[129] In such a global marketplace, relying on a state-based regulatory system creates increasing tensions both in the ability of U.S.-based insurers to compete abroad, and in allowing greater participation of foreign insurers in U.S. markets.

The state-based insurance regulatory system evidences a number of potential inefficiencies. In particular, the state-based structure results in the inevitable duplication of regulatory functions and increased costs associated with multiple, non-uniform regulatory regimes. Even with the efforts of the National Association of Insurance Commissioners ("NAIC") to foster greater uniformity through the development of model laws and other coordination efforts, ultimate regulatory authority still rests with individual states.[130] For insurers operating on a national basis, this requires not only being subject to licensing and regulatory examinations in all states where the insurer operates, but also operating under different laws in each state. For example, some of the differing state laws focus on consumer protection issues, such as required approvals of policy forms, filing procedures, and allowable premium charges. Some aspects of state-level oversight, especially maintaining a clear view of local market activities, can add value to consumer protection regulation. The next section of the report discusses issues associated with consumer protection regulation in the optimal framework and the role of the states.

In terms of prudential financial regulation, some progress in modernizing state regulation has occurred as exemplified by the development of uniform solvency standards through the NAIC's Accreditation Program ("Accreditation Program"), initiated in the early 1990s. The Accreditation Program requires an independent team to review each state's insurance regulatory agency to assess compliance with certain designated NAIC Financial Regulation Standards.[131] Nonetheless, each individual state where an insurer operates still possesses prudential financial oversight, which makes it difficult within the state system to evaluate fully the risks of national insurers.

Having states solely responsible for prudential insurance regulation has also led to the creation of state-level guarantee funds. While prudential regulation of insurers is broadly viewed as a mechanism to protect consumers by ensuring that an insurer has the financial capacity to pay claims, such regulation does not prevent insolvencies in all cases. Until the 1960s, policyholders experiencing an insured loss were largely left without any explicit protection upon an insurer's failure or inability to pay claims. This led to the creation of various types of state-level guarantee funds, and today all states provide a guarantee fund association system that steps in upon the insolvency of an insurer and pays policyholder claims up to specified statutory limits.

One way to address the inefficiencies in the state-based insurance regulatory system is to establish a new FII charter. Similar to the FIDI charter, a key characteristic of the FII charter should be its clear focus on retail consumer products with some type of government guarantee. In terms of a government guarantee, a state-level guarantee system could be explicitly maintained in this framework. Alternatively, much like the structure for FIDIs set forth above, in the long run a uniform and consistent federally established guarantee structure could accompany a system of federal oversight. PFRA should be responsible for the financial regulation of FIIs. The following are some issues associated with the establishment of a FII charter and a potential Federal Insurance Guarantee Fund ("FIGF"). If a state-level guarantee system were maintained, similar issues regarding the types of insurance that could be sold under the FII charter and the structure of the state-level guarantee system would have to be addressed.

Basic Structure of FII Charter

The basic structure of the FII charter should mirror aspects described above for the FIDI charter. In particular, the FII charter should be open to all corporate forms, have field preemption over state laws, and be subject to the same types of restrictions on affiliate transactions as a FIDI charter.

Types of Insurance

If a FII charter and a guarantee system were established in the optimal structure, they should be linked together. Only insurance products sold under a FII charter should receive the benefit of a federal assurance of access to guarantee coverage. Other insurance products in the optimal structure could be sold by FFSPs, as described below, and states should still retain the ability to charter insurers.[132]

The key aspect in determining the types of insurance products sold through a FII charter and the access given to guarantee coverage should be a link to retail consumers (e.g., individuals and small businesses). More specifically, the FII and guarantee framework should include personal insurance products providing some type of protection from catastrophic loss. Such personal insurance products could include property (e.g., fire, dwelling, homeowners, renters, personal property), personal automobile, liability (e.g., general, umbrella), and life insurance (all products, individual and group). These types of personal insurance products should form the bulk of the products eligible for a federal guarantee. Further consideration could be given to including other types of personal insurance products in the guarantee system. Similarly, the FII and FIGF framework could include certain commercial insurance products (e.g., commercial property, business interruption, and liability) sold to small businesses. Apart from types of insurance available for guarantee coverage, decisions should also be made regarding levels of coverage (e.g., dollar limits based on type of product or the policyholder's net worth). Any new federal guarantee fund would mirror some aspects of the current state-level guarantee system covering certain retail products up to specified limits, while not covering other policies not focused on retail consumers (e.g., surplus lines market or large commercial businesses). A key difference would be that the FIGF would set consistent national standards for types of policies, as opposed to those standards being determined at the state level.

FIGF Structure

If a federal guarantee for certain insurance products were provided, a decision would also need to be made on the level of the guarantee. The current state-level guarantee system provides different levels of guarantee depending on the state where the policyholder or the insured property is located. In most cases, dollar limits on the amounts of coverage vary by type of policy. Limits would have to be implemented as part of the process of determining the products included in the FIGF, with the goal to provide an adequate level of protection for average retail consumers.

If a FIGF is established, it could be pre-funded (similar to the current FDIC structure) as well as have the ability to cover any shortfalls through post-insolvency assessments on all FIIs (resembling the current structure of the FDIC and most state guarantee funds). As described in the next section, if a FIGF is established it should be administered by the reconstituted FDIC. This new agency could consider other issues, such as the need for separate funds for property and casualty and life insurance (or other subsets).

Role of the Federal Deposit Insurance Corporation

The FDIC should primarily function as an insurer in the optimal structure. Much as the FDIC operates today, it should have the authority to set risk-based premiums, charge ex-post assessments, act as a receiver for failed FIDIs, and possess some back-up examination authority over those institutions. In terms of back-up examination authority, the FDIC should possess the ability to maintain an on-site presence, join in PFRA's examination functions, and undertake special examinations in circumstances where the potential tapping of insurance funds exists. With changes in the federal deposit insurance fund (i.e., the requirement to have a FIDI charter for federal deposit insurance), the FDIC no longer needs to be the primary supervisor of state-chartered nonmember banks. Finally, some degree of coordination among the FDIC, PFRA, and the Federal Reserve must occur. In that regard, PFRA should have to consult with the FDIC and the Federal Reserve in the promulgation of new regulations.

If a FIGF is established, the FDIC should be reconstituted as the Federal Insurance Guarantee Corporation ("FIGC") in charge of not only the deposit insurance fund, but also the FIGF. Under such a structure, the FIGC should have similar authority over FIIs as it does over FIDIs. In addition, given the separation between FIDIs and FIIs, the FIGC should be required to maintain a separate deposit insurance fund and FIGF. Whether or not additional separation of funds within the FIGF is necessary (as is currently done in state guarantee funds between property and casualty and life) could be considered in the development of the FIGF, or additional authority could be provided to the FIGC to consider this issue.

Prudential Regulation for Government-Sponsored Enterprises

The scope of prudential regulation for GSEs in the optimal structure should also be considered. The federal government created GSEs, privately owned companies, to accomplish a particular public purpose. Today, three GSEs, the Federal National Mortgage Association ("Fannie Mae"), the Federal Home Loan Mortgage Corporation ("Freddie Mac"), and the FHLB System, focus on housing while two GSEs, the Federal Agriculture Mortgage Corporation ("Farmer Mac") and the Farm Credit System, focus on agriculture. Fannie Mae and Freddie Mac are publicly traded firms operating in the secondary mortgage market through a credit guarantee business and a mortgage investment business. Twelve cooperatively owned regional banks that primarily raise funds in the capital markets and serve as alternative funding source for members (primarily insured depository institutions) comprise the FHLB System. Farmer Mac is a publicly-traded firm operating in the secondary market for agricultural loans while the Farm Credit System is a cooperative system comprised of direct agricultural lending institutions. In general, each GSE's public purpose relates to enhancing liquidity and improving the availability of funds to particular sectors of the economy. As of December 31, 2007, GSEs' total assets were $3.1 trillion, and the GSEs had an additional $3.6 trillion in off-balance sheet credit guarantees.[133]

The GSEs' unique structure does not fit well within the optimal structure. No explicit guarantee backs the GSEs' obligations. However, government sponsorship provides each GSE with a set of benefits not available to other financial institutions. Taken together, the statutory benefits provided to the GSEs, along with the financial markets' misperception that GSEs are backed by the federal government, have provided the GSEs with three advantages in comparison to other financial institutions: lower funding costs, the ability to operate with less capital, and lower direct costs. These cost advantages also enhance the GSEs' liquidity, principally by subsidizing their access to capital market financing. In theory, the GSEs use their subsidies to attract private capital, which is then directed to some particular market sector underserved or not served by private firms.

Given the existing market misperception that the federal government stands behind the GSEs' obligations, the optimal structure implies that PFRA should not regulate the GSEs. PFRA's regulation of the GSEs would likely serve to strengthen that misperception even further. Nonetheless, given that the federal government has charged the GSEs with a specific mission, some type of prudential regulation would be necessary to ensure the accomplishment of that mission.

To address these challenging issues in the near-term, the idea of a separate regulator conducting prudential oversight of the GSEs should be considered. A separate regulator would be an important signaling device that the GSEs do not have government guarantees. In order to ensure that the GSEs operate in a safe and sound manner, that regulator should have powers similar to those provided to PFRA. In addition to these safety and soundness powers, that regulator should limit the GSEs' activities to those necessary to accomplish their public purpose. The Federal Reserve as market stability regulator should have the same ability to evaluate the GSEs' activities as it has for other federally chartered entities in the optimal structure.

The optimal structure provides a flexible framework for regulating many of the wholesale financing activities of Fannie Mae, Freddie Mac, the FHLB System, and Farmer Mac, while also addressing the retail lending activities of the Farm Credit System. In the long term, there should be a continued evaluation of the need for separate GSE charters.

BUSINESS CONDUCT REGULATOR

Key Functions of the Business Conduct Regulator

The primary function of the business conduct regulator in the optimal structure is to focus on the interactions between financial institutions and financial services consumers. More specifically, at the level of individual transactions, the business conduct regulator should focus on transactions and interactions with retail consumers, both individuals and small businesses.

Business conduct is fundamentally linked to consumer protection. A key element of any consumer protection regulatory framework is ensuring that consumers receive adequate information about the terms of financial transactions. One of the primary functions of the business conduct regulator should be developing adequate disclosures for all types of financial products and services. Currently, various federal, state, and SROs supervising banking, insurance, futures, and securities activities have responsibility for promulgating and implementing consumer disclosure regulations and standards. Having one agency responsible for all financial products should allow for the development of appropriate disclosures across products that have converged across these industry lines.

Another key element of the business conduct regulator's responsibilities should be ensuring that financial institutions do not conduct business practices in an unfair, deceptive, or discriminatory manner. Responsibilities of the business conduct regulator in this area should focus on how financial institutions interact with consumers through sales and marketing practices, which include ensuring that institutions do not provide financial services on a discriminatory basis. As with disclosures, having one agency responsible for all financial products should bring greater consistency to these areas of business conduct regulation where overlapping requirements currently exist.

The business conduct regulator should also have authority for the chartering and licensing of various types of financial service providers. The chartering and licensing function should be designed to ensure that individuals or companies engaged in the provision of financial services possess the financial capacity and expertise to engage in such transactions. In general, the requirements for financial capacity and managerial expertise should vary by the type of financial product being sold. Initial requirements to obtain a charter or license should include demonstration of financial capacity and managerial expertise, and requirements to maintain a charter or license should include in many situations an ongoing demonstration of financial capacity and managerial expertise. This type of monitoring, often referred to as "fit and proper" requirements, should differ from the type of financial safety and soundness regulation applied to financial institutions by the prudential financial regulator. In particular, the business conduct regulator should not have extensive supervisory and regulatory oversight over an institution's financial condition, but rather should be limited to ensuring satisfaction of the financial and managerial expertise conditions. This type of financial monitoring should not be designed to provide full protection to consumers (such as with explicit government guarantees), but rather to provide appropriate standards for firms to be able to enter the financial services industry and sell their products and services to customers. Financial institutions regulated by the prudential financial regulator should automatically be granted authority to enter into activities permitted by the prudential regulator, but the business conduct regulator should regulate the business conduct aspects of those activities.

Finally, the business conduct regulator's authority in the optimal structure should be limited to the areas described above: disclosures, business practices, chartering and licensing, and enforcement. The business conduct regulator should not have the ability to broadly prohibit products, limit entry through excessive licensing requirements, or control prices. In general, business conduct requirements that are too rigid can result in less competition, less innovation, and diminished flexibility to adapt to market conditions. For example, broad prohibitions on products should only be considered in circumstances where disclosures and regulation of business practices prove insufficient. Price controls are even more problematic. While less common in banking and securities markets, price controls remain prevalent in insurance markets. Following the fundamental principles of economics, price controls lead to economically inefficient shortages or surpluses, with shortages evidenced by the size of residual markets for insurance in some states.

In summary, in the optimal structure a new business conduct regulator, CBRA, should be created. CBRA should be responsible for business conduct regulation across all types of financial firms. As described above, business conduct regulation in the optimal framework includes the regulation of key aspects of consumer protection such as disclosures, business practices, and chartering and licensing. CBRA should be responsible for implementing uniform national business conduct standards in these areas.

Key long-term issues associated with the business conduct regulatory framework are presented below.

Key Long-Term Issues

Consolidate Business Conduct Regulation for Financial Services

In the current regulatory framework multiple federal and state authorities govern the business conduct of financial institutions. The ultimate authority often depends on the type of financial service provided and the type of financial institution charter.

In the banking and general consumer lending area, typically a single federal agency or some combination of federal agencies has federal responsibility for developing regulations regarding disclosures and other business conduct practices. For example, the Federal Reserve has sole authority to develop regulations surrounding the disclosure of certain credit terms required under the Truth in Lending Act ("TILA"), the U.S. Department of Housing and Urban Development has the responsibility for developing regulations implementing the Real Estate Settlement Procedures Act ("RESPA"), and several agencies jointly develop regulations surrounding the privacy of consumer information. Despite differences among various federal laws, the general enforcement structure follows the chartering structure of individual institutions. For example, for the general provisions of TILA, regulators enforce these against their respective federally chartered institutions and the FTC enforces against all non-depository lenders.[134] States also pass various business conduct laws related to banking and general lending. In general, the applicability of state law varies based on a number of factors associated with charter type. The current multi-agency business conduct oversight structure creates uneven enforcement, potential enforcement gaps, disputes over jurisdiction, and regulatory inconsistency.

In insurance, other than in a few exceptions, the states solely oversee business conduct regulation. Some key aspects of state-based business conduct regulation include policy form approval, insurance rate approval, unfair trade practices (including discrimination), and unfair claims settlement practices. As described earlier, the state-based structure results in inevitable duplication in regulatory functions and increased costs associated with multiple non-uniform regulatory regimes. In terms of business conduct regulation, an insurer must seek separate state approvals in order to sell an insurance product nationwide. This state-by-state approval process can impact the availability of a product to consumers and cause product differences due to varying state requirements. States have made efforts to improve this process: thirty-one states have jointly established some uniform standards, rules, and processes for streamlined filings and approvals for certain products (e.g., life insurance, annuities, disability income, and long-term care insurance). Still, this agreement only covers a subset of insurance products and many states are not participating.[135]

In the futures and securities marketplace the SROs and the federal agencies undertake most business conduct regulation. In terms of state responsibilities, the National Securities Markets Improvement Act of 1996 ("NSMIA") reduced complexity and duplicative regulation among federal and state securities regulators. NSMIA limited the states' regulatory authority to particular areas (e.g., investment advisers with less than $25 million under management) and to enforce state laws against fraud.[136] State responsibilities with regard to futures have not been an issue because states have not had the authority to regulate futures markets. Most of the issues in futures and securities regulation relate to overlapping or uncertain federal jurisdiction as products have developed. Tensions also remain in some aspects of the overlapping federal and state enforcement authority.

To address the deficiencies of the current business conduct regulatory structure, existing business conduct laws and regulatory authority for all types of retail financial products and services should be consolidated under one structure. Consolidation of business conduct regulation should allow for the development of national standards for disclosures and business practices associated with retail financial products and services. The newly developed national standards should apply to all retail financial transactions, whether undertaken by institutions chartered or licensed at the federal or state level. This broad application takes on greater importance as the optimal structure provides a number of federal chartering options preempting state law (a continuing role for the states will be described later in this chapter). These options include the FIDI and FII charters described earlier and the FFSP charter option described later in this chapter.

The goal of consolidating business conduct regulation for financial services within CBRA is to enhance competitiveness through the establishment of national business conduct standards, as opposed to multiple standards being established and enforced by multiple financial regulators under the current system. The consolidation of business conduct regulation should also provide flexibility to ensure that as products converge across traditional lines of financial services, a single business conduct regulator provides consumers with a consistent set of information and protections. While there are numerous structural and technical issues to consider, examples of business conduct functions that CBRA should have authority to administer are presented below.

Banking and Lending

The existing business conduct regulatory framework for banking and nonbank consumer finance institutions includes a significant number of federal laws and implementing regulations. In general, business conduct laws applicable to banking and lending fall into three broad categories: disclosure, sales and marketing practices (including laws and regulations addressing unfair and deceptive practices), and anti-discrimination laws.

In the disclosure area, CBRA should become responsible for TILA, RESPA, the Truth in Savings Act, and other similar laws. In addition, greater consideration could be given to rationalizing the disclosure process as part of this consolidation. For example, with respect to mortgages, both TILA and RESPA provide separate and important disclosures. Combining regulatory authority over disclosures in one agency could make efforts to harmonize and improve the mortgage disclosure process easier to accomplish.

In the sales and marketing practices area, a key provision of current law is Section 5(a) of the FTC Act, broadly prohibiting "unfair or deceptive acts or practices in or affecting commerce." In this case, the FTC Act defines "unfair" practices as those that "cause or are likely to cause substantial injury to consumers that are not reasonably avoidable by consumers themselves and not outweighed by countervailing benefits to consumers or to competition." Providing CBRA authority to develop regulations and enforce Section 5(a) of the FTC Act,[137] or constructing an alternative structure related to unfair and deceptive practices, should be an essential part of CBRA's authority. In addition, CBRA should be responsible for implementing other laws in this area, such as the Fair Credit Billing Act, the Fair Credit Reporting Act, the Fair Debt Collection Practices Act, and those related to consumer privacy.

Finally, CBRA should have authority over laws designed to prevent discrimination such as the Equal Credit Opportunity Act, which prohibits discrimination against an applicant for credit because of age, sex, marital status, religion, race, color, national origin, or receipt of public assistance. CBRA should also be responsible for other related laws, such as the financing aspects of the Fair Housing Act and the Home Mortgage Disclosure Act.

Insurance

Similar to its authority over banking and lending regulation, CBRA should have the authority to regulate insurance business conduct issues associated with disclosures, business practices, and discrimination. Unlike banking regulation, because states have had the responsibility for insurance regulation, a large body of current federal law specifically targeted at insurance business conduct does not exist.

Consistent with insurance business conduct regulation at the state level, CBRA should have authority over a number of key areas. For example, state-based regulations surrounding policy forms are somewhat analogous to a disclosure regime. Policy forms provide the terms and conditions of the insurance contract. States have used regulation of the policy form approval process broadly to mandate certain types of coverage or to allow for specific exclusions. As it relates to policy forms, CBRA's primary responsibility should be developing standard disclosures so that consumers can compare an insurance policy's pricing and coverage provisions.

In terms of general business practices, most states either have insurance laws prohibiting unfair trade practices or overall state consumer protection laws. Generally, insurance-specific laws prohibiting unfair trade practices address issues such as misrepresentations about policies; statements about the insurance business which are untrue, deceptive, or misleading; and any knowing or willful false or fraudulent statement or representation with reference to any application for insurance. These laws also address issues of discrimination, both in terms of contractual issues (e.g., unfair discrimination in premiums, amount of coverage, refusing to insure or renew, or canceling policies), or on the basis of race, color, creed, national origin, sex, or marital status. State law also specifically addresses claims-handling procedures. The NAIC has adopted a model Unfair Claims Settlement Practices Act, which each state has adopted in some form. Such laws protect claimants from improper claims practices given the unequal position of the insured suffering an underlying financial loss. These types of laws governing insurance business practices should form the bulk of CBRA's authority. In some areas, if current federal law were applied to insurance it might be sufficient to provide the necessary authority; in other cases new federal legislation might be required.

Finally, one area of state-based business conduct that CBRA should not have authority over is price controls. The degree to which states regulate insurance rates depends on the type of insurance product and the particular insurance buyer. Rate regulation is most common in personal lines of insurance (e.g., homeowners' and personal automobile insurance). Commercial insurance (other than workers' compensation) is generally subject to a lesser degree of rate regulation. Life insurance and surplus line insurance products are not subject to rate regulation.

States generally do not formulate mandatory rates for their licensed insurers. Instead insurers determine the rates they want to use in a particular state in which they are licensed, and then must comply with the applicable state rate and form regulatory requirements. In general, insurers must be able to justify their rates, either by the use of their own loss data and projections, or by the use of rating information and loss cost factors developed by a state regulator-accepted national insurance advisory organization, such as the Insurance Services Organization.

In its early years, state insurance regulation focused on the adequacy and levels of rates necessary to prevent solvency problems. In the optimal framework PFRA should address that issue. However, today states generally use rate regulation to hold down costs for consumers.

One of the fundamental principles of economics is that price controls result in inefficient outcomes. If the mandated price is set above the market clearing price, the result will be a surplus; if the mandated price is set below the market clearing price, the result will be a shortage. Insurance markets with strict price controls generally evidence shortages. When they are unable to charge an adequate rate for their product, insurers generally tighten their underwriting standards. In addition, rate restrictions limit insurers' abilities to price on the basis of measurable differences. Prices not accurately reflecting differences in risk effectively force low-risk consumers to subsidize high-risk consumers. These factors generally lead to a lack of coverage availability in some insurance markets, and a corresponding increase in state-run residual markets (i.e., state-sponsored mechanisms that serve as an insurance market of last resort).

Futures and Securities

Like banking and insurance, in the futures and securities market CBRA should primarily focus on business conduct issues associated with retail consumers. However, unlike banking and insurance, given the inherent link between futures and securities firms and their respective exchanges, issues related to business conduct are broader. As described earlier, in the optimal structure the newly established regulators should focus on issues unique to financial institutions. In that regard the corporate finance regulator should remain responsible for general issues related to corporate oversight in public securities markets, while CBRA should be responsible for the regulation and oversight of financial institutions and the futures and securities markets.

As described below, CBRA should also be responsible for the licensing of a wide range of financial firms. That licensing function should define the types of institutions and activities over which CBRA should have authority in the futures and securities area. As described in Chapter V, an intermediate-term recommendation is to merge the regulation of futures and securities. In the long term, CBRA should take over the majority of these functions. Since the sound functioning of exchanges clearly impacts the stability of financial markets, CBRA should have to consult with the Federal Reserve in the development of licensing requirements and oversight responsibilities.

The new licensing regime set forth below allows for a fundamental re-evaluation of the current dividing lines in futures and securities regulation. Whatever the structure of the licensing regime, the types of business conduct areas identified in current securities laws and regulations provide a framework for CBRA's authority. For example, broker-dealers are subject to regulatory standards for operational ability, professional conduct, testing and training, fraud and manipulation, and duties to customers (e.g., best execution and investor suitability). Investment companies are subject to regulations surrounding disclosure practices (initial and ongoing), valuation methodologies, and governance standards. Investment advisers are subject to regulation to protect investors by broadly prohibiting fraud and deception. Similarly, under current futures laws and regulations, financial institutions engaged in futures transactions are subject to a wide range of disclosure, reporting, recordkeeping, and ethical requirements, depending on the nature of their activities.

Federal Financial Services Provider Charter

As noted above, a key aspect of business conduct regulation is ensuring that financial institutions have and maintain minimum qualifications to enter certain lines of business. A chartering function administered by CBRA should accomplish this function.

To implement the chartering function, a new federal financial services provider ("FFSP") charter should be established. The FFSP charter should be flexible enough to incorporate a wide range of financial services providers. The establishment of a FFSP charter should result in the creation of appropriate national standards, in terms of financial capacity, expertise, and other requirements, that must be satisfied to enter the business of providing financial services. While there are numerous structural and technical issues associated with the establishment of a FFSP charter, some key issues to consider are presented below.

Scope of the FFSP Charter

A FFSP charter should be available for a wide range of financial activities. While there are a number of differences between the optimal structure and objectives-based regulation in other countries, the licensing framework adopted in Australia provides a good starting point. The Australian licensing framework generally requires applicants to specify the types of financial services provided, which in turn leads to different requirements. For example, the financial requirement for a firm only providing financial advice is less than what applies to a firm providing custody services.[138]

Taking into consideration differences between the Australian framework and the optimal structure, a FFSP charter could be available for several types of activities: brokerage and dealing in futures and securities transactions, investment management, investment advice, general insurance products (i.e., not guaranteed by the FIGF), and general lending. Much like the Australian licensing framework, each of the financial activities authorized under a FFSP charter should have its own unique set of "fit and proper" minimum requirements. For example, the minimum financial capacity and expertise to provide securities brokerage services should differ from the requirements necessary for general insurance.

As in the Australian framework, the minimum requirements should also be flexible enough to accommodate requirements resulting from membership in various exchanges or clearing organizations. CBRA, in consultation with the Federal Reserve, should have the authority to approve these requirements for certain types of charters, potentially impacting market stability (e.g., market makers and clearing participants).

In addition to meeting the appropriate financial requirements to obtain a FFSP charter, these firms should also have to remain in compliance with appropriate standards and provide regular updates on financial condition to CBRA, Federal Reserve, and as part of their standard public disclosures as appropriate. Upon the violation of appropriate financial requirements, CBRA (either directly or through SROs) should be able to take actions such as rescinding the charter or placing the firm into bankruptcy.

Special Provisions Applied to Some FFSP Charters

Because in many cases FFSPs will be responsible for holding or managing customer assets, clear segregation of customer accounts should be required for certain activities (e.g., securities brokerage). Segregation of customer assets is a primary means of protecting customer assets in the current U.S. futures and securities framework. However, due to issues associated with risks that customers and regulators may have difficulty monitoring (such as outright fraud or theft), some potential risk exposure still exists.

The Australian framework addresses this issue through a licensing requirement that firms with retail customers maintain professional indemnity insurance coverage as an added protection.[139] In the U.S. securities industry, in addition to a general requirement mandating customer accounts be segregated, the Securities Investor Protection Corporation ("SIPC") provides an additional level of protection for customer assets. While other structures like those employed in Australia could be used to accomplish a purpose similar to SIPC, the optimal framework could maintain a structure like SIPC. SIPC could be recast as part of an SRO structure, and current features such as a line of credit with the federal government and government representation on the SIPC Board should be re-evaluated. Other than those changes, SIPC could function much like it does today by working with CBRA to ensure that customer accounts in an insolvent firm would have an appropriate degree of protection.

Applicability of State Law

Similar to FIDIs and FIIs, FFSPs should be provided field preemption over state laws. Other state laws associated with general business practices (e.g., contracts, torts, taxation, or zoning) should continue to apply. As described below, state authorities should continue to have a role in the development and enforcement of business conduct regulations.

While this may seem to be a broad grant of federal preemption, in some cases this structure resembles the current structure. As noted above, NSMIA has already greatly limited the role of the states in securities regulation and states have little role in futures regulation. Business conduct regulation in many states is inapplicable for non-retail insurance products (e.g., reinsurance, surplus lines, and large policyholders). In other cases, such as general retail lending, the general business conduct rules developed by CBRA should apply to FFSPs.

Rule Writing, Compliance, and Enforcement

CBRA's responsibilities for business conduct regulation in the optimal structure should be very broad. CBRA should have authority to develop and enforce business conduct regulations for all retail financial services and products, and for other aspects of business conduct. In comparison to the current business conduct oversight system, CBRA's responsibilities should take the place of the Federal Reserve and other insured depository institution regulators, state insurance regulators, and some aspects of the Commodity Futures Trading Commission, the SEC, and the FTC.

A number of models could be considered to implement CBRA's rule writing, compliance, and enforcement responsibilities. CBRA could employ a model, similar to the current approach in banking regulation, under which it would be solely responsible for these functions. However, given CBRA's scope of responsibilities, that structure would not likely be practical. CBRA could also employ, or in some instances be required to employ, a structure similar to the current futures and securities regime that relies on SROs for many aspects of regulatory implementation and oversight. Given the breadth and scope of CBRA's responsibilities, some aspect of self-regulation should form an important component of implementation. Given its significance and effectiveness, the current SRO model for futures and securities should be preserved. That model could be considered for other areas, or the structure could be flexible enough to allow for certain modifications, such as maintaining rule writing authority with CRBA, while relying on an SRO model for compliance and enforcement.

Providing an extensive amount of detail about the extent of rule writing, compliance and enforcement programs is beyond the scope of this report. The goal, however, is not to weaken any existing program but an attempt to achieve some consensus across differing but converging product lines.

Role of the States

As described above, CBRA should be responsible for setting national standards for a wide range of business conduct laws across all types of financial services providers. The national standards established by CBRA should apply to all financial services firms, whether federally or state-chartered. In addition, field preemption should be provided to

FIDIs, FIIs, and FFSPs, preempting state business conduct laws directly relating to the provision of financial services.

In the optimal structure, states should still retain clear authority to enact laws and take enforcement actions against state-chartered financial service providers as long as the state laws do no conflict with federal laws. In practice, the standards set by CBRA will be applicable exclusively to federally chartered financial services providers but should represent a floor for state-chartered financial services providers.

As noted previously, state authorities can play an important role in business conduct regulation. The more localized focus of state authorities often allows for more in-depth knowledge of local business practices. In considering the future role of the states, the optimal structure seeks to acknowledge more clearly than the current regulatory structure that a national market for financial products exists, while at the same time preserving an appropriate role for state authorities to respond to local conditions.

To address these issues, two aspects of the role of the states should be considered.

Input into Rulemaking

State authorities could be given a formalized role in CBRA's rulemaking process as a means of building off of their extensive local experience. Creating a State Advisory Board ("SAB") with a specific mandate to be a regular and transparent mechanism for providing input into the rulemaking process represents one way to accomplish this. Such a process could be used to bring issues of importance and relevance to the states to CBRA's attention. Given CBRA's wide responsibilities across all financial services, the composition of the SAB should likely have to be similarly broad, drawing on state regulatory experience across all financial services and states' attorneys general experience in business conduct areas.

Role in Compliance and Enforcement

As noted above, the business conduct regulations established by CBRA should form a appropriate national standard applicable to all financial services providers, whether operating under federal or state charters.

States could also play a role in enforcement. As noted above, states should continue to exercise authority under state laws that apply to state-chartered financial service providers. In addition to that inherent function, state officials could also be given the authority to monitor compliance and enforce CBRA's regulations for state-chartered financial services providers. Providing state officials with the authority to monitor and enforce compliance with federal regulations helps to avoid gaps in the implementation of these regulations.

Finally, states could also be granted some limited authority to address business conduct issues associated with federally chartered financial institutions. For example, given the experience of state officials with state-chartered financial institutions or other locally based knowledge of business conduct issues (e.g., complaints regarding certain business practices in local areas), state officials could bring these issues to CBRA's attention. Based upon that local information, state officials could be given the authority to proceed with full investigations and enforcement actions if approved by CBRA. An alternative to this grant of authority to state officials should be for CBRA (or the appropriate SRO) to use such information to further investigate compliance issues and take enforcement actions as necessary. In both cases, the goal should be to build off the local knowledge of state officials and to provide an appropriate role for states in business conduct oversight.

Chapter 7

CONCLUSION

The United States has the strongest and most liquid capital markets in the world. This strength is due in no small part to the U.S. financial services industry regulatory structure, which promotes consumer protection and market stability. However, recent market developments have pressured this regulatory structure, revealing regulatory gaps and redundancies. These regulatory inefficiencies may serve to detract from U.S. capital markets competitiveness.

In order to ensure the United States maintains its preeminence in the global capital markets, the Department of the Treasury ("Treasury") sets forth the aforementioned recommendations to improve the regulatory structure governing financial institutions. Treasury has designed a path to move from the current functional regulatory approach to an objectives-based regulatory regime through a series of specific recommendations. The short-term recommendations focus on immediate reforms responding to the current events in the mortgage and credit markets. The intermediate recommendations focus on modernizing the current regulatory structure within the current functional system.

The short-term and intermediate recommendations will drive the evolution of the U.S. regulatory structure towards the optimal regulatory framework, an objectives-based regime directly linking the regulatory objectives of market stability regulation, prudential financial regulation, and business conduct regulation to the regulatory structure. Such a framework best promotes consumer protection and stable and innovative markets.

APPENDIX

APPENDIX A – FEDERAL REGISTER NOTICE

DEPARTMENT OF THE TREASURY BILLING CODE 4811-42
Review by the Treasury Department of the Regulatory Structure Associated with Financial Institutions.

AGENCY: Department of the Treasury, Departmental Offices.

ACTION: Notice; request for comments.

SUMMARY: The Treasury Department is undertaking a broad review of the regulatory structure associated with financial institutions. To assist in this review and obtain a broad view of all perspectives, the Treasury Department is issuing this notice seeking public comment.

DATES: Comments should be submitted electronically and received by Wednesday, November 21, 2007.

ADDRESSES: Please submit comments electronically through the Federal eRulemaking Portal – "Regulations.gov." Go to http://www.regulations.gov, select "Department of the Treasury – All" from the agency drop-down menu, then click "Submit." In the "Docket ID" column, select "TREAS-DO-2007-001 8" to submit or view public comments and to view supporting and related materials for this notice. The "User Tips" link at the top of the Regulations.gov home page provides information on using Regulations.gov, including instructions for submitting or viewing public comments, viewing other supporting and related materials, and viewing the docket after the close of the comment period.

Please include your name, affiliation, address, e-mail address and telephone number(s) in your comment. Where appropriate, comments should include a short Executive Summary (no more than five single-spaced pages). All statements, including attachments and other supporting materials, received are part of the public record and subject to public disclosure. You should submit only information that you wish to make available publicly.

FOR FURTHER INFORMATION CONTACT: Jeffrey Stoltzfoos, Senior Advisor, Office of the Assistant Secretary for Financial Institutions, (202) 622-2610 or Mario Ugoletti, Director, Office of Financial Institutions Policy, (202) 622-2730 (not toll free numbers).

SUPPLEMENTARY INFORMATION: The Treasury Department is currently engaged in a number of initiatives associated with maintaining the competitiveness of United States capital markets. One of those initiatives is evaluating the regulatory structure associated with financial institutions.

The regulatory structure for financial institutions in the United States has served us well over the course of our history. Much of the basic regulatory structure associated with financial institutions was established decades ago. While there have been important changes over time in the way financial institutions have been regulated, the Treasury Department believes that it is important to continue to evaluate our regulatory structure and consider ways to improve efficiency, reduce overlap, strengthen consumer and investor protection, and ensure that financial institutions have the ability to adapt to evolving market dynamics, including the increasingly global nature of financial markets.

The Treasury Department's review of regulatory structure will focus on all types of financial institutions: commercial banks and other insured depository institutions; insurance companies; securities firms; futures firms; and other types of financial intermediaries.

The Treasury Department is soliciting comments to assist in this review. The Treasury Department would be particularly interested in comments on the specific questions set forth below, or on other issues related to the regulatory structure associated with financial institutions. We are also interested in specific ideas or recommendations as to how we can improve our current regulatory structure.

I. GENERAL ISSUES

1.1. What are the key problems or issues that need to be addressed by our review of the current regulatory structure for financial institutions?

1.2. Over time, there has been an increasing convergence of products across the traditional "functional" regulatory lines of banking, insurance, securities, and futures.

What do you view as the significant market developments over the past two decades (e.g. securitization, institutionalization, financial product innovation and globalization) and please describe what opportunities and/or pressures, if any, these developments have created in the regulation of financial institutions?

1.2.1. Does the "functional" regulatory framework under which banking, securities, insurance, and futures are primarily regulated by respective functional regulators lead to inefficiencies in the provision of financial services?

1.2.2. Does the "functional" regulatory framework pose difficulties for considering overall risk to the financial system? If so, to what extent have these difficulties been resolved through regulatory oversight at the holding company level? 1.2.3 Many countries have moved towards creating a single financial market regulator (e.g., United Kingdom's Financial Services Authority; Japan's Financial Services Agency; and Germany's Federal Financial Supervisory Authority (BaFin)). Some countries (e.g., Australia and the Netherlands) have adopted a twin peaks model of regulation, separating prudential safety and soundness regulation and conduct-of-business regulation. What are the strengths and weaknesses of these structural approaches and their applicability in the United States? What ideas can be gleaned from these structures that would improve U.S. capital market competitiveness?

1.3. What should be the key objectives of financial institution regulation? How could the framework for the regulation of financial institutions be more closely aligned with the objectives of regulation? Can our current regulatory framework be improved, especially in terms of imparting greater market discipline and providing a more cohesive look at overall financial system risk? If so, how can it be improved to achieve these goals? In regards to this set of questions, more specifically:

1.3.1. How should the regulation of financial institutions with explicit government guarantees differ from financial institutions without explicit guarantees? Is the current system adequate in this regard?

1.3.2. Is there a need for some type of market stability regulation for financial institutions without explicit Federal Government guarantees? If so, what would such regulation entail?

1.3.3. Does the current system of regulating certain financial institutions at the holding company level allow for sufficient amounts of market discipline? Are there ways to improve holding company regulation to allow for enhanced market discipline?

1.3.4. In recent years, debate has emerged about "more efficient" regulation and the possibility of adopting a "principles-based" approach to regulation, rather than a "rules-based" approach. Others suggest that a proper balance between the two is essential. What are the strengths, weaknesses and feasibility of such approaches, and could a more "principles-based" approach improve U.S. competitiveness?

1.3.5. Would the U.S. financial regulatory structure benefit if there was a uniform set of basic principles of regulation that were agreed upon and adopted by each financial services regulator?

1.4. Does the current regulatory structure adequately address consumer or investor protection issues? If not, how could we improve our current regulatory structure to address these issues?

1.5. What role should the States have in the regulation of financial institutions? Is there a difference in the appropriate role of the States depending on financial system protection or consumer and investor protection aspects of regulation?

1.6. Europe is putting in place a more integrated single financial market under its Financial Services Action Plan. Many Asian countries as well are developing their financial markets. Often, these countries or regions are doing so on the basis of widely adopted international regulatory standards. Global businesses often cite concerns about the costs associated with meeting diverse regulatory standards in the numerous countries in which they operate. To address these issues, some call for greater global regulatory convergence and others call for mutual recognition. To what extent should the design of regulatory initiatives in the United States be informed by the competitiveness of U.S. institutions and markets in the global marketplace? Would the U.S. economy and capital market competitiveness be better served by pursuing greater global regulatory convergence?

II. SPECIFIC ISSUES

2.1. Depository Institutions

2.1.1. Are multiple charters for insured depository institutions the optimal way to achieve regulatory objectives? What are the strengths and weaknesses of having charters tied to specific activities or organizational structures? Are these distinctions as valid and important today as when these charters were granted?

2.1.2. What are the strengths and weaknesses of the dual banking system?

2.1.3. What is the optimal role for a deposit insurer in depository institution regulation and supervision? For example, should the insurer be the primary regulator for all insured depository institutions, should it have back-up regulatory authority, or should its functions be limited to the pricing of deposit insurance, or other functions?

2.1.4 What role should the central bank have in bank regulation and supervision? Is central bank regulatory authority necessary for the development of monetary policy?

2.1.5. Is the current framework for regulating bank or financial holding companies with depository institution subsidiaries appropriate? Are there other regulatory frameworks that could or should be considered to limit the transfer of the safety net associated with insured depository institutions?

2.1.6. What are the key consumer protection elements associated with products offered by depository institutions? What is the best regulatory enforcement mechanism for these elements?

2.2. Insurance

2.2.1. What are the costs and benefits of State-based regulation of the insurance industry?

2.2.2. What are the key Federal interests for establishing a presence or greater involvement in insurance regulation? What regulatory structure would best achieve these goals/interests?

2.2.3. Should the States continue to have a role (or the sole role) in insurance regulation? Insurance regulation is already somewhat bifurcated between retail and wholesale companies (e.g., surplus lines carriers). Does the current structure work? How could that structure be improved?

2.2.4. States have taken an active role in some aspects of the insurance marketplace (e.g., workers' compensation and residual markets for hard to place risks) for various policy reasons. Are these policy reasons still valid? Are these necessarily met through State (as opposed to federal) regulation?

2.3. Securities and Futures

2.3.1. Is there a continued rationale for distinguishing between securities and futures products and their respective intermediaries?

2.3.2. Is there a continued rationale for having separate regulators for these types of financial products and institutions?

2.3.3. What type of regulation would be optimal for firms that provide financial services related to securities and futures products? Should this regulation be driven by the need to protect customers or by the broader issues of market integrity and financial system stability?

2.3.4. What is the optimal role for the states in securities and futures regulation?

2.3.5. What are the key consumer/investor protection elements associated with products offered by securities and futures firms? Should there be a regulatory distinction among retail, institutional, wholesale, commercial, and hedging customers?

2.3.6. Would it be useful to apply some of the principles of the Commodity Futures Modernization Act of 2000 to the securities regulatory regime? Is a tiered system of regulation appropriate? Is it appropriate to make distinctions based on the relative sophistication of the market participants and/or the integrity of the market?

Dated: October 11, 2007
Taiya Smith
Executive Secretary of the Treasury

APPENDIX B – REVIEW OF PAST TREASURY AND ADMINISTRATION REGULATORY REFORM REPORTS

Synthesized below are the five most recent reports regarding financial services regulatory reform that the Treasury or the Administration has issued. Although many of these reports often explored regulatory technicalities (e.g., deposit rate ceilings), the analysis provided below focuses on the broad structural reforms these reports recommended and the reasoning contributing to these recommendations.

Commission on Financial Structure and Regulation (1971)

In 1970, President Richard M. Nixon created the Commission on Financial Structure and Regulation to "review and study the structure, operation, and regulation of the private financial institutions in the United States, for the purpose of formulating recommendations that should improve the functioning of the private financial system."[140] The problems in the U.S. financial system exposed by the volatile economic period of the 1 960s, with high inflation, severely fluctuating interest rates, and a lack of liquidity at many financial institutions leading to their subsequent restrictions on customer loans, particularly for residential mortgages and small business, prompted the formation of the Commission. The Commission was made up of private sector members and chaired by Reed O. Hunt, former Chairman of the Board, Crown Zellerbach Corporation, and subsequently named, the "Hunt Commission."[141]

The Hunt Commission studied the functional specialization, the effects of deposit rate regulations, chartering and branching, problems of deposit insurance, reserves and taxation, the effects of regulation on mortgage markets and residential construction, competitive problems, and, finally, the framework of the financial regulatory agencies of commercial banks, mutual savings banks, savings and loan associations, credit unions, private pension plans, and reserve life insurers.[142]

In 1971, the Hunt Commission released *The Report of the President's Commission on Financial Structure and Regulation* urging the adoption of "more responsible" fiscal policies and, more pertinent to Treasury's current study, reforms in the regulatory structure surrounding the banking industry.[143] The Hunt Commission recommended the consolidation of the federal examination and supervisory functions over financial institutions into two separate agencies. To improve state banking regulation and eliminate duplicative examinations, the Hunt Commission recommended that the Office of the Administrator of State Banks ("OASB") should examine and supervise state-chartered thrift institutions, such as insured commercial banks, mutual savings banks, and savings and loan associations (if deposits subject to third party payment orders aggregate more than 10 percent of total deposit liabilities), taking over these functions from the Federal Reserve and the Federal Deposit Insurance Corporation ("FDIC").[144]

The Hunt Commission recommended retitling the Office of the Comptroller of the Currency ("OCC") as the Office of the National Bank Administrator (the "ONBA") and establishing the ONBA as an independent agency separate from Treasury. In addition to retaining all the authority of the OCC with respect to national banks, the ONBA should supervise all federally chartered thrift associations, such as mutual commercial banks, mutual savings banks, and savings and loan associations (if deposits subject to third party payment orders aggregate more than 10 percent of total deposit liabilities).[145] These two consolidating acts should have several benefits: enhancement of the uniformity and efficiency in examination, supervision, and enforcement relating to financial institutions; and more acutely focusing the Federal Reserve on monetary policy, bank holding companies, and international finance[146]

In order to promote uniformity in insurance treatment among depository institutions, the Hunt Commission recommended that a new agency, the Federal Deposit Guarantee Administration (the "FDGA"), be established to incorporate the FDIC, the Federal Savings and Loan Insurance Corporation (the "FSLIC"), and the insurance function of the National Credit Union Administration (the "NCUA").[147] Five trustees (i.e., a director of the FDGA as Chairman, the Administrator of State Banks, the Administrator of National Banks, the Federal Home Loan Bank Board ("FHLBB") Chairman, and the Administrator of the NCUA) should govern the FDGA, diminishing the incentive to maximize the value of the insurance fund.[148] The FDGA should administer the FDIC, whose Director positions should be eliminated. At the same time, each of the entities within the FDGA should be able to respond to problems within its specialized institutional area.[149]

In order that insured depository institutions be able to adapt to changing market conditions and not be inhibited in their growth by the particular regulatory constraints of their charter relating to assets, liabilities, and services, the Hunt Commission also recommended that any such depository institution have the ability to alter its charter to that of any other institution.[150]

The Hunt Commission also recommended that the Federal Reserve, the OCC, and the FDIC remain outside the budgetary controls of the Office of Management and Budget (the "OMB") and the ONBA, the OASB, the FHLBB, and the NCUA be made independent of the federal budgetary process[151]

Blueprint for Reform: The Report of the Task Group on Regulation of Financial Services (1984)

In 1982, President Ronald Reagan created the Task Group on Regulation of Financial Services ("Task Group") to review federal financial services regulation and make legislative recommendations to increase regulatory effectiveness, promote competition, and reduce unnecessary costs.[152] The Task Group, chaired by Vice President George H.W. Bush, included the Secretary of the Treasury, the Attorney General, the OMB Director, the

Assistant to the President for Policy Development, the Chairman of the Council of Economic Advisors, the Chairmen of the Federal Reserve, the FDIC, the FHLBB, the Securities and Exchange Commission ("SEC"), the Commodity Futures Trading Commission, and the NCUA, and the Comptroller of the Currency.[153]

In 1984, the Task Group released its *Blueprint for Reform: The Report of the Task Group on Regulation of Financial Services*, setting forth the six objectives of its recommendations: First, the recommendations should encourage regulation by function, or "functional regulation"—"to regulate each common activity or product by a single agency under a common set of rules, irrespective of the type of institution involved"[154]— so as to ease the regulatory disparity (and regulatory arbitrage) and the anti-competitive effects that institutions engaging in the same activity or function face. The Task Group noted that functional regulation was not appropriate in all areas, conceding that safety and soundness and operations regulation should be handled by a single agency, but activities common to many firms should be regulated by a functionally suited regulato[155]

Other objectives of the Task Group were to reduce competitive barriers where not absolutely necessary to preserve safety and soundness. The Task Group reasoned that competitive barriers often lead to higher prices and reduced alternative services and products for consumers, ultimately effecting the efficiency of the economy as a whole.[156] In addition, the Task Group strove for recommendations to reduce unnecessary regulations for which ultimately consumers pay.[157]

Recommendations also sought to streamline and clarify the responsibilities in the regulatory structure, while preserving the checks and balances among regulators. Noting the fact that the regulatory system does not face the same competitive pressures to reduce waste and inefficiencies as the private sector, the Task Group noted that checks and balances among regulators attempt to provide these pressures.[158] The Task Group also recognized a need to preserve the dual regulatory banking system, holding this system out as "one of the finest examples of cooperative federalism in the nation's history."[159]

In attempting to meet its objectives, the Task Group provided the following structural reforms: The Task Group recommended eliminating the examination and supervisory powers over non-member state banks of the FDIC and creating a new "Federal Banking Agency" (the "FBA") within Treasury, incorporating and enhancing the OCC, to regulate all national banks.[160] The Comptroller of the Currency should become the Director of the FBA.[161] The Federal Reserve should provide federal regulation of state-chartered banks, except regulation of many state-chartered banks and savings and loan associations should be transferred to better state regulatory agencies with the Federal Reserve's maintaining residual authority.[162] The Task Group proposed a "certification program" for the most qualified state regulators so that federal supervision could be concentrated on the institutions (and regulators) most in need and state regulators should be incentivized to improve their supervisory practices.[163]

Attempting to eliminate the inefficiencies in reporting to two regulators, the Task Group recommended that, instead of the Federal Reserve's supervising all bank holding companies, the subsidiary bank regulator should in almost all cases also be the bank holding company supervisor.[164] This would mean that the FBA, the Federal Reserve, or the "certified" state banking regulator would supervise the bank holding company and its subsidiary bank. The Federal Reserve should remain the supervisor for bank holding companies of the largest domestic banks, those with significant international operations, and foreign-owned institutions.[165] The Federal Reserve should transfer its authority to decide permissible activities for banks to the newly created FBA.[166]

The supervisory, examination, and regulatory authority of the FDIC should be transferred to other agencies so that its mandate should be focused entirely on providing deposit insurance and regulating the deposit insurance system.[167] The FDIC should supervise all troubled institutions posing the most risk to the financial system.[168] With the FSLIC, the FDIC should be required to establish minimum capital requirements and accounting standards for insurance.

The FHLBB should still regulate thrift institutions, but given the expansion beyond housing and housing-related activities of thrift institutions, certain thrift institutions not meeting a portfolio asset test based on investments in housing-related financial instruments should be forced to convert their charter to a national or state-chartered bank and be more appropriately functionally regulated.[169] These newly chartered banking institutions should be required to obtain FDIC insurance.[170]

In order to further streamline regulation, the Task Group recommended that all securities and antitrust matters relating to depository institutions be regulated by the SEC and the Department of Justice, respectively.[171] At the time of the Task Group's recommendations, the OCC, the FDIC, the Federal Reserve, and the FHLBB enforced the securities and antitrust laws against their regulated entities.

Report of the Presidential Task Force on Market Mechanisms (1988)

Responding to concerns surrounding the stock market decline in October 1987, President Ronald Reagan issued an Executive Order creating The Presidential Task Force on Market Mechanisms ("Task Force").[172] The Executive Order charged the Task Force with analyzing the financial condition of the securities markets, including problems affecting the markets' short-term liquidity and long-term solvency, and issuing a report recommending solutions to these problems.[173] Secretary of the Treasury Nicholas F. Brady served as Chairman along side four private sector members.[174]

In January 1988, the Task Force issued its *Report of the Presidential Task Force on Market Mechanisms*, attributing the failure of three separate markets—markets for stocks, stock index futures, and stock options—"to act as one," and consequently recommending greater unity in various market mechanisms.[175] For the Task Force, the "guiding objective" of any regulatory changes should be to "enhance the integrity and competitiveness of U.S. financial markets."[176] The Task Force focused on "the individual marketplaces and the interrelationship of existing market mechanisms, including the instruments traded, the strategies employed and the regulatory structures."[177] The Task Force did not take into account, but did acknowledge, that other factors besides market mechanisms might have contributed to the market decline.

The Task Force set out the various interlinking mechanisms of the markets, including the following: financial instruments; the dominance of the same financial institutions in the trading of these financial instruments both in their principal and agent capacities; trading strategies, such as index arbitrage and other inter-market hedging activities; and clearing procedures.[178] The Task Force reasoned that, "Certain important conclusions should be drawn from the behavior of the markets for stocks, stock index futures, and options in mid-October. First and foremost, these apparently separate markets are in an economic sense one market. They are linked by instruments, participants, trading strategies and clearing flows. Nonetheless, institutional and regulatory structures interfere with the linkages among them and hinder their smooth and efficient operation."[179]

In setting out its recommendations, the Task Force concluded, "[I]t is only prudent to design mechanisms to protect investors, the market's infrastructures, the financial system and the economy from the destructive consequence of violent market breaks."[180] The Task Force recommended that one agency should coordinate the limited, but critical, regulatory issues which have an impact across market segments, to work towards the unity of clearing systems across marketplaces, harmonization of margin requirements across markets, creation and implementation of circuit breaker mechanisms, and the creation of information systems to monitor transactions in related markets.[181] Although admitting that neither its resources nor mandate allowed it to consider this one agency, the Task Force surmised that the Federal Reserve should be the appropriate agency.

Modernizing the Financial System: Recommendations for Safer, More Competitive Banks (1991)

Under the Financial Institutions Reform, Recovery, and Enforcement Act of 1989, Congress directed Treasury to produce recommendations in consultation with the depository institution regulatory agencies, the OMB, and the private sector to reform and strengthen the federal deposit insurance system.[182] In February 1991, Treasury issued *Modernizing the Financial System: Recommendations for Safer, More Competitive Banks* (the "Green Book").[183] Guiding this report were two principles: Deposit insurance reforms must enhance both the banking system's safety and soundness and the industry's competitiveness.[184] In developing reforms, Treasury addressed then-current issues affecting the banking industry: reduced competitiveness and financial strength caused by outdated restrictions on banking activities; overextension of deposit insurance; a fragmented regulatory system with duplicative regulation; and an undercapitalized deposit insurance fund.[185] The "four fundamental reforms" of the Green Book were lifting restrictions on banking activities and allowing nationwide banking and commercial ownership of banks; reining in the overextended deposit insurance and improving supervision with strengthened capital requirements; streamlining the regulatory structure with one federal regulator for a given banking entity; and recapitalizing the Bank Insurance Fund.

Two sets of recommendations focused on modernizing and streamlining financial services regulation.[186] First, given the erosion in the traditional banking franchise, the report recommended removing the restrictions "protecting" banks from competition, such as permitting well-capitalized banks to have financial affiliates through the creation of financial services holding companies.[187] These financial affiliates could engage in any financial activity, including securities, insurance, and mutual fund activities, although the financial services holding companies could not engage in these activities.[188] At the same time, securities, insurance, and mutual fund companies could affiliate with well-capitalized banks,[189] and commercial firms could own financial services holding companies with appropriate firewalls.[190]

This proposal had three benefits: This "blending of banking, finance and commerce" should foster a stronger financial services system with consumer and taxpayer benefits.

A more attractive, expanded franchise possibility should allow firms with undercapitalized banks to attract capital. To prevent putting the taxpayer at risk with the potential for expanded deposit insurance and a federal safety net to cover these affiliated institutions, the recommendation included certain safeguards: only well-capitalized banks would be eligible to engage in these newly permissible activities through financial services holding companies; unlike banks, financial affiliates and financial services holding companies would not have access to the deposit insurance system; capital-based supervision would focus on banks; financial affiliates would be separately capitalized; financial activities would be regulated by function, rather than by institution allowing for a more efficient and effective regulatory framework; funding and disclosure firewalls would be created between the bank and its affiliates or holding company; and the bank regulator would perform "umbrella oversight" of the financial services holding company to understand affiliate risk and protect the insured bank.[191]

In order to produce "greater accountability, efficiency, and consistency of regulation and supervision, through a reduction in the number of regulators; improved consumer benefits from the reduced duplication and overlap; and the separation of the regulator from the insurer," Treasury recommended a restructuring of banking regulation.[192] Treasury based its proposals upon those in the 1984 *Blueprint for Reform* and, consequently, like this prior report, called for the streamlining of the four federal banking regulators into two: the Federal Reserve being responsible for all state-chartered banks and their bank holding companies (removing the FDIC's authority); a new Federal Banking Agency under Treasury assuming the responsibilities of the OCC, the OTS, and the Federal Reserve's supervisory powers over bank holding companies).[193] The second structural reform called for consolidating all deposit insurance functions for banks and thrifts into the FDIC.[194]

American Finance for the 21st Century (1997)

Under the Riegle-Neal Interstate Banking and Branching Efficiency Act of 1994, Congress directed the Secretary of the Treasury to review the strengths and weaknesses of the financial services system, and, in particular, the adequacy of regulation to meet market developments.[195] In November 1997, Treasury published *American Finance for the 21st Century*.[196]

The purpose of the report was to identify the most important market developments, policy issues those developments raise, and provide a regulatory framework for adapting to those developments.[197] The report laid out the four trends reshaping the financial services industry: "advances in information and communication technology; globalization; financial innovation; and stronger competition unleashed by the removal of counterproductive restrictions."[198] The report then described how these changes would impact "finance's three major functions: payments, intermediation, and the spreading of risk."[199] Payments would become increasingly electronic-driven, not paper-driven.

Disintermediation would lower prices for consumers at the same time as offering more choice.[200] With growing securitization, there is greater risk dispersion.

The policy issues dominating the report were: removing impediments to competition;[201] protecting taxpayers (and the deposit insurance system);[202] the use of electronic money;[203] preserving competition to prevent concentration and rupture.[204] The report devotes one of its five chapters to a discussion of risk,[205] including focusing on the clearance and settlement systems (in particular, Fedwire and CHIPS) and an historical analysis of regulatory attempts at risk containment and recommendations on such containment.[206]

This report is different than previous Treasury and Administration reports due to the broad-based philosophical tone of its recommendations, calling for a paradigmatic shift in regulatory policy. The report recommends the following policy principles: "hospitality to innovation, use of market mechanisms to pursue policy goals, avoidance of micro management in pursuit of stability, and a preference for targeted policies over expansive and uniform mandates."[207] In addition, policy recommendations shied away from micromanagement of entire sectors, and focused on specific areas where needs arise, such as targeting the underserved.[208]

What guided the report was a belief that financial services regulation in the twenty-first century needed to distance itself from the Depression-era model focused on "market segmentation and failure prevention" and approach a model focused on "competition and failure containment."[209] The policy recommendations emerging from this report all share the premise of this model: "[I]n an increasingly competitive financial world, periodic upsets in financial markets—sometimes very large ones—are inevitable, and the foremost goal of policy should be not to prevent such upsets but to *contain* them. That means, to the greatest extent possible, identifying, isolating, and disposing of trouble spots so that they do not endanger the stability of the whole system, and doing so without at the same time requiring the federal government, and thus taxpayers, to extend blanket guarantees against loss."[210]

A "containment policy" thus influences the recommendations of the report.[211] Specific containment recommendations include: isolating troubled institutions before they can lead to systemic damage, exemplified by the Federal Deposit Insurance Corporation Improvement Act of 1991 authorizing federal regulators to take "prompt corrective action" against weakly capitalized banks;[212] reducing informational gaps among regulators and markets regarding systemic risk, including placing a "heart monitor" at financial institutions as well as securities firms and insurers to alert regulators instantaneously of capital vulnerability, and requiring financial institutions, securities firms, and insurers to disclose continuously (and possibly to the public) their counterparty and creditor exposures;[213] relying on market participants to apply discipline and bolster government regulation and supervision, including expanding the Federal Reserve's precommitment policies, where banks specify the amount of potential losses from trading activities, to all risk-exposing activities, and requiring banks belonging to large banking organizations to back a portion of their assets with uninsured subordinated debt;[214] progressing towards instantaneous settlement of transactions, including real-time gross settlement of CHIPS transactions and T+1 for securities transactions;[215] and further scrutinizing the level of margin required for exchange-traded and over-the-counter derivatives.[216]

APPENDIX C – EXISTING REGULATORY STRUCTURE FOR SUBPRIME MORTGAGE ORIGINATION

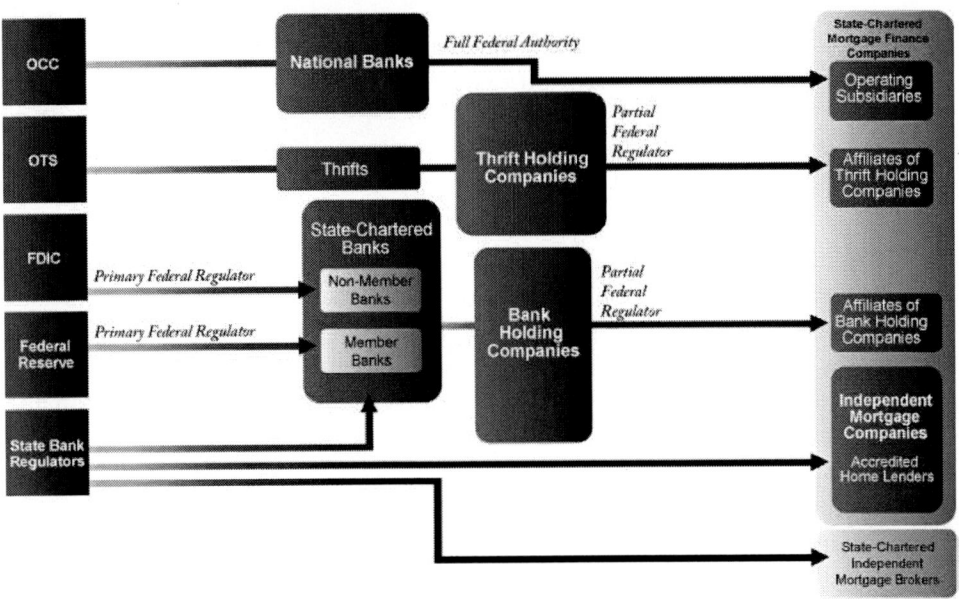

APPENDIX D – DESCRIPTIONS OF SELECT U.S. PAYMENT AND SETTLEMENT SYSTEMS FEDERAL RESERVE BANK SYSTEMS

Fedwire Funds Service

The Fedwire Funds Service is a real-time gross settlement system. This means that payments are continuously settled on an individual, order-by-order basis without netting. When a depository institution initiates a Fedwire funds transfer, it irrevocably authorizes the Federal Reserve to debit its Federal Reserve account for the amount of the transfer. The Federal Reserve then credits the account of the receiving depository institution on its books. This immediate finality of payment is the major distinguishing characteristic of the Fedwire Funds Service. In 2007, the Fedwire Funds Service processed about 537,000 transfers per day valued at nearly $2.7 trillion.

Fedwire Securities Service

The Fedwire Securities Service, also known as the National Book-Entry System ("NBES"), is a real-time, delivery-versus-payment ("DVP"), gross settlement system that allows for the immediate, simultaneous transfer of government and mortgage-backed securities against payment. A DVP system ensures that the final transfer of securities occurs if and only if the final transfer of funds occurs. The Fedwire Securities Service consists of a safekeeping function and a transfer and settlement function. The safekeeping function involves the electronic storage of securities holdings records in custody accounts; the transfer and settlement function involves the electronic transfer of securities between parties, either free or against a settlement payment. In 2007, the Fedwire Securities Service processed nearly 98,800 transfers per day valued at about $2.0 trillion.

National Settlement Service

The National Settlement Service ("NSS") is a multilateral settlement service for depository institutions that settle for participants in clearinghouses, financial exchanges, and other clearing and settlement groups. Settlement agents acting on behalf of those depository institutions electronically submit settlement files, which are processed by the service on receipt. NSS first posts all debit entries, ensuring that each settling bank has sufficient funds or capacity in its Federal Reserve account. Once all debits have been made, NSS then posts all credits to the Federal Reserve accounts of settling banks in credit positions. Entries are final and irrevocable when posted. Key private-sector systems that use NSS include the Depository Trust Company ("DTC") and the National Securities Clearing Corporation ("NSCC") for end-of-day cash settlement (with DTC acting as settlement agent for NSCC), the Fixed Income Clearing Corporation ("FICC") for funds-only settlement (with DTC acting as settlement agent for FICC), the Electronic Payments Network ("EPN"), which is the only large private-sector automated clearing house ("ACH") operator, and several large national and regional check clearinghouses.[217] In 2007, NSS processed about 2,000 transfers per day valued at about $61 billion.

FedACH Service

The FedACH service is the Federal Reserve Banks' ACH service through which they provide depository institutions with ACH operator services. The ACH is an electronic payment system in which batched debit and credit payments are exchanged among business, consumer, and government accounts. The ACH is used for pre-authorized recurring payments, such as payroll payments, Social Security payments, mortgage payments, and utility payments. It is also used for non-recurring payments, such as payments initiated through the telephone, for the conversion of checks into ACH payments at lockboxes and at points of sale. The Federal Reserve Banks offer value-added ACH informational and risk management services as well as the ability to send outbound cross-border ACH payments through its FedACH International service (this service currently actively covers Canada, Mexico, and four European countries). In 2007, FedACH processed about 37 million transactions per day with an average aggregate value of about $58 billion.

Private Sector Systems

Clearing House Interbank Payments System
The Clearing House Interbank Payment Systems ("CHIPS") is a bank-owned large-value payment system that provides real-time final settlement of payments. It is owned and operated by The Clearing House, which is owned by the largest U.S. banks or the U.S.-based affiliates of major foreign banks. Since it was launched in 1970, CHIPS has undergone several modifications to reduce the risks it presented to the payments system. Most recently, on January 22, 2001, CHIPS was converted from an end-of-day, multilateral net settlement system to one that provides final settlement for all payment orders as they are released. Under real-time final settlement, CHIPS payment instructions are settled against a positive current position in the CHIPS account held at the Federal Reserve Bank of New York ("FRBNY") or simultaneously offset by incoming payments or both. Payment instructions that are submitted but that remain unsettled at the end of the day (known as the residual) are netted on a multilateral basis. CHIPS participants in a net debit position fund their residual net positions through Fedwire funds transfers to the CHIPS account at FRBNY. In 2007, CHIPS processed about 348,000 transfers per day valued at about $1.9 trillion.

CLS Bank
CLS Bank ("CLSB") is a special purpose bank, chartered as an Edge Act corporation by the Federal Reserve, that simultaneously settles payment instructions for foreign exchange transactions in eligible currencies. CLSB commenced live operations on September 9, 2002, initially settling foreign exchange transactions among seven currencies. CLSB added four more currencies in 2003 and another four more in 2004.[218] Organizationally, the CLS Group consists of a top-tier Swiss and a second-tier U.K. holding company, with an operating subsidiary (CLS Services) in London and a banking subsidiary (CLSB) in New York. The Federal Reserve supervises CLSB and regulates its holding companies. In 2007, CLSB processed an average of about 370,000 sides with an average daily gross value of about $3.7 trillion (USD equivalent).

Electronic Payments Network
EPN is the only private-sector ACH operator in the United States, and it settles the same type of batched debit and credit transactions as FedACH. Like CHIPS, it is owned and operated by The Clearing House. The Federal Reserve Banks and EPN rely on each other to process inter-operator transactions, which are transactions in which the originating and receiving depository institutions are serviced by the different ACH operators. Inter-operator transactions are settled by the Federal Reserve Banks while EPN uses the Federal Reserve Banks' NSS to settle ACH transactions that are processed solely on its network. In 2006, EPN processed an average of 19.1 million transactions per day worth about $50.2 billion.

The Depository Trust and Clearing Corporation
The Depository Trust and Clearing Corporation ("DTCC") is a holding company with three principal Securities and Exchange Commission ("SEC")- registered clearing agency subsidiaries, DTC, NSCC, and FICC, which is composed of two divisions,

the Government Securities Division ("GSD") and the Mortgage-Backed Securities Division ("MBSD").[219] These entities provide the primary infrastructure for the clearance, settlement, and custody of the vast majority of equity, corporate debt, municipal bond, money market instruments, and government securities transactions in the United States. DTCC is owned by its users – major banks, broker-dealers, and other financial institutions. Overseeing the company is an eighteen member board of directors elected by the participant owners of DTCC.

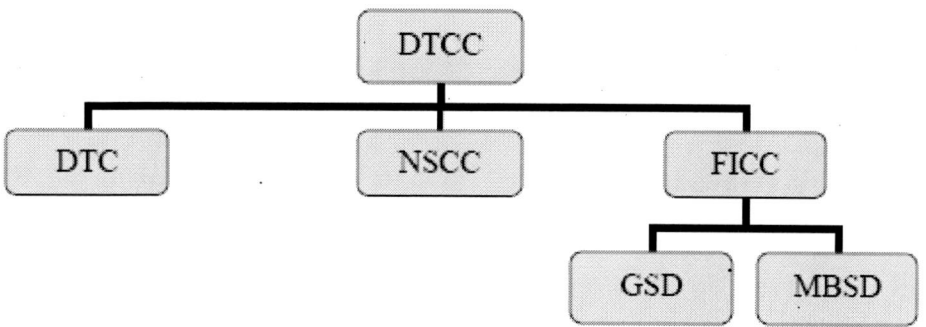

The Depository Trust Company

DTC is a central securities depository for settling trades in corporate, municipal, and mortgage-backed securities and provides a wide range of ancillary services for its participating banks and broker/dealers. DTC is a limited purpose trust company under New York State banking law, a member of the Federal Reserve System, and a SEC- registered clearing agency. The Federal Reserve, the New York State Banking Department, and the SEC supervise DTC. In 2007, DTC settled about $1 trillion per day in book-entry securities transactions.

National Securities Clearing Corporation

NSCC currently processes nearly all broker-to-broker equity, corporate, and municipal bond trades in the U.S. Its principal activities are centralized clearance, settlement, and post-trade information services for equities, bonds, mutual fund, and annuity transactions. Its members include brokers, dealers, banks, mutual funds, insurance carriers, and other financial intermediaries. NSCC is a SEC-registered clearing agency. In 2007, NSCC processed transactions valued at about $1.1 trillion per day.

Fixed Income Clearing Corporation

FICC is designed to ensure orderly settlement in the government and mortgage-backed securities marketplaces. FICC operates through two divisions – the GSD and the MBSD, each offering their own services to their own members pursuant to separate rules and procedures. FICC is a SEC-registered clearing agency.

GSD is a central counterparty providing automated real-time trade comparison, netting, and settlement services for brokers, dealers, banks, and other financial institutions trading in the U.S. government-securities marketplace. In 2007, the daily average value of transactions that GSD processed was about $4 trillion.

MBSD provides automated post-trade comparison, position netting, risk management, and pool notification services to the mortgage-backed securities ("MBS") market (e.g., Government National Mortgage Association, Federal Home Loan Mortgage Corporation, and Fannie Mae MBS programs). MBSD, however, is not a central counterparty; therefore, it does not guarantee trades that it compares and nets. FICC is currently pursuing an initiative, targeted to be completed in 2010, to convert MBSD into a central counterparty that will net and novate a subset of MBS transactions processed by MBSD. MBSD's users include banks, government-sponsored enterprises, institutional investors, insurers, international organizations, investment managers, inter-dealer brokers, mortgage originators, private investment companies, and broker-dealers. In 2007, the monthly average value of transactions that MBSD processed was about $7.9 trillion.

Society for Worldwide Interbank Financial Telecommunication SCRL

The Society for Worldwide Interbank Financial Telecommunications SCRL ("SWIFT") provides secure, standardized financial messaging services and other related services to its member financial institutions, their market infrastructures, and their end-user communities. SWIFT is a user-owned, limited liability cooperative organized under Belgian law. Its headquarters is located in Belgium with operational centers in the Netherlands and the United States. SWIFT supplies secure messaging services to 8,300 financial institutions in more than 200 countries and over 100 banking and securities market infrastructures for clearing and settlement. In 2007, SWIFT processed about fourteen million messages per day. While U.S. payment and settlement systems generally do not rely upon SWIFT services directly, U.S. financial institutions are among the heaviest users of SWIFT services for correspondent banking communications.

APPENDIX E – COMMODITY FUTURES MODERNIZATION ACT CORE PRINCIPLES

Core Principles for Contract Markets:

1) In general.--To maintain the designation of a board of trade as a contract market, the board of trade shall comply with the core principles specified in this subsection. The board of trade shall have reasonable discretion in establishing the manner in which it complies with the core principles.

2) Compliance with rules.--The board of trade shall monitor and enforce compliance with the rules of the contract market, including the terms and conditions of any contracts to be traded and any limitations on access to the contract market.

3) Contracts not readily subject to manipulation.--The board of trade shall list on the contract market only contracts that are not readily susceptible to manipulation.

4) Monitoring of trading.--The board of trade shall monitor trading to prevent manipulation, price distortion, and disruptions of the delivery or cash-settlement process.

5) Position limitations or accountability.--To reduce the potential threat of market manipulation or congestion, especially during trading in the delivery month, the board of

trade shall adopt position limitations or position accountability for speculators, where necessary and appropriate.

6) Emergency authority.--The board of trade shall adopt rules to provide for the exercise of emergency authority, in consultation or cooperation with the Commission, where necessary and appropriate, including the authority to—

a. Liquidate or transfer open positions in any contract;
b. Suspend or curtail trading in any contract; and
c. Require market participants in any contract to meet special margin requirements.

7) Availability of general information.--The board of trade shall make available to market authorities, market participants, and the public information concerning—

a. The terms and conditions of the contracts of the contract market; and
b. The mechanisms for executing transactions on or through the facilities of the contract market.

8) Daily publication of trading information.--The board of trade shall make public daily information on settlement prices, volume, open interest, and opening and closing ranges for actively traded contracts on the contract market.

9) Execution of transactions.--The board of trade shall provide a competitive, open, and efficient market and mechanism for executing transactions.

10) Trade information.--The board of trade shall maintain rules and procedures to provide for the recording and safe storage of all identifying trade information in a manner that enables the contract market to use the information for purposes of assisting in the prevention of customer and market abuses and providing evidence of any violations of the rules of the contract market.

11) Financial integrity of contracts.--The board of trade shall establish and enforce rules providing for the financial integrity of any contracts traded on the contract market (including the clearance and settlement of the transactions with a derivatives clearing organization), and rules to ensure the financial integrity of any futures commission merchants and introducing brokers and the protection of customer funds.

12) Protection of market participants.--The board of trade shall establish and enforce rules to protect market participants from abusive practices committed by any party acting as an agent for the participants.

13) Dispute resolution.--The board of trade shall establish and enforce rules regarding and provide facilities for alternative dispute resolution as appropriate for market participants and any market intermediaries.

14) Governance fitness standards.--The board of trade shall establish and enforce appropriate fitness standards for directors, members of any disciplinary committee, members of the contract market, and any other persons with direct access to the facility (including any parties affiliated with any of the persons described in this paragraph).

15) Conflicts of interest.--The board of trade shall establish and enforce rules to minimize conflicts of interest in the decision-making process of the contract market and establish a process for resolving such conflicts of interest.

16) Composition of boards of mutually owned contract markets.--In the case of a mutually owned contract market, the board of trade shall ensure that the composition of the governing board reflects market participants.

17) Recordkeeping. --The board of trade shall maintain records of all activities related to the business of the contract market in a form and manner acceptable to the Commission for a period of 5 years.

18) Antitrust considerations.--Unless necessary or appropriate to achieve the purposes of this Act, the board of trade shall endeavor to avoid—

   a. Adopting any rules or taking any actions that result in any unreasonable restraints of trade; or
   b. Imposing any material anticompetitive burden on trading on the contract market.

Core Principles for Derivative Clearing Organizations:

1) In general.--To be registered and to maintain registration as a derivatives clearing organization, an applicant shall demonstrate to the Commission that the applicant complies with the core principles specified in this paragraph. The applicant shall have reasonable discretion in establishing the manner in which it complies with the core principles.

2) Financial resources.--The applicant shall demonstrate that the applicant has adequate financial, operational, and managerial resources to discharge the responsibilities of a derivatives clearing organization.

3) Participant and product eligibility. --The applicant shall establish—

   a. Appropriate admission and continuing eligibility standards (including appropriate minimum financial requirements) for members of and participants in the organization; and
   b. Appropriate standards for determining eligibility of agreements, contracts, or transactions submitted to the applicant.

4) Risk management.--The applicant shall have the ability to manage the risks associated with discharging the responsibilities of a derivatives clearing organization through the use of appropriate tools and procedures.

5) Settlement procedures.--The applicant shall have the ability to—

   a. Complete settlements on a timely basis under varying circumstances;
   b. Maintain an adequate record of the flow of funds associated with each transaction that the applicant clears; and
   c. Comply with the terms and conditions of any permitted netting or offset arrangements with other clearing organizations.

6) Treatment of funds.--The applicant shall have standards and procedures designed to protect and ensure the safety of member and participant funds.

7) Default rules and procedures.--The applicant shall have rules and procedures designed to allow for efficient, fair, and safe management of events when members or

participants become insolvent or otherwise default on their obligations to the derivatives clearing organizations.

8) Rule enforcement.--The applicant shall—

a. Maintain adequate arrangements and resources for the effective monitoring and enforcement of compliance with rules of the applicant and for resolution of disputes; and
b. Have the authority and ability to discipline, limit, suspend, or terminate a member's or participant's activities for violations of rules of the applicant.

9) System safeguards.--The applicant shall demonstrate that the applicant—

a. Has established and will maintain a program of oversight and risk analysis to ensure that the automated systems of the applicant function properly and have adequate capacity and security; and
b. Has established and will maintain emergency procedures and a plan for disaster recovery, and will periodically test backup facilities sufficient to ensure daily processing, clearing, and settlement of transactions.

10) Reporting.--The applicant shall provide to the Commission all information necessary for the Commission to conduct the oversight function of the applicant with respect to the activities of the derivatives clearing organization.

11) Recordkeeping. --The applicant shall maintain records of all activities related to the business of the applicant as a derivatives clearing organization in a form and manner acceptable to the Commission for a period of 5 years.

12) Public information.--The applicant shall make information concerning the rules and operating procedures governing the clearing and settlement systems (including default procedures) available to market participants.

13) Information-sharing.--The applicant shall—

a. Enter into and abide by the terms of all appropriate and applicable domestic and international information-sharing agreements; and
b. Use relevant information obtained from the agreements in carrying out the clearing organization's risk management program.

14) Antitrust considerations.--Unless appropriate to achieve the purposes of this Act, the derivatives clearing organization shall avoid—

a. Adopting any rule or taking any action that results in any unreasonable restraint of trade; or
b. Imposing any material anticompetitive burden on trading on the contract market.

REFERENCES

[1] See Appendix B for background on prior Executive Branch studies.
[2] Treasury notes that the PWG, the Federal Reserve Bank of New York, and the OCC have previously stated that market discipline is the most effective tool to limit systemic risk. See Agreement among PWG and U.S. Agency Principals on Principles and Guidelines Regarding Private Pools of Capital (Feb. 2007). See also PWG, HEDGE FUNDS, LEVERAGE, AND THE LESSONS OF LONG-TERM CAPITAL MANAGEMENT 24- 25, 30 (Apr. 1999); PWG, OVER-THE-COUNTER DERIVATIVES MARKETS AND THE COMMODITY EXCHANGE ACT 34-35 (Nov. 1999).
[3] See Appendix B for background on prior Executive Branch studies.
[4] The existing regulatory structure for subprime mortgage origination demonstrates this point. See Appendix C.
[5] See http://www.treas.gov/offices/domestic-finance/regulatory-blueprint.
[6] Ben S. Bernanke, Chairman, Federal Reserve, Speech to the Federal Reserve Bank of Kansas City's Economic Symposium: Housing, Housing Finance, and Monetary Policy (Aug. 31, 2007).
[7] Jerry W. Markham, *Banking Regulation: Its History and Future*, 4 N.C. BANKING INST. 221, 7 (Apr. 2000).
[8] While the Commodity Futures Trading Commission Act was adopted in 1974, authority did not transfer from the USDA to the CFTC until 1975.
[9] See Appendix E.
[10] See Appendix E.
[11] Open-end funds (e.g., mutual funds) may issue additional shares without restriction, and shareholders are generally free to sell their shares at any time. Closed-end funds issue a fixed number of shares, often through an initial public offering, and are listed and traded as stock on a stock exchange. Investors in unit investment trusts hold either joint or proportional interests in a portfolio of securities that remains fixed and unmanaged for the life of the fund.
[12] Security futures products are regulated as both securities and futures and include futures on individual securities (e.g., single-stock futures) as well as on certain narrow indexes of securities, plus options on such futures.
[13] 8 Wall. 168, 19 L.Ed. 357 (1869).
[14] 322 U.S. 533 (1944).

[15] U.S. Gen. Accounting Office, Insurer Failures: Property/Casualty Insurer Insolvencies And State Guaranty Funds, Gao/Ggd-87-100 (Jul. 1987).

[16] U.S. Gen. Accounting Office, Insurance Regulation: Problems In The State Monitoring Of Property/Casualty Insurer Insolvency, Gao/Ggd-89-129 (Sept. 1989).

[17] U.S. Gen. Accounting Office, Regulatory Initiatives Of The National Association Of Insurance Commissioners, Gao/Ggd-01 -885r (Jul. 2001).

[18] U.S. Gen. Accounting Office, Insurance Regulation: The Naic Accreditation Program Can Be Improved, Gao/Ggd-01-948 (Aug.31, 2001).

[19] 15 U.S.C. §675 1 (A)

[20] U.S. Gen. Accounting Office, Financial Regulatory Coordination: The Role And Functioning Of The President's Working Group, Gao/Ggd-00-46 (Jan. 2000).

[21] H.R. Rep. No. 110-441, at 36 (2007) (citing statistics from the Mortgage Bankers Association).

[22] See Appendix C.

[23] Federally regulated mortgage lenders and their employees are subject to an extensive scheme of federal supervision of their lending practices and compliance with applicable laws and regulations.

[24] The structure of the MOC would incorporate some aspects of the structure and operations of the Appraisal Subcommittee ("the Subcommittee") of the Federal Financial Institutions Examination Council. Congress created the Subcommittee under Title XI of the Financial Institutions Reform, Recovery and Enforcement Act of 1989 to monitor the activities of the Appraisal Foundation, a group that sets generally accepted appraisal standards and qualification standards for state-certified and licensed appraisers, and the activities of state appraiser regulatory agencies. The Subcommittee does not oversee or regulate appraisers themselves. If the Subcommittee finds that a particular state's appraiser regulation and certification program is inadequate, then, under the banking agencies' regulations, all appraisers in that state are no longer eligible to do appraisals for depository institutions. This draconian and un-calibrated authority is impractical, and it has not been used. The MOC would be vested with broader and more calibrated authorities to set uniform minimum standards for, evaluate, and address weaknesses in, state systems.

[25] Treasury also seriously considered recommending the creation of a self-regulatory organization ("SRO") in order to improve licensing and oversight of participants in the mortgage origination process. In such a model, a new SRO or an existing SRO, such as the Financial Industry Regulatory Authority, would be vested with licensing and oversight responsibility. Establishing such a structure would require a significant staff presence and continued oversight from a federal body to approve rulemaking. It would also require significant preemption of state law. Treasury's recommendation accomplishes a similar goal of enhancing enforcement while leveraging off of the existing framework.

[26] The funding for the MOC's personnel and other operational costs should derive from nominal assessments on mortgage originators that will be required to be registered through the NMLSR.

[27] This need not preclude states from adding additional standards for mortgage lenders subject to state jurisdiction.

[28] The definition of "creditor" in TILA does not include a party that functions only as a broker and is not the party to whom the debt is initially payable.
[29] Although the Federal Trade Commission may enforce TILA with respect to lenders that are not specifically allocated to another agency under the statute, it has no ongoing supervisory or regulatory role with respect to those lenders.
[30] "Affiliate" for these purposes does not include a subsidiary of a depository institution, which, as noted above, is generally supervised and regulated in the same manner as its parent; instead, "affiliate" means a related company owned by the same holding company.
[31] State attorneys general have some authority to enforce HOEPA provisions; however, state attorneys general do not have authority to enforce the non-HOEPA mortgage-related provisions of TILA. Furthermore, the particular state authorities for licensing and monitoring originators and brokers are not authorized to enforce any of the mortgage provisions of TILA.
[32] Section 13(3) of the Federal Reserve Act.
[33] Section 13(3) of the Federal Reserve Act.
[34] For a history of thrift regulation, see Chapter III.
[35] Fhlb System, A Guide To The Federal Home Loan Bank System 8 (1987).
[36] Among other requirements, the BHC Act (and the BHC Act Amendments of 1970) prohibited bank holding companies from entering other lines of business without the Federal Reserve's prior approval.
[37] The purpose of the FFIEC as described in the statute is to "prescribe uniform principles and standards for the Federal examination of financial institutions by the [federal depository institution regulators] and make recommendations to promote uniformity in the supervision of those financial institutions." 12 U.S.C § 3301.
[38] "While [direct investment in] windmill farms and other exotic investments made for interesting reading, high-risk development loans and the resultant mortgages on the same properties were most likely the principal cause for thrift failures after 1982." FDIC, *History of the Eighties, Lessons for the Future*, Vol. 1, p. 180 (1997).
[39] Jerry W. Markham, *Banking Regulation: Its History and Future*, 4 N.C. BANKING INST. 221, 7 n. 153 (Apr. 2000).
[40] Section 104(b) of CEBA, 12 U.S.C. § 1467a(c)(3). As described below, the Gramm-Leach-Bliley Act of 1999 repealed the unitary savings and loan holding company exemption subject to grandfathering.
[41] Jerry W. Markham, *Banking Regulation: Its History and Future*, 4 N.C. BANKING INST. 221, 8 (Apr. 2000).
[42] The FDIC also is the primary federal supervisor of state-chartered banks that are not members of the Federal Reserve System.
[43] For a discussion of this view, see George J. Benston and George G. Kaufman, *Deposit Insurance Reform in the FDIC Improvement Act: The Experience to Date*, ECONOMIC PERSPECTIVES 5-10 (1998); Frederick S. Mishkin, *Evaluating FDICIA* In RESEARCH IN FINANCIAL SERVICES 17-33 (George G. Kaufman ed., 1997).
[44] The five categories triggering PCA are: well capitalized, adequately capitalized, undercapitalized, significantly undercapitalized, and critically undercapitalized.
[45] McFadden Act, Pub. L. No. 69-639, 44 Stat. 1224 (1927).

[46] Unitary thrift holding companies registered before May 4, 1999.
[47] The QTL test requires that at least 65 percent of an institution's portfolio assets be qualified thrift investments, primarily residential mortgages and related investments. The QTL test was relaxed somewhat in 1996 by expanding the list of qualified investments to include small business loans, and by increasing the amount of consumer-oriented loans that can be counted as qualifying assets. Since the passage of the Economic Growth and Regulatory Paperwork Reduction Act of 1996, thrifts can also qualify for QTL status by passing the Internal Revenue Service's "domestic building and loan association" test.
[48] 12 C.F.R § 559.4 authorizes federally chartered thrift service corporations to acquire real estate for prompt development or subdivision in accordance with a prudent program of property development. Service corporations also may provide management and other real estate-related services. In addition to pre-approved activities, thrifts can apply to the OTS for approval of activities on a case-by-case basis. HOLA Section 5(c)(4)(B) limits the thrift's investment in the service corporation's securities to 3 percent of the thrift's assets. Any investment exceeding 2 percent of the thrift's assets must serve primarily community, inner city, or community development purposes.
[49] Federal courts have interpreted field preemption to occur when Congress has "occupied the field" available to state regulation. In other words, Congress has legislated in a manner in which it is clear that it intended for the federal government, or its agent, to have the ability and authority to govern areas of commerce across state lines. See C.F. Muckenfuss, Iii And Robert C. Eager, Preemption Under The Home Owners Loan Act (Feb. 2003).
[50] Thrifts include federal and state-chartered S and Ls, state-chartered savings banks, and uninsured institutions.
[51] Federal Housing Finance Board, Quarterly Report (Sept. 2007).
[52] A 1997 Treasury proposal to unify bank and thrift regulation provides the basis for this proposal.
[53] Ots, Fact Book 2006 (Eighty-four state-chartered thrifts as of year-end 2006).
[54] Fdic, Statistics At A Glance (Four hundred twenty-six as of Sept. 30, 2007).
[55] For example, the Depository Trust Company, a securities settlement system, is a state-chartered limited- purpose trust company, and its affiliates, the National Securities Clearing Corporation and the Fixed Income Clearing Organization, are SEC-registered clearing agencies. The Continuous Linked Settlement Bank, a foreign-exchange settlement system, is a federally chartered Edge Act corporation, and SWIFT, a financial services messaging and network provider, has no specific financial regulatory charter or license.
[56] On March 13, 2008, the President's Working Group on Financial Markets released a Policy Statement on Financial Market Developments ("Policy Statement"). The Policy Statement called for an industry cooperative to assemble a well-designed processing system and infrastructure for all OTC derivatives, including credit default swaps and collateralized debt obligations. Such a system will promote standardization, moderate excessive complexity, and accurate valuation of these financial instruments. The PWG recognizes that the heightened price volatility and increasing trading volumes of OTC derivatives necessitates a well-functioning,

comprehensive infrastructure. Consideration should be given as to whether this would be a systemically important payment and settlement system that should come under the authority of the Federal Reserve.

[57] U.S. Gen. Accounting Office, The Commodity Exchange Act: Issues Related To The Commodity Futures Trading Commission's Reauthorization, Gao/Ggd-99-74, 19 (May 1999) ("While the U.S. futures market has experienced substantial growth, it has also evolved far beyond its agricultural origins. In 1975, agricultural commodities accounted for nearly 80 percent of the total U.S. exchange trading volume. In 1988, financial instruments and currencies accounted for nearly 70 percent of the total U.S. exchange trading volume, with agricultural commodities accounting for about 15 percent of the trading volume and other commodities, such as energy and metals, accounting for the remaining volume.").

[58] Congress did not formally amend the Securities Act and Securities Exchange Act expanding the definition of "security" to include "option" until 1982. See LOUIS LOSS AND JOEL SELIGMAN, FUNDAMENTALS OF SECURITIES REGULATION 266 (4th ed. 2001).

[59] Thomas A. Russo and Marlisa Vincignerra, *Financial Innovation and Uncertain Regulation: Selected Issues Regarding new Product Development*, 69 TEX. L. REV. 1431 (May 1991).

[60] Board of Trade of Chicago v. SEC, 677 F.2d 1137 (7th Cir. 1982), *vacated as moot*, 459 U.S. 1026 (1982).

[61] Treasury notes that in March 2008 the CFTC and the SEC signed a mutual cooperation agreement which, among other things, establishes principles to guide the agencies' consideration of products with securities and futures components. See Press Release, SEC, SEC, CFTC Sign Agreement to Enhance Coordination, Facilitate Review of New Derivative Products (Mar. 11, 2008), available at http://www.sec.gov/news/press/2008/2008-40.htm

[62] Chicago Mercantile Exchange v. SEC, 883 F.2d 537, 544 (7th Cir. 1989).

[63] The merger of exchanges raises potential antitrust issues, which are beyond the scope of this report. See James M. Falvey and Andrew N. Kleit, *Commodity Exchanges and Antitrust*, 4 BERKELEY BUS. L.J. 123 (Spring 2007) and Department of Justice, Comment Letter: Review of the Regulatory Structure Associated with Financial Institutions (Jan. 31, 2008).

[64] James L. Bothwell, Director, Financial Institutions And Market Issues, General Government Division, U.S. Gen. Accounting Office, Financial Market Regulation: Benefits And Risks Of Merging Sec And Cftc, Gao/T-Ggd-95-153 (May 3, 1995), at 3 ("A single U.S. regulatory agency for financial markets should be able to better monitor systemic risk across our increasingly linked markets, as well as to more effectively conduct cross-market surveillance.").

[65] The CFMA also established core principles derivative trading execution facilities ("DTEF"). No DTEF is currently registered with the CFTC.

[66] Cftc Staff Task Force, A New Regulatory Framework 3 (Feb. 2000).

[67] A complete listing of these core principles can be found in the Appendix.

[68] CFTC STAFF TASK FORCE, A NEW REGULATORY FRAMEWORK *ii* (Feb. 2000).

[69] See Appendix E.

[70] See Appendix E.

[71] See Appendix E.

[72] Regulation of Clearing Agencies, Exchange Act Release No. 34-16900 (June 1980).

[73] The first phrase of Core Principle 11, *Financial Integrity of Contracts*, would not be applicable in the securities context, but the second part of the principle would.

[74] Section 19(b)(1), 15 U.S.C. §78s(b)(1).

[75] Section 19(b)(2), 15 U.S.C. §78s(b)(2).

[76] Section 19(b)(3)(A), 15 U.S.C. §78s(b)(3)(A) and Rule 19b-4.

[77] Proposed Rule Changes of Self-Regulatory Organizations; Annual Filing of Amendments to Registration Statements of National Securities Exchanges, Securities Associations, and Reports of the Municipal Securities Rulemaking Board (proposed Dec. 20, 1994).

[78] Amendment to Rule Filing Requirements for Self-Regulatory Organizations Regarding New Derivative Securities Products, Exchange Act Release No. 34-40761 (Dec. 8. 1998).

[79] Amendment to Rule Filing Requirements for Self-Regulatory Organizations Regarding New Derivative Securities Products, Exchange Act Release No. 34-40761, at 6-7 (Dec. 8. 1998).

[80] Proposed Rule Changes of Self-Regulatory Organizations, Release No. 34-43 860 (Jan. 2001).

[81] SEC Proposed Rule: Proposed Rule Changes of Self-Regulatory Organizations, Exchange Act Release No. 34-43 860 (proposed Jan. 2001), at 3-4.

[82] SEC Proposed Rule: Proposed Rule Changes of Self-Regulatory Organizations, Exchange Act Release No. 34-43 860 (proposed Jan. 2001), at 3-4.

[83] Regulation NMS, Exchange Act Release No. 34-51808 (June 9, 2005).

[84] Section 19(b)(3)(A), 15 U.S.C. §78s(b)(3)(A).

[85] Note that in October 2004 the SEC did issue a rule requiring that SROs file electronically their proposed rule changes with the SEC and that SROs publish their proposals on their websites. Final Rule: Proposed Rule Changes of Self-Regulatory Organizations, Exchange Act Release No. 34-50486 (Oct. 4, 2004).

[86] LOUIS LOSS AND JOEL SELIGMAN, FUNDAMENTALS OF SECURITIES REGULATION 40-42 (4th ed. 2001).

[87] See Proposed Rule: Exchange-Traded Funds, Securities Act Release No. 33-890 1 (Mar. 11, 2008).

[88] Alan L. Beller, *Some Thoughts Regarding Capital Markets Regulatory Reform*, C.V. STARR LECTURE, New York Law School (Feb. 21, 2007), at 6 (noting that the federal securities law "too often prohibits the offering of particular products or the execution of particular transactions. These prohibitions are not fraud- based. Many of them derive from the substantive prohibitions of the Investment Company Act or the treatment of different categories of financial instruments under the U.S. securities and commodities laws. These prohibitions should be eliminated where they can be consistent with investor protection...A business is being developed in London and not in New York solely for regulatory reasons. Is there really no regulatory regime under which transactions involving these products cannot be responsibly carried out in the United States?...The SEC has never attempted a broad modernization of its rules

under or its administration of the Investment Company Act. The SEC succeeded in using its broad exemptive authority in 2005 to achieve far-reaching modernization of the rules for capital formation under a different regulatory regime, the Securities Act of 1933").

[89] Division Of Investment Management, Sec, Protecting Investors: A Half Century Of Investment Company Regulation 332-45 (May 1992).

[90] *Id.*, at 189.

[91] *Id.* at 215. See also David S. Ruder, Chairman of the Board, Mutual Fund Directors Forum, Comment Letter (Mar. 20, 2008).

[92] 15 U.S.C. §78c(4), (5).

[93] 15 U.S.C. §80b-2(a)(11).

[94] 15 U.S.C. §80b-3.

[95] 15 U.S.C. §80b-3a.

[96] NASD Manual, Rule 2110: Standards of Commercial Honor and Principles of Trade.

[97] 15 U.S.C. §78g.

[98] Such a broker-dealer is excluded from the definition of "investment adviser" to which the requirements of the Advisers Act apply. Advisers Act §202(a)(11), 15 U.S.C. §80b-2 (a)(11).

[99] Proposed Rule: Certain Broker-Dealers Deemed Not to Be Investment Advisers, Exchange Act Release No. 34-42099 (proposed 1999) citing Opinion of General Counsel Relating to Section 202(a)(11)(C) of the Investment Advisers Act of 1940, Investment Advisers Act Release No. 2 (Oct. 28, 1940).

[100] Committee On Compensation Practices, Report Of The Committee On Compensation Practices 1 (Apr. 10, 1995).

[101] *Id.* at 10.

[102] Proposed Rule: Certain Broker-Dealers Deemed Not to Be Investment Advisers, Exchange Act Release No. 34-42099 (proposed 1999). Note that the SEC was also considering "execution-only programs" (i.e. discount brokerage programs) and whether they potentially triggered Advisers Act registration for full service accounts. The SEC noted, "[T]he introduction of execution-only services at a lower commission rate may trigger application of the [Advisers] Act to the full service accounts for which the broker provides some investment advice. This is because the difference between full service and execution-only commission rates represents a clearly definable position of a brokerage commission that is attributable, at least in part, to investment advice. We have viewed such a two-tiered fee structure as an indication of 'special compensation' under the Advisers Act."

[103] Proposed Rule: Certain Broker-Dealers Deemed Not to Be Investment Advisers, Exchange Act Release No. 34-42099, at 5 (1999).

[104] For a history of insurance regulation, see Chapter III.

[105] Board Of Governors Of The Federal Reserve System, Flow Of Funds Accounts Of The United States (Mar. 2007).

[106] For a discussion of a single consolidated regulatory approach, see Chapter VI.

[107] For a discussion of state insurance regulation, see Chapter III.

[108] Several recent industry-supported studies have been released, including: University Of Massachusetts Isenberg School Of Management, Consumer Ramifications Of

An Optional Federal Charter For Life Insurers (2004) (surveying some 129 insurers and finding that the costs of the current regulatory system amounted to an average of $2.7 million per company, or about $3,559 per 1,000 policyholders).

[109] Treasury views this recommendation as distinct from the debate regarding the creation of a national catastrophe fund as a backstop to certain catastrophic losses. Treasury continues to oppose the creation of such a federal backstop. Treasury believes this recommendation, which calls for the elimination of price controls, goes a long way towards eliminating the root cause of the problem behind the desire for a backstop fund.

[110] Treasury recognizes that there are currently pending bills in both the House (H.R. 3200) and Senate (S. 40) entitled "The National Insurance Act of 2007" that would create an OFC and establish an ONI. It is not Treasury's intent at this time to opine on the details or merits of the pending legislation, but rather to set forth general guidelines as to the basics that it believes any ultimate legislation should contain in establishing an ONI and creating an OFC. That said, there are many positive attributes to these bills as they address many of the concepts raised in this report.

[111] *Competition and Effective Regulation of Insurance Rates: Hearing Before the H. Committee on Financial Services, Subcomm. on Capital Markets, Insurance, and Government Sponsored Enterprises*, 109th Cong. (June 16, 2005) (statement of Nat Shapo, Illinois Director of Insurance (1999 to 2003) (reviewing the history of rate regulation and stating that "Illinois has achieved great success by regulating rates through competition....Even though the Director has no authority to review rate levels, rates are surely regulated in Illinois: Instead of government passing on the proper price a seller can pay in a competitive market, personal lines auto and homeowners rates are regulated by the most ruthless force in a capitalist economy, the pressures of supply and demand. The results are impressive. Illinois has consistently had the most or nearly the most carriers writing auto and home insurance of any state in the country. And prices have been stable and moderate, ranking either in the middle of the state rankings or below average").

[112] The bills pending before Congress and referenced in Footnote 110 retain the state guarantee system.

[113] Naic, Insurance Department Resources Report (2006).

[114] This is known as the National Association of Registered Agents and Brokers or "NARAB" approach, discussed earlier.

[115] For more detailed summaries of these approaches, see Jacopo Carmassi and Richard J. Herring, *The Structure of Cross-Sector Financial Supervision*, Wharton School Of Business Financial Institutions Center Working Papers (2007); Jeroen J.M. Kremers, Dirk Schoenmaker ,and Peter J. Wierts, *Cross-Sector Supervision: Which Model?,* Brookings-Wharton Papers On Financial Services (2003); Richard K. Abrams and Michael W. Taylor, *Issues in the Unification of Financial Sector Supervision,* International Monetary Fund Working Papers No. 00/2 13 (Dec. 1, 2000); Giorgio Di Giorgio and Carmine Di Noia, *Financial Regulation and Supervision in the Euro Area: A Four-Peak Proposal*, Wharton School Of Business Financial Institutions Center Working Papers (2001); U.S. Gen. Accounting Office, Financial Regulation: Industry Changes Prompt Need To Reconsider U.S. Regulatory Structure (Oct. 2004); And U.S. Gov't Accountability Office, Financial Regulation:

Industry Trends Continue To Challenge The Federal Regulatory Structure (Oct. 2007).

[116] For a more complete discussion of the concept of macro-prudential regulation and supervision see Claudio Borio, *Towards a Macroprudential Framework for Financial Supervision and Regulation?*, in Bank For International Settlements Working Papers No. 128 (Feb. 2003); and Thomas M. Hoenig, President of the Federal Reserve Bank of Kansas City, Speech at the Meeting for Heads of Supervision to the Bank for International Settlements: Exploring the Macro-Prudential Aspects of Financial Sector Supervision (Apr. 27, 2004). Unlike in the optimal framework, some view the macro-prudential role as expanding prudential oversight to a broader set of financial institutions.

[117] See Agreement Among Pwg And U.S. Agency Principals On Principles And Guidelines Regarding Private Pools Of Capital (Feb. 2007). See Also Pwg, Hedge Funds, Leverage, And The Lessons Of Long-Term Capital Management 24-25, 30 (Apr. 1999); Pwg, Over-The-Counter DerivATIVES MARKETS AND THE COMMODITY EXCHANGE ACT 34-3 5 (NOV. 1999).

[118] See Reg.A, 12 CFR 201.4 (d).

[119] For more information on the operation of the discount window and the emergency credit authority, see Brian F. Madigan and William R. Nelson, *Proposed Revision to the Federal Reserve's Discount Window Lending Programs*, FED. RES. BULL. (July 2002); and James Clouse and David H. Small, The *Scope of Monetary Policy Actions Authorized Under the Federal Reserve Act*, 5 THE B.E. J. OF MACROECON. Issue 1, Art. 6 (2005).

[120] Federal Reserve Release, Federal Reserve Board Discount Rate Action (Aug. 17, 2007), *available at* http://www.federalreserve.gov/newsevents/ press/monetary/ 20070817a.htm.

[121] Federal Reserve Statistical Release II.4. 1.

[122] Federal Reserve Release, Federal Reserve and Other Central Banks Announce Measures Designed to Address Elevated Pressures in Short-Term Funding Markets (Dec. 12, 2007), *available at* http://www.federalreserve.gov/newsevents/ press/monetary/ 20071212a.htm.

[123] For additional background on prudential regulation, see Frederic S. Mishkin, *Prudential Supervision: Why Is It Important and What are the Issues?*, in Prudential Supervision: What Works And What Doesn't 1-29 (Frederick S. Mishkin ed., 2001).

[124] For a detailed history of banking regulation, see Chapter III.

[125] Occ, Activities Permissible For A National Bank, Cumulative (2006).

[126] 12 U.S.C. §§371c, 371c-1.

[127] For recent discussion, see a series of articles in the Proceedings From The Federal Reserve Bank Of Chicago's 43rd Annual Conference On Bank Structure And Competition (May 2007). Other surveys include Christine E. Blair, *The Future of Banking in America*, 16 Fdic Banking Rev. no. 4 (2004); Anthony Saunders, *Banking and Commerce: An Overview of the Public Policy Issues*, J. Banking and Fin. 231-54 (1994); Gerald E. Corrigan, *The Banking-Commerce Controversy Revisited*, Quarterly Review, Federal Reserve Bank Of New York (Spring 1991).

[128] For a discussion of the history of commercial affiliations with insured depository institutions, see Cantwell F. Muckenfuss and Robert C. Eager, *The Separation of*

Banking and Commerce Revisited, in Proceedings From The Federal Reserve Bank Of Chicago's 43rd Annual Conference On Bank Structure And Competition 39-60 (May 2007). For specific issues related to unitary thrifts, see Christine E. Blair, *The Future of Banking in America*, 16 Fdic Banking Rev. no. 4, 112 (2004); and James B. Thomson, *Unitary Thrifts; A Performance Analysis*, 37 Federal Reserve Bank Of Cleveland, Econ. Rev. 2, 2-14 (2001).

[129] Reinsurance Association Of America, Offshore Reinsurance In The U.S. Market (2006).
[130] See Chapter III.
[131] See Chapter III.
[132] For additional details on both of these issues, see Section: Business Conduct Regulator.
[133] Financial statements of the individual GSEs.
[134] There is an exception to this general enforcement framework within the TILA that permits state attorneys general to bring a civil action in federal district court to enforce provisions that were enacted as part of the Home Ownership and Equity Protection Act on 1994. The state attorneys general must provide written notice to the appropriate federal regulator.
[135] For a description of state insurance regulation, see Chapter III.
[136] For a description of NSMIA, see Chapter III.
[137] 15 U.S.C. §§ 41-58
[138] For additional information on the financial requirements in Australia's licensing framework, see Australian Securities And Investment Commission Regulatory Guide 166.
[139] For additional information on these types of requirements in the Australian framework see Australian Securities And Investment Commission Regulatory Guide 126.
[140] The Commission On Financial Structure and Regulation, The Report Of The President's Commission On Financial Structure and Regulation 1 (Dec. 1971).
[141] *Id.* at 8. Other members included Alan Greenspan, President, Townsend-Greenspan and Co., Inc., Ralph S. Regula, Attorney-State Senator, Ohio, and Lane Kirkland, Secretary-Treasurer, AFL-CIO.
[142] *Id.* at 2.
[143] *Id.* at 8. The Hunt Commission provided several recommendations relating to the regulation of interest rate ceilings on deposits.
[144] *Id.* at 87, 91.
[145] *Id.* at 87, 91.
[146] *Id.* at 91.
[147] *Id.* at 87, 91.
[148] *Id.* at 91-92.
[149] *Id.* at 88, 91.
[150] *Id.* at 89, 92.
[151] *Id.* at 89, 94-95.
[152] The Task Group On Regulation Of Financial Services, Blueprint For Reform: The Report Of The Task Group On Regulation Of Financial Services (July 1984).
[153] *Id.* at 8.
[154] *Id.* at 40.

[155] *Id.* at 41 ("While functional regulation promotes equality of regulatory treatment and reduces overall government duplication, it can also result in a particular type of firm (e.g. savings and loan, credit union, etc.) having to deal with a variety of special-purpose agencies rather than a single agency. This can result in added regulatory costs for such types of firms because they must deal with more than one agency. Therefore, application of functional regulation in any particular case requires a balancing of the costs and benefits that would result, and a recognition that functional regulation may not be suitable in every area. As a result, the overall public interest will most likely be obtained through a mix of institutional and functional regulatory programs, rather than a system consisting exclusively of either type of regulation. Under such a system depository institutions and securities or commodities firms would continue to have most of their internal operations and safety and soundness concerns handled by a single agency, while activities common to many different types of firms or specialized issues would be handled by the appropriate functionally oriented agency.")

[156] *Id.* at 41.

[157] *Id.* at 41-42.

[158] *Id.* at 43 ("While checks and balances are an essential element in regulatory organization, beyond a certain point the creation of checks and balances may result in a system that is too highly fragmented to be able to operate coherently. Therefore, achieving the optimum regulatory organization requires a balancing of the benefits of reducing overlap and improving consistency and the costs of bureaucratic centralization, which may include excessive rigidity and slowness to adapt to changing situations. Complete consolidation and chaotic fragmentation represent the opposite extremes in regulatory organization, and both involve significant potential costs to the public.").

[159] *Id.* at 44.

[160] *Id.* at 11.

[161] *Id.* at 71.

[162] *Id.* at 50.

[163] *Id.* at 50.

[164] *Id.* at 11.

[165] *Id.* at 12.

[166] *Id.* at 11.

[167] *Id.* at 63.

[168] *Id.* at 63.

[169] *Id.* at 62.

[170] *Id.* at 62.

[171] *Id.* at 64.

[172] Executive Order 12614 (Nov. 5, 1987), amended by Executive Order 12621 (Dec. 29, 1987).

[173] Executive Order 12614 ("The Task Force shall review relevant analyses of the current and long-term financial condition of the Nation's securities markets; identify problems that may threaten the short-term liquidity or long-term solvency of such markets; analyze potential solutions to such problems that will both assure the continued functioning of free, fair, and competitive securities markets and maintain

investor confidence in such markets; and provide appropriate recommendations to the President, to the Secretary of the Treasury, and to the Chairman of the Board of Governors of the Federal Reserve System."), amended by Executive Order 12621 (Dec. 29, 1987).

[174] The four other members were James C. Cotting, Robert G. Kirby, John R. Opel, and Howard M. Stein.

[175] Presidential Task Force On Market Mechanisms, Report Of The Presidential Task Force On Market Mechanisms vi (Jan. 1988).

[176] *Id.* at vi.

[177] *Id.* at 2.

[178] *Id.* at 55.

[179] *Id.* at 57.

[180] *Id.* at 57.

[181] *Id.* at vii.

[182] The Financial Institutions Reform, Recovery, and Enforcement Act of 1989, P.L. 101-73 (Section 1001).

[183] U.S. Treasury Department, Modernizing The Financial System: Recommendations For Safer, More Competitive Banks ix (Feb. 1991).

[184] *Id.* at ix.

[185] *Id.* at ix.

[186] Deposit insurance reforms included strengthening the role of bank's capital in determining safety and soundness, such as increased capital-based supervision with rewards for well-capitalized banks, prompt corrective action for undercapitalized banks, early resolution for failing banks, improved capital measurement, and improved independent auditor reporting; capital-based insurance premiums; capital-based expanded activities; capital adjusted for interest rate risk; reducing the overextended deposit insurance system, such as reducing coverage of multiple insured accounts; eliminating pass-through coverage for pension plan deposits and Bank Investment Contracts; eliminating brokered deposits coverage; eliminating non-deposit creditor coverage; limiting coverage of uninsured depositors; restricting risky activities of federally insured state-chartered banks, such as direct investment in real estate and other commercial ventures and other activities which national banks are restricted from undertaking; authorizing full nationwide banking for holding companies and interstate branching for banks; reforming credit unions, such as changing the accounting treatment of insurance fund and reorganizing the National Credit Union Administration Board; recapitalizing the Bank Insurance Fund to provide sufficient resources, take into account any impact on banking system, rely on industry funds, and use generally accepted accounting principles. *Id.* at xiii-xvii.

[187] *Id.* at 54-55, XVIII-9-12.

[188] *Id.* at 56.

[189] *Id.* at 56.

[190] *Id.* at 56.

[191] *Id.* at 57-61.

[192] *Id.* at 67.

[193] *Id.* at 68.

[194] *Id.* at 69.

[195] The Riegle-Neal Interstate Banking and Branching Efficiency Act, Pub. L. No. 103-328, §210 (1994).
[196] Robert E. Litan With Jonathan Rauch, American Finance For The 21st Century (Nov. 17, 1997).
[197] *Id.* at 3.
[198] *Id.* at 42-53. (Highlighting the "digitization of finance" with the creation and growth of securitization, automated teller machines, credit cards, smart cards; the growth in the foreign exchange markets, international interbank lending, international intermarket trading, international equity mutual funds, and American consumers' banking with foreign institutions underscoring the globalization of the financial services industry; two leading trends in financial innovation—securitization and derivatives; the increase in competition among financial services providers due to the removal of legal restrictions, such as liberalization of branching authority, blurring of historical boundaries among financial services providers.).
[199] *Id.* at 53.
[200] *Id.* at 56.
[201] *Id.* at 74-77.
[202] *Id.* at 77-81.
[203] *Id.* at 81-88.
[204] *Id.* at 8 8-96.
[205] *Id.* at 97 ("Risk is the essence of finance; and it is the essence, too, of government's regulation of finance. The first chapter of this report argued that government's core responsibilities in finance are three: protecting consumers, protecting taxpayers, and reducing systemic risk. Of those, many might consider the last the most important.")
[206] *Id.* at 115-124.
[207] *Id.* at 8.
[208] *Id.* at 7.
[209] *Id.* at 4 ("[T]he time has arrived for federal policy to embrace competition in financial services wholeheartedly and open-mindedly. It is no longer necessary to view competition as the enemy of marketplace stability or to preslice and segregate entire markets to protect consumers or investors. Indeed, competition is a simple yet powerful tool that federal policy has embraced in virtually every economic sphere *except* in some important sectors of finance. True, a good deal has been done in recent years to open financial services to competition and innovation. But policy change has lagged behind market change, and there is more left to do. In making this case, the report does not suggest that freewheeling competition is by itself the solution to all marketplace problems. Rather it argues that for too long government policies have deprived consumers of the full benefits of an innovative, robustly competitive marketplace, and that the goal of policy in the coming century should be to encourage rather than to suppress competition and innovation in finance.").
[210] *See id.* at 6.
[211] *See id.* at 126, 147-50 for other recommendations, including the development of international accounting standards; extending access to credit through specialized and focused institutions, such as Community Development Financial Institutions; and encouraging the unbanked to create bank accounts through, among other things, non-traditional entities, such as fast food restaurants; encouraging people to trust

financial institutions and encouraging these institutions to offer their services to the unserved; using incentives and market forces to expand access rather than statutory mandates.

[212] *Id.* at 116-117.
[213] *Id.* at 117-119.
[214] *Id.* at 119-123.
[215] *Id.* at 124.
[216] *Id.* at 9.
[217] The Options Clearing Corporation also uses the NSS.
[218] The following fifteen currencies can be settled in CLSB: Australian Dollar, Canadian Dollar, Danish Krone, Euro, GB Pound, Hong Kong Dollar, Japanese Yen, Korean Won, New Zealand Dollar, Norwegian Krone, Singapore Dollar, South African Rand, Swedish Krona, Swiss Franc, and US Dollar.
[219] The DTCC structure also includes Omgeo LLC, a joint-venture with Thomson Financial, providing post-trade pre-settlement services to broker-dealers, investment managers, and custodians. Omgeo is conditionally exempt from clearing agency registration, but is regulated and examined by the SEC. The holding company, DTCC, also includes two unregulated U.S. subsidiaries, Deriv/SERV LLC and DTCC Solutions LLC and one non-U.S. subsidiary, EuroCCP, which is located in London and regulated by the U.K. Financial Services Authority.

INDEX

A

abusive, 66, 68, 169
academic, 105
academics, 24, 94
access, vii, 1, 7, 15, 21, 31, 42, 60, 70, 71, 72, 82, 85, 90, 115, 117, 120, 123, 125, 126, 127, 135, 137, 139, 162, 168, 169, 185
accountability, 162, 168
accounting, 19, 47, 48, 54, 112, 118, 160, 177, 184, 185
accounting standards, 47, 160, 185
accreditation, 56
achievement, 41
acquisitions, 29, 30, 108
actuarial, 54
adjustment, 125
administration, 93, 179
administrative, 11, 49, 92, 93
advertising, 54, 57, 100, 107
affiliates, 6, 14, 16, 29, 31, 33, 36, 66, 69, 76, 122, 133, 134, 135, 161, 162, 166, 176
age, 143
agent, 98, 160, 165, 169, 176
agents, 9, 45, 47, 56, 106, 107, 109, 165
aggregates, 14, 122
agricultural, 10, 37, 38, 40, 41, 88, 139, 177
agricultural commodities, 10, 37, 38, 40, 88, 177
agriculture, 138
aid, 33, 101
air, 35
Alexander Hamilton, 27
alternative, 7, 26, 70, 80, 93, 119, 127, 139, 143, 148, 159, 169
ambiguity, 88
amendments, 37, 38, 39, 42, 45, 47, 51, 74, 93
analysts, 99
annual review, 55

annuities, 9, 59, 105, 106, 133, 142
anticompetitive, 170, 171
antitrust, 52, 53, 91, 118, 134, 160, 177
antitrust laws, 52, 160
application, 31, 42, 142, 144, 179, 183
appraisals, 174
appropriations, 33, 97, 101
arbitrage, 76, 89, 114, 159, 160
arbitration, 44
argument, 10, 90
articulation, 127
Asian, 155
Asian countries, 155
assessment, 98, 121
assets, vii, 1, 4, 7, 17, 21, 22, 29, 30, 32, 33, 37, 38, 39, 40, 41, 53, 55, 75, 77, 79, 80, 100, 102, 104, 130, 131, 135, 139, 146, 158, 163, 176
assignment, 100
assumptions, 130
asymmetric information, 128
attacks, 54
Attorney General, 158
auditing, 48, 52, 112, 118
Australia, 3, 12, 22, 113, 115, 117, 145, 146, 154, 182
authority, 2, 4, 6, 7, 8, 9, 10, 11, 13, 14, 15, 16, 18, 19, 23, 25, 26, 28, 29, 30, 31, 33, 34, 35, 36, 37, 38, 39, 46, 47, 48, 49, 50, 51, 52, 53, 55, 65, 66, 67, 68, 69, 70, 71, 72, 74, 75, 77, 78, 82, 84, 86, 87, 90, 91, 93, 94, 95, 98, 99, 103, 107, 108, 109, 111, 112, 113, 116, 117, 119, 120, 121, 122, 123, 124, 125, 126, 127, 128, 130, 132, 134, 135, 136, 138, 140, 141, 142, 143, 144, 145, 146, 147, 148, 156, 158, 159, 160, 162, 169, 171, 173, 174, 175, 176, 177, 179, 180, 181, 185
availability, 35, 79, 91, 139, 142, 144
avoidance, 163

B

balance sheet, 14, 70, 71, 72, 122, 139
bank account, 185
bank failure, 28
Bank of England, 3, 22
banking, 2, 4, 8, 12, 18, 23, 24, 26, 27, 28, 29, 30, 31, 32, 33, 35, 36, 44, 51, 56, 69, 73, 74, 76, 77, 78, 80, 81, 82, 84, 104, 112, 113, 126, 130, 131, 133, 134, 135, 140, 141, 143, 144, 147, 154, 156, 157, 159, 160, 161, 162, 163, 166, 167, 168, 174, 181, 184, 185
banking industry, 74, 80, 130, 157, 161
bankruptcy, 55, 96, 146
banks, vii, 1, 4, 8, 14, 15, 16, 21, 23, 27, 28, 29, 30, 31, 32, 33, 34, 35, 36, 40, 50, 52, 53, 73, 74, 76, 77, 78, 79, 80, 81, 82, 83, 84, 85, 98, 105, 107, 113, 119, 126, 130, 131, 132, 133, 138, 139, 154, 157, 158, 159, 161, 162, 163, 165, 166, 167, 168, 175, 176, 184
barrier, 32
barriers, 53, 105, 107, 131, 132, 159
Basel II, 4, 23, 113
basis points, 126
BD, 98
behavior, 41, 123, 124, 125, 129, 160
Belgium, 168
benefits, 3, 10, 22, 32, 53, 65, 68, 69, 75, 77, 79, 85, 86, 91, 107, 115, 132, 134, 139, 143, 156, 158, 162, 183, 185
Best Practice, 84
bifurcation, 2, 10, 77, 88
blocks, 108
blurring, 71, 185
board members, 101
Board of Governors, 26, 28, 34, 71, 124, 126, 128, 184
bondholders, 48
bonds, 9, 30, 75, 89, 106, 167
borrowers, 6, 32, 66
borrowing, 15, 16, 71, 126, 127, 128
bottom-up, 120
branching, 76, 77, 157, 184, 185
breakdown, 105
brokerage, 12, 45, 99, 100, 102, 103, 146, 179
buildings, 30, 75
burglary, 59
business model, 84, 103, 111, 129, 133
buyer, 60, 144

C

Canada, 165
capacity, 18, 110, 136, 140, 145, 146, 165, 171
capital markets, 1, 2, 3, 4, 5, 19, 21, 22, 23, 63, 65, 111, 139, 151, 153
capitalist, 180
caps, 35
cash payments, 43, 89
catastrophe insurance, 110
CEA, 37, 38, 39, 40, 41, 42, 43, 88, 89, 96, 97
central bank, 3, 13, 22, 34, 82, 84, 85, 111, 114, 115, 117, 119, 120, 156, 181
centralized, 59, 167
certification, 42, 95, 159, 174
certifications, 48, 101
CFTC, 5, 10, 11, 12, 18, 36, 38, 39, 40, 41, 42, 43, 44, 64, 72, 88, 89, 90, 91, 95, 96, 97, 173, 177
channels, 111, 117, 120
citizens, 107
civil action, 182
Civil War, 2, 27, 28, 130
classes, 15, 123, 124
Clayton Act, 53
clients, 98, 100, 102
Co, 61, 182
collateral, 10, 15, 61, 71, 86, 109, 126, 127
Columbia, 44, 53, 56, 60, 105
commerce, 30, 32, 35, 37, 52, 53, 54, 76, 78, 104, 109, 134, 135, 143, 162, 176
Commerce Clause, 52
commercial bank, vii, 1, 8, 21, 28, 29, 30, 31, 32, 33, 34, 79, 80, 82, 130, 133, 134, 154, 157, 158
commodity, 37, 38, 39, 40, 41, 42, 43, 89
Commodity Exchange Act, 10, 37, 38, 39, 64, 88, 177
commodity futures, 43
Commodity Futures Trading Commission, 5, 36, 38, 41, 64, 88, 147, 159, 173, 177
communication, 5, 63, 64, 65, 116, 122, 162
communities, 119, 168
community, 32, 33, 35, 63, 67, 68, 82, 131, 132, 176
compensation, 9, 48, 59, 98, 101, 102, 106, 144, 156, 179
competence, 58, 99, 101
competition, 9, 16, 56, 92, 94, 105, 106, 107, 118, 132, 134, 141, 143, 158, 161, 162, 163, 180, 185
competitive advantage, 29, 74, 77

competitiveness, 1, 3, 5, 9, 19, 21, 22, 36, 63, 65, 92, 94, 95, 108, 119, 131, 136, 142, 151, 153, 154, 155, 160, 161
complement, 14, 45, 120, 121
complexity, 3, 4, 22, 23, 46, 58, 88, 129, 142, 176
compliance, 6, 9, 15, 18, 19, 31, 41, 42, 52, 55, 58, 67, 69, 91, 101, 105, 106, 119, 124, 128, 136, 146, 147, 148, 168, 171, 174
components, 4, 6, 23, 66, 120, 127, 177
composition, 78, 91, 148, 170
Comptroller of the Currency, 5, 26, 33, 34, 65, 73, 75, 121, 158, 159
concentration, 77, 90, 134, 163
conceptual model, 2, 24, 111
confidence, 5, 16, 48, 64, 71, 83, 112, 117, 120, 184
conflict, 89, 91, 100, 148
conflict of interest, 91
confusion, 103
Congress, iv, 2, 7, 10, 11, 27, 28, 29, 30, 32, 33, 35, 36, 37, 38, 39, 45, 46, 47, 53, 54, 55, 64, 67, 73, 74, 75, 76, 80, 81, 88, 94, 97, 101, 102, 104, 108, 109, 113, 119, 130, 131, 161, 162, 174, 176, 177, 180
consensus, 7, 147
consent, 41, 49
consolidation, 54, 97, 114, 115, 142, 143, 157, 183
Constitution, 52
constraints, 77, 80, 158
construction, 77, 80, 157
consulting, 109, 133
consumer choice, 104, 107
consumer goods, 107
consumer protection, vii, 1, 3, 4, 5, 10, 12, 13, 17, 19, 21, 22, 23, 35, 36, 57, 63, 65, 68, 78, 105, 106, 107, 112, 113, 114, 115, 117, 118, 128, 136, 140, 141, 143, 151, 156
consumers, vii, 1, 5, 8, 16, 21, 23, 32, 35, 36, 58, 61, 66, 75, 78, 89, 104, 106, 107, 110, 111, 112, 113, 115, 117, 128, 130, 136, 137, 138, 140, 142, 143, 144, 159, 163, 185
consumption, vii, 1, 21
contingency, 15, 41, 123
contractions, 85
contracts, 37, 38, 39, 40, 41, 42, 43, 48, 58, 89, 91, 92, 100, 107, 132, 147, 168, 169, 170
control, 31, 33, 35, 39, 55, 60, 79, 92, 141
convergence, 4, 10, 12, 23, 31, 76, 88, 90, 97, 103, 105, 111, 113, 131, 154, 155
conversion, 80, 81, 165
corporate finance, 13, 19, 111, 112, 118, 122, 145
corporate governance, 19, 112, 118

corporate responsibility, 48
corporations, 77, 84, 126, 127, 176
correlations, 120
cost saving, 105
cost-benefit analysis, 119
cost-effective, 12, 103, 104
costs, 4, 10, 22, 55, 68, 87, 101, 105, 106, 136, 139, 142, 144, 155, 156, 158, 174, 180, 183
costs of compliance, 105
cotton, 38
Court of Appeals, 89, 103
courts, 97, 176
coverage, 9, 12, 34, 54, 60, 95, 96, 103, 106, 107, 130, 137, 138, 143, 144, 146, 184
covering, 50, 57, 137
creativity, 91
credit, 2, 5, 7, 15, 16, 19, 23, 25, 26, 28, 32, 34, 35, 36, 43, 52, 63, 68, 70, 71, 72, 78, 79, 84, 85, 87, 96, 99, 100, 123, 125, 126, 127, 130, 131, 134, 138, 141, 143, 146, 151, 157, 165, 166, 176, 181, 183, 184, 185
credit card, 32, 35, 185
credit market, 7, 19, 70, 72, 125, 126, 131, 151
credit rating, 52
credit unions, 2, 28, 32, 34, 36, 78, 131, 157, 184
creditors, 68, 69
crimes, 48
criticism, 30, 101
cross-border, 165
currency, 27, 40
customers, 8, 17, 18, 32, 43, 50, 56, 83, 90, 91, 96, 99, 100, 101, 107, 112, 118, 128, 132, 140, 145, 146, 156

D

database, 56
debt, 25, 27, 28, 48, 51, 68, 79, 80, 125, 129, 163, 167, 175, 176
decision making, 124
decision-making process, 169
decisions, 33, 34, 72, 82, 137
defense, 101
definition, 31, 75, 98, 175, 177, 179
delivery, 38, 107, 164, 168
demand, 33, 61, 75, 180
Department of Agriculture, 37, 88
Department of Commerce, 61
Department of Housing and Urban Development, 141
Department of Justice, 119, 160, 177
deposits, 26, 28, 29, 31, 33, 34, 74, 75, 82, 83, 96, 158, 182, 184

derivatives, 11, 38, 39, 40, 41, 43, 64, 83, 89, 91, 92, 93, 163, 169, 170, 171, 176, 185
desire, 15, 126, 180
developed countries, 84, 105
differentiation, 102
digitization, 185
direct cost, 139
direct costs, 139
direct investment, 175, 184
directives, 61
disability, 9, 53, 59, 105, 106, 142
disaster, 171
discipline, 12, 13, 14, 16, 112, 115, 116, 117, 119, 121, 123, 129, 155, 163, 171, 173
disclosure, 18, 35, 43, 45, 47, 48, 52, 68, 100, 120, 122, 140, 141, 143, 145, 153, 162
discounts, 102
discretionary, 30
discrimination, 18, 35, 142, 143, 144
discriminatory, 54, 57, 59, 107, 140
dislocation, 4, 23, 113
dispersion, 4, 23, 129, 163
disputes, 4, 13, 23, 88, 89, 101, 113, 114, 117, 119, 142, 171
disseminate, 125
distortions, 72
distribution, 25, 52, 94
District of Columbia, 44, 53, 56, 60, 105
divergence, 45
diversification, 47, 79, 80, 133, 134
diversity, 24, 25
division, 29, 56
dominance, 2, 10, 88, 160
draft, 6, 46, 59, 64, 95
duplication, 2, 4, 23, 24, 36, 73, 82, 113, 134, 136, 142, 162, 183
duration, 25, 124
duties, 18, 50, 52, 145

E

earnings, 80
e-commerce, 54
economic activity, vii, 1, 21, 83, 104, 135
economic efficiency, 130
economic growth, vii, 1, 2, 3, 21, 22, 24, 104, 135
economic stability, 120
economics, 88, 141, 144
election, 32, 132
eligibility standards, 170
emerging issues, 101
Employee Retirement Income Security Act, 53

employees, 45, 67, 102, 132, 174
empowered, 37, 108
end-users, 25
energy, 37, 39, 40, 42, 177
England, 3, 22
Enron, 48
environment, 51, 91, 92, 93
Equal Credit Opportunity Act, 35, 143
equality, 183
equities, 167
equity, 18, 49, 51, 64, 75, 96, 167, 185
equity market, 49, 64
ERISA, 53
erosion, 161
ethics, 101
Euro, 180, 186
Europe, 155
European Commission, 61
European Union, 54, 61
evolution, 19, 30, 52, 92, 104, 116, 151
examinations, 9, 14, 16, 33, 36, 54, 61, 72, 82, 87, 99, 101, 116, 122, 125, 128, 136, 138, 157
exchange markets, 49, 185
exchange rate, 39
exchange rates, 39
exclusion, 39, 43, 98
execution, 18, 41, 42, 43, 50, 91, 99, 145, 177, 178, 179
Executive Branch, 173
Executive Office of the President, 109
Executive Order, 5, 36, 63, 64, 65, 160, 183
exercise, 10, 109, 134, 148, 169
expert, iv, 68
expertise, 6, 18, 47, 65, 67, 68, 101, 108, 109, 135, 140, 145, 146
exposure, 14, 90, 120, 122, 123, 125, 128, 134, 136, 146

F

failure, 30, 46, 54, 75, 103, 120, 129, 136, 160, 163
fair housing, 35
Fair Housing Act, 143
fairness, 54
family, 80, 131
family members, 131
Fannie Mae, 79, 138, 139, 168
farms, 30, 75, 175
fast food, 185
FDIC, 5, 6, 8, 19, 26, 29, 30, 31, 32, 33, 34, 36, 56, 65, 67, 74, 75, 76, 78, 80, 81, 82, 131, 138, 158, 159, 160, 162, 175

February, 161
federal budget, 158
Federal Deposit Insurance Act, 34
Federal Deposit Insurance Corporation, 5, 26, 30, 34, 65, 74, 76, 81, 107, 131, 138, 158, 163
federal funds, 126, 127
federal government, 17, 49, 52, 53, 74, 106, 110, 111, 130, 135, 138, 139, 146, 163, 176
federal law, 6, 37, 44, 46, 53, 82, 141, 143, 144, 148
Federal Open Market Committee, 28
Federal Register, 24, 153
Federal Reserve, 2, 5, 6, 7, 8, 13, 14, 15, 18, 26, 28, 29, 30, 31, 32, 33, 34, 35, 36, 64, 65, 66, 67, 68, 69, 70, 71, 72, 76, 78, 81, 82, 83, 84, 85, 86, 87, 104, 111, 113, 117, 118, 119, 120, 121, 122, 123, 124, 125, 126, 127, 128, 133, 135, 138, 139, 141, 145, 146, 147, 158, 159, 160, 161, 162, 163, 164, 165, 166, 167, 173, 175, 177, 179, 181, 182, 184
Federal Reserve Bank, 8, 28, 34, 36, 65, 82, 85, 87, 121, 164, 165, 166, 173, 181, 182
Federal Reserve Board, 181
Federal Trade Commission, 6, 35, 78, 119, 175
Federal Trade Commission Act, 35, 78
federalism, 2, 27, 159
fee, 94, 102, 179
fees, 33, 48, 56, 87, 92, 97, 100, 101, 102, 119
FHLBs, 74
finance, vii, 1, 3, 13, 19, 21, 22, 27, 28, 33, 74, 81, 111, 112, 118, 123, 143, 145, 158, 162, 173, 185
Financial Accounting Standards Board, 47
financial crises, 2, 4, 23, 83, 87
financial instability, 2, 70, 122
financial institution, vii, 1, 2, 3, 4, 8, 12, 13, 14, 15, 16, 19, 21, 22, 23, 24, 32, 39, 52, 58, 73, 75, 76, 79, 80, 82, 83, 85, 86, 92, 105, 107, 111, 112, 113, 114, 115, 116, 117, 118, 119, 120, 121, 122, 123, 124, 125, 127, 128, 129, 131, 132, 133, 139, 140, 141, 145, 148, 151, 153, 154, 155, 157, 158, 160, 163, 167, 168, 175, 181, 186
financial institutions, vii, 1, 2, 3, 4, 8, 12, 13, 14, 15, 16, 19, 21, 22, 23, 24, 32, 39, 52, 73, 80, 82, 83, 85, 86, 92, 105, 107, 111, 112, 113, 114, 115, 116, 117, 118, 119, 120, 121, 122, 123, 124, 125, 127, 128, 129, 131, 132, 133, 139, 140, 141, 145, 148, 151, 153, 154, 155, 157, 158, 160, 163, 167, 168, 175, 181, 186
financial intermediaries, 15, 25, 83, 90, 97, 102, 126, 154, 167
financial loss, 52, 144

financial markets, 2, 3, 5, 7, 22, 36, 64, 70, 83, 85, 100, 101, 121, 127, 139, 145, 154, 155, 160, 163, 177
financial oversight, 17, 114, 115, 118, 136
financial performance, 56, 79
financial regulation, 4, 7, 8, 12, 13, 17, 19, 23, 24, 54, 55, 113, 115, 116, 118, 125, 128, 132, 135, 136, 137, 151
financial resources, 100
financial sector, 5, 64, 104, 108, 119, 135
Financial Services Action Plan, 155
Financial Services Authority, 3, 22, 114, 154, 186
financial soundness, 26, 50
financial stability, 27, 35, 54, 82, 120, 123, 129
financial support, 16, 134
financial system, 4, 5, 7, 11, 13, 15, 16, 23, 35, 65, 66, 70, 72, 73, 80, 83, 84, 85, 86, 90, 95, 104, 108, 111, 112, 113, 114, 115, 117, 120, 121, 123, 126, 127, 129, 130, 154, 155, 156, 157, 160, 161
financing, 77, 126, 139, 143
fines, 33, 45, 99
fingerprinting, 58
fire, 59, 137
firewalls, 134, 162
firms, 9, 11, 12, 13, 16, 17, 18, 25, 26, 30, 32, 36, 45, 48, 50, 51, 52, 53, 56, 76, 86, 93, 98, 99, 101, 102, 103, 107, 108, 112, 113, 114, 116, 117, 118, 122, 125, 128, 129, 134, 135, 138, 139, 140, 141, 145, 146, 147, 154, 156, 159, 162, 163, 183
fitness, 58, 91, 169
flexibility, 26, 41, 56, 75, 76, 87, 91, 101, 132, 141, 142
floating, 29
flow, 7, 72, 170
focusing, 11, 12, 13, 14, 57, 59, 95, 111, 117, 120, 125, 158, 163
food, 185
foreign banks, 34, 166
foreign exchange, 166, 185
foreign exchange market, 185
foreign firms, 9
FRA, 16, 137
fragmentation, 183
franchise, 161, 162
fraud, 18, 36, 37, 44, 45, 46, 47, 48, 50, 75, 99, 101, 108, 142, 145, 146, 178
Freddie Mac, 79, 138, 139
FTC, 6, 18, 35, 36, 53, 66, 78, 119, 141, 143, 147
fulfillment, 43, 45
functional approach, 4, 23, 90
fund transfers, 83

funding, vii, 1, 4, 7, 8, 9, 12, 15, 21, 22, 33, 57, 72, 75, 79, 80, 95, 97, 101, 106, 119, 123, 127, 130, 131, 135, 139, 162, 174
funds, vii, 1, 8, 9, 16, 18, 21, 25, 28, 29, 30, 35, 39, 43, 48, 56, 57, 64, 71, 74, 75, 79, 83, 84, 85, 86, 87, 91, 93, 94, 96, 100, 106, 107, 126, 127, 128, 129, 136, 138, 139, 164, 165, 166, 167, 169, 170, 173, 184, 185
futures, vii, 1, 2, 4, 10, 11, 12, 18, 21, 23, 24, 26, 31, 36, 37, 38, 39, 40, 41, 42, 43, 44, 51, 52, 73, 83, 88, 89, 90, 91, 95, 96, 97, 113, 117, 140, 142, 144, 145, 146, 147, 154, 156, 160, 161, 169, 173, 177
futures markets, 37, 38, 40, 41, 88, 90, 95, 96, 142

G

GAAP, 47
GAO, 55, 56, 64
General Accounting Office, 90
generally accepted accounting principles, 47, 184
geography, 28
Germany, 154
global markets, 3, 109
globalization, 3, 10, 22, 54, 88, 90, 92, 105, 154, 162, 185
goals, 2, 10, 12, 13, 24, 45, 109, 111, 116, 134, 155, 156, 163
governance, 19, 27, 48, 49, 51, 91, 94, 101, 112, 118, 145
government, vii, 1, 2, 8, 12, 13, 16, 17, 21, 24, 28, 30, 32, 39, 45, 46, 49, 50, 52, 53, 61, 68, 72, 74, 75, 79, 84, 89, 98, 101, 106, 110, 111, 112, 114, 115, 117, 118, 129, 130, 132, 133, 135, 137, 138, 139, 140, 146, 155, 163, 164, 165, 167, 168, 176, 180, 183, 185
Government Accountability Office, 55
government securities, 50, 84, 98, 167
governors, 53
grains, 37, 38
grants, 31
Great Depression, 2, 7, 28, 49, 73, 74, 130
gross domestic product, 83
groups, 51, 131, 165
growth, vii, 1, 2, 3, 21, 22, 24, 38, 79, 90, 94, 95, 102, 104, 135, 158, 177, 185
GSA, 50
guidance, 15, 108, 123, 125
guidelines, 119, 180
guiding principles, 119

H

handling, 18, 90, 144
harmonization, 12, 97, 103, 161
health, 4, 23, 56, 57, 113, 120, 128, 129
health insurance, 56, 57
heart, 55, 163
hedge funds, 18, 64
hedging, 129, 156, 160
high-risk, 60, 144, 175
holding company, 6, 14, 16, 17, 29, 30, 54, 69, 75, 76, 77, 108, 122, 133, 134, 135, 154, 155, 159, 162, 166, 175, 186
home ownership, 79
homeowners, 9, 106, 137, 144, 180
Hong Kong, 186
hospitality, 163
host, 131, 133
House, 38, 55, 166, 180
housing, 32, 35, 74, 75, 77, 80, 81, 115, 138, 160
Housing and Urban Development, 141
hybrid, 39, 40
hybridization, 88

I

id, 49, 66, 173, 177, 185
idiosyncratic, 8, 84, 85, 128
Illinois, 106, 180
implementation, 10, 13, 16, 18, 41, 46, 51, 56, 61, 109, 114, 134, 147, 148, 161
in situ, 129
incentive, 158
incentives, 6, 68, 186
inclusion, 7, 130
income, 9, 27, 33, 94, 105, 106, 131, 142
income tax, 131
increased competition, 134
indebtedness, 25
independence, 48
indication, 179
industrial, 26
industry, vii, 1, 2, 3, 5, 7, 12, 13, 17, 18, 19, 21, 22, 23, 24, 28, 30, 32, 37, 38, 44, 47, 50, 51, 53, 56, 57, 59, 67, 69, 73, 74, 75, 79, 80, 81, 89, 94, 95, 97, 100, 101, 102, 103, 104, 105, 106, 111, 112, 114, 115, 118, 130, 135, 136, 140, 146, 151, 156, 157, 161, 162, 176, 179, 184, 185
ineffectiveness, 134
inefficiency, 78
inflation, 28, 157

information and communication technology, 162
information sharing, 36, 65, 91, 122
information systems, 161
information technology, 4, 22, 129
infrastructure, 85, 167, 176
injury, iv, 143
innovation, 1, 2, 3, 4, 10, 11, 21, 22, 23, 24, 79, 88, 91, 92, 93, 95, 101, 104, 105, 106, 129, 134, 141, 154, 162, 163, 177, 185
insight, 72
inspection, 99
instability, 2, 14, 70, 121, 122, 125
institutionalization, 4, 23, 154
institutions, vii, 1, 2, 3, 4, 5, 6, 7, 8, 11, 12, 13, 14, 15, 16, 17, 18, 19, 21, 22, 23, 24, 25, 26, 27, 29, 30, 32, 33, 34, 35, 36, 39, 52, 66, 67, 68, 69, 70, 71, 72, 73, 74, 75, 76, 77, 78, 79, 80, 81, 82, 83, 84, 85, 86, 90, 92, 93, 105, 107, 111, 112, 113, 114, 115, 116, 118, 119, 120, 121, 122, 123, 124, 125, 126, 127, 128, 129, 130, 131, 132, 133, 135, 138, 139, 140, 141, 142, 143, 145, 148, 151, 153, 154, 155, 156, 157, 158, 159, 160, 162, 163, 165, 166, 167, 168, 174, 175, 176, 181, 183, 185
instruments, 8, 27, 32, 37, 38, 39, 40, 43, 52, 83, 85, 86, 160, 167, 176, 177, 178
insurance, 2, 4, 8, 9, 10, 12, 13, 16, 17, 18, 19, 23, 24, 26, 28, 30, 31, 32, 33, 34, 36, 52, 53, 54, 55, 56, 57, 58, 59, 60, 61, 64, 71, 73, 74, 75, 76, 81, 82, 95, 96, 104, 105, 106, 107, 108, 109, 111, 112, 113, 115, 117, 118, 129, 130, 132, 133, 135, 136, 137, 138, 140, 141, 142, 143, 144, 146, 147, 154, 156, 157, 158, 160, 161, 162, 163, 167, 179, 180, 182, 184
insurance companies, 154
intangible, 41
integration, 54
integrity, 5, 11, 36, 41, 42, 44, 49, 63, 64, 65, 85, 91, 92, 95, 101, 156, 157, 160, 169
intensity, 41
interactions, 43, 99, 122, 125, 140
interest rates, 39, 41, 75, 84, 157
intermediaries, 4, 15, 23, 25, 37, 39, 43, 44, 45, 83, 90, 97, 99, 100, 102, 126, 154, 156, 167, 169
internal controls, 48, 51, 92
Internal Revenue Service, 176
international markets, 9, 89, 105, 106
International Monetary Fund, 180
interpretation, 46, 92
interstate, 29, 30, 37, 46, 53, 59, 76, 86, 105, 184
interstate commerce, 37, 53
intervention, 54

intrastate, 46
intrinsic, 4, 22
Investigations, 55
investigative, 38
investment, vii, 1, 7, 11, 12, 16, 21, 26, 28, 29, 30, 32, 46, 47, 48, 75, 76, 88, 92, 93, 94, 97, 98, 99, 100, 101, 102, 103, 112, 114, 117, 118, 125, 129, 130, 131, 139, 142, 146, 168, 173, 175, 176, 179, 184, 186
investment bank, 28, 29, 30, 76
investors, vii, 1, 4, 12, 21, 22, 39, 44, 45, 47, 48, 49, 79, 86, 88, 92, 93, 94, 97, 99, 101, 103, 125, 145, 161, 168, 185
ISO, 59

J

January, 67, 93, 103, 160, 166
Japan, 114, 154
Japanese, 186
jurisdiction, 4, 9, 22, 37, 38, 39, 40, 41, 42, 46, 53, 69, 88, 89, 90, 106, 113, 134, 142, 174
jurisdictions, 4, 11, 22, 23, 88, 89, 92, 94, 115

K

Korean, 186

L

language, 64
large-scale, 85
law, 27, 29, 37, 44, 45, 46, 47, 51, 53, 61, 67, 69, 78, 80, 81, 82, 85, 87, 94, 108, 134, 141, 142, 143, 144, 167, 168, 174, 178
laws, 6, 7, 9, 10, 16, 18, 33, 34, 43, 44, 45, 46, 47, 48, 49, 50, 51, 52, 53, 54, 55, 56, 57, 58, 66, 67, 68, 69, 78, 82, 84, 88, 89, 96, 97, 98, 99, 100, 102, 105, 106, 109, 131, 132, 136, 137, 141, 142, 143, 145, 147, 148, 160, 174, 178
lawyers, 98
lead, 10, 56, 61, 86, 87, 101, 104, 109, 114, 115, 116, 123, 126, 133, 141, 144, 154, 159, 163
leadership, 2, 49
legislation, 6, 11, 12, 28, 29, 30, 53, 55, 57, 66, 67, 76, 88, 94, 95, 106, 107, 109, 144, 180
legislative, 3, 22, 28, 39, 44, 46, 64, 74, 76, 108, 110, 158
lender of last resort, 15, 16, 120, 123, 126, 127
lenders, 6, 35, 36, 66, 69, 141, 174, 175

lending, 6, 7, 15, 18, 28, 32, 34, 35, 66, 67, 68, 69, 70, 71, 72, 75, 77, 79, 80, 82, 84, 90, 114, 115, 124, 126, 127, 130, 131, 132, 133, 139, 141, 143, 146, 147, 174, 185
liability insurance, 9, 56, 106
liberalization, 185
licenses, 57, 108
licensing, 6, 9, 17, 44, 45, 54, 56, 57, 58, 66, 67, 68, 69, 86, 87, 105, 106, 109, 112, 118, 136, 140, 141, 145, 146, 174, 175, 182
limitation, 80
limitations, 35, 71, 77, 81, 94, 126, 131, 168
limited liability, 168
links, 114
liquidation, 55, 57, 108
liquidity, 4, 7, 13, 15, 23, 25, 28, 31, 32, 51, 56, 70, 71, 72, 74, 79, 82, 84, 85, 87, 96, 111, 117, 120, 123, 125, 126, 127, 139, 157, 160, 183
loans, 6, 7, 8, 28, 32, 66, 68, 74, 75, 77, 78, 79, 80, 126, 134, 139, 157, 175, 176
local government, 39
London, 166, 178, 186
long-term, 9, 14, 16, 17, 59, 105, 106, 116, 119, 121, 125, 141, 142, 160, 183
long-term care insurance, 9, 105, 106, 142
losses, vii, 1, 21, 29, 54, 60, 75, 76, 97, 104, 107, 163, 180
lower prices, 163
loyalty, 100

M

machines, 185
macroeconomic, 13, 29, 111, 117, 119, 120
magnetic, iv
main line, 98
management, 4, 13, 14, 15, 16, 22, 28, 30, 32, 46, 47, 48, 53, 54, 58, 77, 86, 87, 91, 92, 94, 96, 98, 112, 114, 115, 118, 122, 123, 125, 128, 129, 142, 146, 163, 165, 168, 170, 171, 176
management practices, 14, 92, 122, 125, 128
mandates, 49, 163, 186
manipulation, 18, 36, 37, 39, 42, 49, 50, 91, 92, 96, 99, 145, 168
marital status, 143, 144
market, 2, 3, 4, 5, 6, 7, 8, 10, 11, 12, 13, 14, 15, 16, 17, 18, 19, 22, 23, 24, 28, 29, 33, 34, 36, 37, 39, 41, 42, 43, 44, 47, 49, 50, 51, 54, 56, 57, 58, 59, 60, 61, 63, 64, 65, 66, 67, 68, 70, 71, 72, 73, 74, 78, 79, 80, 83, 88, 90, 91, 92, 93, 94, 95, 96, 101, 103, 104, 105, 106, 107, 108, 111, 112, 113, 114, 115, 116, 117, 118, 119, 120, 121, 122, 123, 124, 125, 126, 127, 128, 129, 130, 132, 133, 135, 136, 137, 138, 139, 141, 144, 146, 148, 151, 154, 155, 156, 157, 158, 160, 161, 162, 163, 167, 168, 169, 170, 171, 173, 177, 180, 185, 186
market discipline, 12, 13, 14, 16, 112, 115, 116, 117, 121, 123, 129, 155, 173
market disruption, 4, 23, 127
market economy, 14, 121
market failure, 12, 115, 116, 130
market segment, 41, 124, 161, 163
market share, 57, 78
market stability, 2, 3, 4, 5, 7, 12, 13, 14, 15, 17, 19, 22, 23, 24, 63, 70, 71, 111, 113, 114, 115, 116, 117, 118, 119, 120, 121, 122, 123, 124, 126, 127, 128, 135, 139, 146, 151, 155
market structure, 49, 91, 92
market-based economies, 3, 22
marketing, 18, 140, 143
markets, vii, 1, 2, 3, 4, 5, 7, 9, 10, 11, 18, 19, 21, 22, 23, 24, 36, 37, 38, 39, 40, 41, 42, 44, 46, 47, 48, 49, 50, 51, 52, 63, 64, 65, 66, 67, 70, 79, 83, 85, 86, 88, 89, 90, 91, 92, 93, 95, 96, 97, 99, 100, 101, 105, 106, 107, 109, 111, 112, 113, 116, 118, 121, 125, 126, 127, 131, 132, 136, 139, 141, 142, 144, 145, 151, 153, 154, 155, 156, 157, 160, 161, 163, 170, 177, 183, 185
Massachusetts, 52, 179
measurement, 184
measures, 4, 23, 30, 39, 71, 76, 113, 125
membership, 5, 31, 32, 63, 65, 80, 81, 101, 131, 132, 146
mergers, 12, 95, 108, 119
messages, 168
metals, 37, 40, 42, 177
Mexico, 165
migration, 4, 23
mining, 44
minority, 103
mirror, 137
misleading, 99, 100, 144
missions, 73, 100
models, 84, 103, 111, 147
modernization, 5, 56, 63, 95, 178
monetary policy, 13, 15, 28, 82, 84, 111, 114, 115, 117, 119, 120, 126, 127, 156, 158
money, 25, 29, 84, 85, 163, 167
moral hazard, 16, 112, 118, 129, 130
moratorium, 39
mortgage, 2, 5, 6, 7, 8, 19, 23, 28, 32, 35, 36, 63, 66, 67, 68, 69, 74, 75, 78, 79, 110, 123, 130, 138, 143, 151, 157, 164, 165, 167, 168, 173, 174, 175, 176

mortgage securitization, 79
mortgages, 6, 7, 32, 66, 68, 75, 79, 123, 130, 143, 157, 175, 176
motivation, 134
movement, 57, 85, 131
multilateral, 43, 109, 165, 166
mutual banks, 82
mutual funds, 18, 29, 48, 93, 167, 173, 185

N

NAIC, 9, 10, 53, 54, 55, 56, 57, 58, 59, 60, 61, 105, 109, 136, 144
NASDAQ, 49
nation, 27, 33, 47, 85, 159
national, 2, 3, 6, 8, 9, 10, 16, 18, 22, 27, 28, 31, 33, 34, 38, 46, 47, 48, 49, 50, 51, 57, 58, 59, 61, 66, 73, 77, 78, 79, 80, 81, 98, 105, 106, 107, 108, 109, 130, 131, 132, 133, 135, 136, 137, 141, 142, 143, 144, 145, 147, 148, 158, 159, 160, 165, 180, 184
National Association of Insurance Commissioners, 9, 53, 105, 136
National Credit Union Administration, 6, 26, 34, 65, 78, 158, 184
national origin, 143, 144
national product, 9, 58, 136
natural, 13, 110, 115
negotiation, 40
Netherlands, 3, 12, 22, 115, 154, 168
network, 74, 166, 176
Nevada, 33
New Jersey, 57
New York, iii, iv, 27, 36, 50, 52, 55, 57, 65, 98, 105, 121, 166, 167, 173, 178, 181
New York Stock Exchange, 50, 98
New Zealand, 186
Nixon, 157
non-profit, 109, 132
non-uniform, 105, 136, 142
normal, 15, 127, 135
North America, 46
not-for-profit, 101
NYSE, 49

O

obligation, 25, 134
obligations, 5, 17, 23, 43, 51, 57, 83, 100, 113, 125, 139, 171, 176
obsolete, 45
OECD, 61

off-exchange trading, 37, 41
Office of Federal Housing Enterprise Oversight, 65
Office of Management and Budget, 158
Office of the U.S. Trade Representative, 61
Office of Thrift Supervision, 5, 26, 33, 65, 73, 75, 78
offshore, 94, 136
Ohio, 182
oil, 30, 75
OMB, 158, 161
online, 32
opacity, 129
open market operations, 33, 34, 126
operator, 165, 166
organization, 10, 11, 43, 48, 52, 53, 74, 85, 92, 93, 108, 109, 124, 144, 169, 170, 171, 174, 183
Organization for Economic Cooperation and Development, 61
organizations, 11, 30, 38, 43, 57, 59, 84, 87, 88, 91, 95, 97, 98, 109, 146, 163, 168, 170, 171
orientation, 77
OTC, 39, 43, 176
oversight, 2, 6, 8, 10, 12, 16, 17, 18, 19, 23, 27, 30, 32, 33, 35, 38, 41, 42, 44, 49, 50, 51, 52, 56, 61, 66, 69, 74, 77, 78, 83, 84, 85, 86, 88, 89, 90, 91, 98, 101, 103, 108, 109, 112, 113, 114, 115, 118, 119, 120, 125, 128, 130, 131, 132, 134, 135, 136, 137, 139, 140, 141, 145, 147, 149, 154, 162, 171, 174, 181
over-the-counter, 11, 39, 64, 93, 163
ownership, 16, 31, 56, 74, 77, 79, 132, 161
ownership structure, 16, 74, 77, 132

P

paper, 46, 80, 162
partnerships, 126, 127
payroll, 165
PCA, 30, 76, 107, 175
PCAOB, 48, 52
peer, 14, 56, 122
peer group, 14, 122
peer review, 56
penalties, 45, 48, 87, 96, 99
pension, 39, 157, 184
pension plans, 157
perception, 103
performance, 56, 79, 96, 100
periodic, 48, 64, 98, 163
permit, 11, 32, 64, 80, 88, 94, 96, 132
personal, 6, 36, 67, 137, 144, 180

philosophical, 96, 163
philosophy, 10, 90, 95
planning, 104
platforms, 4, 23, 90
play, vii, 1, 8, 19, 21, 83, 84, 87, 128, 129, 136, 148
police, 90
policy initiative, 64
policymakers, 1, 21, 64, 65, 101
pools, 51, 64, 79, 117
poor, 14, 30, 57, 121
population, 104, 135
portfolio, 32, 75, 79, 80, 96, 160, 173, 176
portfolios, 78, 79
potatoes, 38
power, 29, 35, 45, 47, 52, 86, 108, 109, 119, 124, 134
powers, 10, 13, 28, 30, 33, 34, 38, 40, 46, 82, 107, 108, 109, 110, 111, 117, 120, 139, 159, 162
preference, 96, 163
premium, 52, 57, 60, 105, 136
premiums, 19, 33, 57, 112, 136, 138, 144, 184
prevention, 49, 163, 169
price ceiling, 29
price competition, 106
price stability, 84
prices, 59, 96, 104, 120, 141, 159, 163, 169, 180
primacy, 52
priorities, 27
privacy, 35, 36, 141, 143
private, 12, 18, 45, 57, 64, 67, 68, 95, 97, 101, 110, 117, 139, 157, 159, 160, 161, 165, 166, 168
private investment, 168
private sector, 67, 68, 157, 159, 160, 161
private-sector, 165, 166
producers, 9, 105, 106, 107, 108
product eligibility, 91, 170
profit, 101, 109, 132
profitability, 97
profits, 106
program, 34, 51, 54, 56, 70, 81, 126, 127, 147, 159, 171, 174, 176
promote, 2, 5, 9, 24, 36, 44, 46, 49, 65, 85, 90, 105, 106, 107, 108, 120, 126, 158, 175, 176
property, iv, 9, 54, 55, 56, 57, 58, 59, 60, 106, 137, 138, 176
property owner, 60
protection, vii, 1, 3, 4, 5, 10, 11, 12, 13, 17, 19, 21, 22, 23, 35, 36, 45, 48, 50, 54, 57, 63, 65, 68, 78, 85, 88, 90, 92, 94, 95, 96, 100, 103, 104, 105, 106, 107, 112, 113, 114, 115, 117,
118, 128, 134, 136, 137, 138, 140, 141, 143, 146, 151, 154, 155, 156, 169, 178
proxy, 131
public, 6, 14, 18, 19, 24, 26, 31, 35, 36, 37, 42, 47, 48, 49, 51, 52, 53, 55, 67, 68, 76, 79, 86, 91, 92, 97, 112, 118, 119, 121, 122, 123, 125, 129, 132, 133, 138, 139, 143, 145, 146, 153, 163, 169, 173, 183
public companies, 48, 52
Public Company Accounting Oversight Board, 48
public interest, 48, 49, 53, 183
public markets, 51, 118
public policy, 36, 76
publishers, 98
Puerto Rico, 44
punitive, 27

Q

qualifications, 145
quality of service, 104

R

race, 143, 144
radical, 54
range, 8, 9, 17, 18, 25, 31, 32, 34, 39, 42, 43, 57, 65, 77, 82, 97, 99, 101, 103, 124, 125, 126, 127, 128, 129, 134, 135, 145, 147, 167
rash, 28, 49, 73
rat, 13, 118, 143
rating agencies, 52
ratings, 52
reading, 175
real estate, 30, 75, 77, 80, 176, 184
reasoning, 89, 157
reciprocity, 54, 58
recognition, 3, 22, 90, 101, 155, 183
reconcile, 96
recovery, 171
reduction, 11, 55, 77, 95, 162
reflection, 63
Reform Act, 52, 76
reforms, 3, 19, 21, 39, 86, 91, 151, 157, 159, 161, 184
regional, 27, 28, 34, 74, 131, 139, 165
Registry, 67
regular, 18, 42, 48, 65, 68, 69, 102, 121, 122, 146, 148
regulation, vii, 1, 2, 3, 4, 5, 6, 7, 8, 9, 10, 11, 12, 13, 14, 16, 17, 18, 19, 21, 22, 23, 24, 27, 29, 31, 32, 35, 36, 37, 38, 40, 41, 42, 44, 45, 46,

47, 49, 50, 51, 52, 53, 54, 55, 56, 57, 58, 59, 60, 61, 63, 71, 74, 77, 78, 80, 81, 84, 85, 86, 87, 88, 89, 90, 91, 95, 97, 98, 100, 101, 102, 103, 104, 105, 106, 107, 108, 109, 110, 111, 112, 113, 114, 115, 116, 118, 119, 120, 121, 125, 128, 129, 132, 133, 134, 135, 136, 137, 138, 139, 140, 141, 142, 143, 144, 145, 147, 148, 151, 154, 155, 156, 157, 158, 159, 160, 161, 162, 163, 174, 175, 176, 179, 180, 181, 182, 183, 185

regulations, 6, 11, 15, 18, 27, 33, 34, 36, 41, 43, 45, 47, 50, 52, 53, 58, 65, 66, 68, 78, 84, 87, 95, 96, 97, 98, 99, 105, 109, 123, 125, 133, 138, 140, 141, 143, 145, 147, 148, 153, 157, 159, 174

regulators, 4, 6, 10, 13, 14, 16, 18, 23, 24, 27, 28, 30, 35, 36, 37, 44, 45, 46, 53, 54, 57, 58, 59, 61, 65, 66, 67, 68, 69, 73, 74, 75, 76, 77, 78, 85, 87, 90, 94, 98, 101, 105, 107, 108, 109, 111, 113, 114, 116, 117, 118, 119, 125, 134, 141, 142, 145, 146, 147, 154, 156, 159, 162, 163, 175

regulatory bodies, 10, 51, 109
regulatory capital, 51
regulatory framework, 2, 12, 16, 17, 19, 24, 94, 111, 116, 121, 125, 129, 130, 140, 141, 143, 151, 154, 155, 156, 162
regulatory oversight, 30, 41, 42, 78, 89, 113, 128, 130, 140, 154
regulatory requirements, 53, 60, 67, 99, 101, 120, 123, 144
rehabilitate, 55
rehabilitation, 55, 57, 108
reinsurance, 10, 61, 108, 109, 136, 147
relationship, 3, 22
relationships, 16, 119, 134, 135
relatives, 131
relevance, 75, 148
religion, 143
research, 99, 129
reserves, 15, 54, 127, 157
residential, 7, 8, 28, 32, 75, 77, 78, 79, 80, 130, 157, 176
resolution, 30, 34, 44, 91, 97, 113, 169, 171, 184
Resolution Trust Corporation, 30, 75
resources, 55, 82, 91, 100, 115, 134, 161, 170, 171, 184
responsibilities, 8, 13, 14, 17, 18, 19, 27, 29, 33, 34, 44, 47, 64, 65, 81, 82, 83, 85, 86, 99, 100, 112, 115, 118, 119, 121, 125, 129, 130, 140, 142, 145, 147, 148, 159, 162, 170, 185
responsiveness, 93
restaurants, 185

restitution, 45
restructuring, 104, 162
retail, 8, 11, 12, 13, 17, 31, 40, 42, 83, 86, 88, 94, 95, 102, 103, 111, 115, 118, 128, 130, 137, 138, 139, 140, 142, 144, 146, 147, 156
retail deposit, 31
retirees, 132
retirement, 34, 53
returns, 75, 86
rewards, 184
Rhode Island, 52
rice, 38, 141, 168
rigidity, 183
risk, 4, 5, 9, 11, 13, 14, 15, 16, 17, 19, 22, 23, 26, 30, 39, 41, 43, 50, 52, 54, 56, 60, 63, 64, 65, 68, 72, 76, 77, 79, 83, 85, 86, 87, 90, 91, 92, 95, 96, 100, 104, 106, 108, 112, 113, 114, 115, 118, 120, 121, 122, 123, 125, 128, 129, 133, 135, 136, 138, 144, 146, 154, 155, 160, 162, 163, 165, 168, 171, 173, 175, 177, 184, 185
risk management, 4, 13, 14, 15, 16, 22, 86, 87, 91, 92, 112, 114, 115, 118, 122, 123, 125, 128, 129, 165, 168, 171
risk profile, 96, 120, 129
risks, vii, 1, 4, 15, 16, 21, 22, 26, 34, 56, 59, 60, 83, 85, 86, 87, 104, 108, 114, 120, 132, 133, 134, 135, 136, 146, 156, 166, 170
risk-taking, 15, 86
rolling, 68

S

safeguard, 104, 135
safeguards, 87, 91, 129, 162, 171
safety, 2, 7, 9, 15, 24, 26, 29, 35, 70, 72, 74, 77, 83, 84, 87, 104, 106, 108, 126, 127, 134, 135, 139, 140, 154, 156, 159, 161, 162, 170, 183, 184
sales, 4, 5, 12, 18, 23, 44, 45, 54, 58, 95, 99, 102, 108, 113, 114, 115, 140, 143
sanctions, 45
SAP, 54
Sarbanes-Oxley Act, 48, 52
satisfaction, 47, 140
savings, vii, 1, 7, 16, 21, 28, 32, 33, 34, 73, 78, 80, 81, 98, 101, 105, 130, 131, 132, 157, 158, 159, 175, 176, 183
savings banks, 33, 34, 80, 81, 157, 158, 176
school, 131
scores, 56
SE, 12, 97
Secretary of Agriculture, 37, 38

Secretary of the Treasury, 5, 10, 27, 34, 36, 64, 81, 109, 119, 124, 157, 158, 160, 162, 184
securities, vii, 1, 2, 4, 8, 10, 11, 12, 18, 19, 21, 23, 24, 25, 26, 28, 30, 31, 32, 36, 37, 38, 39, 40, 43, 44, 45, 46, 47, 48, 49, 50, 51, 52, 53, 56, 68, 73, 76, 79, 80, 83, 84, 88, 89, 90, 91, 92, 93, 95, 96, 97, 98, 99, 100, 102, 104, 107, 112, 113, 117, 118, 127, 128, 129, 130, 133, 135, 140, 141, 142, 144, 145, 146, 147, 154, 156, 160, 161, 163, 164, 167, 168, 173, 176, 177, 178, 183
Securities and Exchange Commission, 5, 36, 49, 64, 87, 88, 90, 95, 112, 113, 159, 166
Securities Exchange Act, 47, 92, 177
security, 4, 23, 35, 40, 42, 43, 47, 51, 79, 88, 89, 96, 99, 113, 129, 171, 177
segmentation, 163
segregation, 11, 87, 95, 96, 100, 146
seigniorage, 27, 33
selecting, 26
Self, 44, 51, 92, 93, 95, 100, 101, 178
self-regulation, 37, 47, 49, 51, 100, 103, 147
Senate, 33, 34, 35, 38, 41, 49, 180
separation, 28, 76, 134, 138, 162
September 11, 54, 60
series, 1, 2, 4, 19, 23, 28, 46, 83, 113, 116, 151, 181
service provider, 18, 140, 148
services, iv, vii, 1, 2, 3, 4, 9, 12, 13, 16, 17, 18, 19, 21, 22, 23, 24, 25, 26, 29, 30, 32, 35, 43, 44, 50, 54, 73, 83, 84, 85, 88, 93, 97, 98, 101, 102, 103, 104, 105, 111, 112, 113, 118, 131, 132, 133, 135, 140, 142, 145, 146, 147, 148, 151, 154, 155, 156, 157, 158, 159, 161, 162, 163, 165, 167, 168, 176, 179, 185, 186
settlements, 170
severe stress, 74
sex, 143, 144
shape, 3, 22
shareholders, 173
shares, 31, 46, 48, 79, 93, 94, 173
sharing, 36, 64, 65, 91, 119, 121, 122, 131, 171
short period, 25
shortage, 144
short-term, 1, 15, 19, 23, 63, 84, 116, 123, 126, 127, 151, 160, 183
short-term interest rate, 84
signaling, 139
similarity, 97
Singapore, 186
Social Security, 165
solutions, 101, 127, 160, 183

solvency, 54, 55, 56, 57, 59, 105, 107, 136, 144, 160, 183
South Africa, 186
specialization, 4, 23, 81, 113, 114, 115, 157
specificity, 78
speed, 56, 59, 92
spillover effects, 119
spillovers, 120
stability, vii, 1, 2, 3, 4, 5, 7, 12, 13, 14, 15, 17, 19, 21, 22, 23, 24, 27, 35, 49, 54, 63, 70, 71, 77, 82, 83, 84, 85, 86, 111, 113, 114, 115, 116, 117, 118, 119, 120, 121, 122, 123, 124, 126, 127, 128, 129, 130, 135, 139, 145, 146, 151, 155, 156, 163, 185
staffing, 114
standardization, 176
standards, 6, 9, 11, 12, 17, 18, 29, 31, 36, 38, 41, 42, 47, 48, 49, 50, 51, 52, 53, 55, 56, 58, 59, 66, 67, 68, 69, 74, 78, 85, 87, 90, 91, 95, 99, 100, 101, 103, 105, 109, 112, 116, 118, 121, 123, 128, 131, 136, 137, 140, 141, 142, 144, 145, 146, 147, 148, 155, 160, 169, 170, 174, 175, 179, 185
state laws, 9, 16, 34, 44, 45, 46, 57, 58, 78, 82, 98, 106, 131, 132, 136, 137, 142, 147, 148
state oversight, 32, 131
state regulators, 6, 36, 57, 59, 61, 66, 78, 159
statistics, 79, 174
statutes, 11, 27, 35, 44, 45, 47, 65, 73, 95, 98
statutory, 10, 12, 31, 35, 38, 39, 52, 54, 55, 57, 58, 65, 78, 86, 87, 88, 100, 101, 103, 109, 110, 136, 139, 186
statutory provisions, 100
stigma, 126
stock, 5, 16, 28, 36, 38, 40, 44, 49, 51, 64, 73, 88, 89, 90, 91, 96, 132, 160, 161, 173
stock exchange, 49, 51, 173
stock price, 96
storage, 91, 165, 169
strains, 9, 135
strategic, 56
strategies, 4, 22, 23, 129, 160
strength, 2, 5, 6, 19, 23, 56, 68, 113, 151, 161
stress, 74, 79
structural reforms, 157, 159
structuring, 101
subjective, 45
subpoena, 46
subsidies, 133, 139
subsidy, 57
suffering, 144
summaries, 180

supervision, 6, 8, 9, 10, 13, 16, 17, 33, 36, 45, 46, 52, 57, 66, 68, 69, 74, 81, 82, 87, 105, 106, 108, 112, 116, 117, 118, 120, 125, 128, 129, 134, 135, 156, 158, 159, 161, 162, 163, 174, 175, 181, 184
supervisor, 8, 14, 34, 76, 138, 159, 175
supervisors, 36, 108, 129
supplements, 48
supply, 42, 84, 180
Supreme Court, 37, 52, 53, 109
surplus, 4, 23, 57, 58, 60, 113, 117, 137, 144, 147, 156
surveillance, 90, 177
systemic risk, 4, 5, 14, 17, 23, 63, 65, 113, 121, 135, 163, 173, 177, 185
systems, 6, 8, 25, 28, 51, 58, 66, 67, 68, 83, 84, 85, 86, 87, 91, 92, 93, 107, 128, 161, 163, 165, 168, 171, 174

T

tangible, 2, 24
task force, 12, 91, 97
taxation, 53, 131, 132, 147, 157
taxes, 57
tax-exempt, 32
taxpayers, 70, 71, 101, 163, 185
TCC, 186
teachers, 98
technical assistance, 109
technological change, 10, 105, 106
technology, 4, 22, 129, 132, 133, 162
telephone, 153, 165
tension, 88
terrorism, 64
terrorist, 54
terrorist attack, 54
testimony, 24
TF, 94
theft, 59, 146
theory, 60, 139
third party, 119, 158
Thomson, 182, 186
threat, 16, 127, 168
threatened, 7, 15
threatening, 17, 54, 123, 135
threshold, 16, 127
thrifts, 2, 7, 8, 28, 29, 30, 31, 32, 33, 34, 35, 36, 73, 74, 75, 76, 77, 78, 79, 80, 81, 130, 162, 176, 182
time, 3, 4, 7, 8, 9, 10, 11, 15, 18, 22, 23, 25, 26, 28, 31, 32, 45, 48, 52, 56, 59, 60, 63, 67, 70, 74, 75, 78, 79, 84, 85, 88, 89, 91, 93, 95, 101, 105, 106, 113, 116, 125, 128, 129, 130, 131, 135, 148, 154, 158, 160, 161, 163, 164, 166, 167, 173, 180, 185
time deposits, 26
time-frame, 85
timing, 52
tolerance, 100
top-down, 120
trade, 18, 24, 37, 38, 40, 42, 44, 51, 61, 83, 89, 91, 92,-94, 96, 99, 142, 143, 167, 168, 169, 170, 171, 186
trade agreement, 61
Trade Representative, 61, 109
trading, 4, 10, 11, 12, 22, 23, 37, 38, 39, 40, 41, 42, 43, 44, 47, 49, 50, 61, 88, 89, 90, 91, 92, 93, 94, 95, 96, 99, 100, 102, 160, 163, 167, 168, 169, 170, 171, 176, 177, 185
trading partners, 61
tradition, 2, 26, 27
training, 18, 50, 99, 101, 145
training programs, 101
transactions, vii, 1, 4, 5, 6, 7, 8, 16, 21, 22, 23, 25, 33, 35, 37, 38, 39, 40, 41, 42, 43, 44, 46, 47, 50, 66, 68, 69, 83, 84, 90, 96, 98, 99, 102, 108, 111, 114, 115, 128, 129, 130, 133, 134, 137, 140, 142, 145, 146, 161, 163, 165, 166, 167, 168, 169, 170, 171, 178
transfer, vii, 1, 8, 21, 25, 26, 34, 43, 47, 81, 83, 84, 85, 88, 128, 134, 135, 156, 160, 164, 169, 173
transformation, 130
transition, 5, 8, 63, 73, 80, 91
transition period, 80
transparency, 70
transparent, 7, 70, 71, 118, 148
Treasury, i, iii, vii, 1, 2, 3, 5, 6, 7, 8, 9, 10, 11, 12, 14, 19, 21, 22, 23, 24, 27, 30, 32, 33, 36, 38, 50, 63, 64, 65, 66, 67, 68, 69, 70, 72, 73, 75, 78, 80, 81, 82, 83, 86, 88, 89, 90, 91, 92, 93, 94, 95, 97, 103, 104, 105, 106, 108, 109, 111, 112, 116, 119, 120, 124, 135, 151, 153, 154, 157, 158, 159, 160, 161, 162, 163, 173, 174, 176, 177, 180, 184
Treasury bills, 38
Treasury Department, 153, 154, 184
trend, 32, 125, 129, 131, 136
triggers, 60
trust, 48, 167, 176, 185
trusts, 48, 93, 173

U

U.S. economy, vii, 1, 21, 28, 83, 104, 155

U.S. history, 9, 135
U.S. Treasury, 38, 89, 184
uncertainty, 38, 39, 52
underwriters, 68, 97
uniform, 6, 8, 10, 17, 34, 36, 46, 53, 55, 56, 57, 58, 59, 66, 67, 74, 78, 84, 105, 109, 136, 137, 141, 142, 155, 163, 174, 175
uninsured, 163, 176, 184
unions, 2, 28, 32, 34, 36, 78, 80, 131, 157, 184
United Kingdom, 3, 12, 22, 89, 112, 114, 115, 154
United States, vii, 1, 2, 3, 6, 8, 10, 12, 16, 19, 21, 22, 26, 27, 28, 29, 37, 41, 44, 46, 47, 50, 53, 59, 66, 80, 82, 83, 84, 88, 90, 92, 94, 98, 105, 108, 109, 112, 113, 115, 116, 119, 128, 129, 130, 131, 134, 135, 151, 153, 154, 155, 157, 166, 167, 168, 178, 179
updating, 92
USDA, 37, 173
Utah, 33

V

vacuum, 129
values, 86
vehicles, 94, 125
vein, 12, 103
venture capital, 18
Vermont, 52
Vice President, 158
victims, 45
violent, 161
voice, 10, 61
volatility, 15, 90, 127, 176
voting, 31
vulnerability, 163

W

war, 28
weakness, 6, 55, 68, 126
web, 27
websites, 178
well-being, 86
wholesale, 25, 111, 139, 156
workers, 9, 59, 106, 144, 156
World Trade Center, 60
World War, 28
World War I, 28
WorldCom, 48
writing, 14, 18, 147, 180

Y

yield, 75

Z

zoning, 132, 147